Responsibility to Protect and Prevent

Anthem Studies in Peace, Conflict and Development

The **Anthem Studies in Peace, Conflict and Development** series publishes high-quality and original research in the areas of conflict analysis, conflict resolution, humanitarianism, peacebuilding, and the complex relationships between security and development. The series addresses academic and professional audiences as it focuses on the causes and dynamics of violent conflicts within and between societies and states, as well as on policies and practices towards conflict management, development and peacebuilding initiatives at various levels.

Series Editor

Ashok Swain – Uppsala University, Sweden

Editorial Board

Responsibility to Protect and Prevent

Principles, Promises and Practicalities

John Janzekovic and Daniel Silander

ANTHEM PRESS

LONDON · NEW YORK · DELHI

Anthem Press
An imprint of Wimbledon Publishing Company
www.anthempress.com

This edition first published in UK and USA 2014
by ANTHEM PRESS
75–76 Blackfriars Road, London SE1 8HA, UK
or PO Box 9779, London SW19 7ZG, UK
and
244 Madison Ave #116, New York, NY 10016, USA

First published in hardback by Anthem Press is 2013

British Library Cataloguing-in-Publication Data
A catalogue record for this book is available from the British Library.

Library of Congress Cataloging-in-Publication Data
The Library of Congress has catalogued the hardcover edition as follows:
Janzekovic, John.
Responsibility to protect and prevent : principles, promises and
practicalities / John Janzekovic and Daniel Silander.
pages cm
Includes bibliographical references and index.
ISBN-13: 978-0-85728-059-6 (hardcover : alk. paper)
ISBN-10: 0-85728-059-7 (hardcover : alk. paper)
1. Responsibility to protect (International law) 2. Humanitarian
intervention. 3. Humanitarian intervention–Libya. 4.
Libya–History–Civil War, 2011– I. Silander, Daniel, 1972– II.
Title.
JZ6369.J258 2013
341.5'84–dc23
2013019628

ISBN-13: 978 1 78308 345 9 (Pbk)
ISBN-10: 1 78308 345 X (Pbk)

This title is also available as an ebook.

CONTENTS

List of Maps   vii
List of Abbreviations   ix

Chapter 1   Introduction   1
Protection and Prevention   3
Structure of the Text   4

**Chapter 2   State versus Human Security:
              The Great Debate**   11
Security, Sovereignty and the State   12
State and Human Security in Weak, Failing or Failed States   17
Human Security During and After the Rwandan Genocide
  and the Balkan Wars   20
The Need for a Human-centric Approach   37
Conclusion   43

Chapter 3   Responsibility: Protection and Prevention   45
Responsibility to Protect (R2P)   46
Intervention and Protection   49
Developments in R2P   50
Intervention, Protection and the War in Kosovo   58
What is a Responsibility to Prevent (R2Prevent)?   65
Protection and Prevention: Where to Now?   71
Conclusion   73

**Chapter 4   State Responsibility, Human
              Security and International Law**   75
The Relevance of International Law to State Behaviour   76
International Humanitarian Laws: Progression and Promises   80
The International Law Commission and State Responsibility   83
Conclusion   87

Chapter 5   Promoting Democratic Norms for
Protection and Prevention   89
Emerging Democracy Norms   90
Democracy Promotion and Human Security   94
R2P through Democratic Norms: The Big Three   98
Popular representation   98
Peace   99
Prosperity   101
Conclusion   102

Chapter 6   Case Study Libya: Moving Principle
into Action?   103
Libya, 2010–11: Revolution and Aftermath   104
The United Nations Security Council and the Application
  of R2P in Libya   106
The Great Powers' Response to the Crisis in Libya   109
Lessons Learned: R2P and the Libyan Crisis   117
Conclusion   121

Chapter 7   Conclusion   123

Appendix I   S/RES/1970 United Nations Resolution 1970
                on Africa (Including Annexes I–II)   127
Appendix II   S/RES/1973 United Nations Resolution 1973
                on the Situation in Libya (Excluding Annexes I–II) 139
Notes   149
Bibliography   167
Index   185

LIST OF MAPS

Map 2.1   Rwanda, Burundi and neighbouring states   22

Map 2.2   Kosovo and neighbouring states   25

Map 2.3   East Timor (Timor-Leste) and neighbouring states   29

Map 2.4   Africa   30

Map 2.5   Somalia and neighbouring states   34

Map 2.6   Chad and neighbouring states   35

Map 2.7   Sudan and neighbouring states   36

Map 3.1   Bosnia–Herzegovina and neighbouring states   59

Map 3.2   Former Yugoslavia and neighbouring states   60

Map 6.1   Libya and neighbouring states   108

All maps courtesy of the University of Texas Libraries, the University of Texas at Austin.

LIST OF ABBREVIATIONS

CDR	Coalition pour la Défense de la République
CIA	Central Intelligence Agency
CIL	Customary International Law
CPI	Corruption Perceptions Index
CRS	Congressional Research Service
DFAIT	Department of Foreign Affairs and International Trade Canada
FRY	Federal Republic of Yugoslavia
GNU	Government of National Unity
HSN	Human Security Network
IBC	Iraqi Body Count
ICAO	International Civil Aviation Organization
ICC	International Criminal Court
ICIDI	Independent Commission on International Development Issues
ICISS	International Commission on Intervention and State Sovereignty
ICJ	International Court of Justice
ICDSI	Independent Commission on Disarmament and Security Issues
IED	Improvised explosive device
IHL	International humanitarian law
IHRL	International Human Rights Law
IICK	Independent International Commission on Kosovo
ILC	International Law Commission (United Nations)
ILO	International Labour Organization
IMF	International Monetary Fund
KLA	Kosovo Liberation Army
MAD	Mutually assured destruction
MRND	Mouvement Républicain National Pour la Démocratie et le Développement

NATO	North Atlantic Treaty Organization
NCP	National Congress Party
NGO	Nongovernmental organization
OAU	Organization of African Unity
OSCE	Organization for Security and Co-operation in Europe
PCIJ	Permanent Court of International Justice
R2P	Responsibility to protect
R2Prevent	Responsibility to prevent
RPF	Rwandan Patriotic Front
SPLM	Sudan People's Liberation Movement
START	Strategic Arms Reduction Treaty
TBBG	Transitional Broad-Based Government
UDHR	Universal Declaration of Human Rights
UN	United Nations
UNAMIR	United Nations Assistance Mission for Rwanda
UNDP	United Nations Development Programme
UNHCR	United Nations High Commissioner for Refugees
UNMIK	United Nations Interim Administration Mission in Kosovo
UNMIS	United Nations Mission in Sudan
UNOSOM	United Nations Operation in Somalia
UNPROFOR	United Nations Protection Force
UNTAES	United Nations Transitional Authority in Eastern Slovenia
UNTAET	United Nations Transitional Administration in East Timor
USSR	Union of Soviet Socialist Republics
WGI	World Bank's Worldwide Governance Indicators
WMDs	Weapons of mass destruction
WOMP	World Order Models Project

Chapter 1

INTRODUCTION

The 2005 UN World Summit was a pivotal event in the formal progression of the responsibility to protect (R2P) principles. Paragraphs 138–9 of the summit's outcome document articulated the fundamental responsibilities of states and the wider international community. The R2P approach was directly applied for the first time by the Security Council to the genocide in Darfur and most recently to the international response in Libya during the Arab Spring uprisings in 2011 and 2012. Since the late 1990s, the concept of R2P has evolved into what supporters now claim is a new type of responsive norm regarding how the international community should react to serious and deliberate human rights violations. The 2001 UN International Commission on Intervention and State Sovereignty co-chaired by Gareth Evans and Mohamed Sahnoun articulated in detail the principles of R2P. These principles were then formally endorsed by the majority of states at the 2005 UN General Assembly World Summit in New York.

At the 2005 summit, the international community almost unanimously endorsed the idea that states have a fundamental responsibility to protect their own citizens, and in most cases the citizens from other states, from gross human rights violations and other mass atrocities.[1] However, the progression of R2P from concept to principle to formal ratification in 2005 has been a very difficult one with a great deal of disagreement over the validity of R2P as a substantive or even a developing norm in international affairs. The disagreement is not that protection or prevention are unimportant, nor is it that the international community does not have at least some responsibility to try to stop extreme human rights violations. The disagreement is primarily about how the protection and prevention principles that underpin the R2P ethos, while theoretically acceptable, are supposed to work in practice. Fundamentally, of what possible use are such principles when governments and policy makers continue to ignore the basic premise of protection?

Some of the major rising powers such as China, India and Russia refuted the overarching concept of R2P primarily because this notion violates the essential principle of state sovereignty. That is, the security of the state must come first and any move towards prioritizing human security over state security threatens the underlying sanctity of statehood itself. Despite such challenges there has been an intensified debate on the practical need to address conflicts that deliberately and repeatedly demonstrate unacceptable state behaviour towards humans.

This is not only a debate about idealizing human rights or substantiating the functions of the state apparatus. This is a debate about the fundamental obligations of a civil and moral society, and how the international community should or even can protect people who are at extreme risk of deliberate violence. The need to prevent violence and to protect people from the excesses of their governments has been preached and argued by many, but the serious application of operational and structural strategies that effectively address the most basic human needs of citizens, particularly in weak states, are significantly more theory than practice. The notion of protection that is enshrined in the R2P ethos attempts to provide some sort of formal structure for how we should ameliorate the effects of mass violence and deprivation.

R2P refers to third-party initiatives aimed at pre-empting the escalation of violence.[2] Such initiatives may be of various kinds, but they are mostly political ventures to prevent violent conflicts rooted in complex networks of religion, ethnicity, identity and culture and in the struggle for power. The Carnegie Commission on Preventing Deadly Conflict, in its final 1999 report *Preventing Deadly Conflict*, identified three broad aims of preventative action: prevent the emergence of violent conflict, prevent ongoing conflicts from spreading and prevent the re-emergence of violence. The commission proposed three fundamental principles underpinning effective prevention strategies; early reaction to signs of trouble, a comprehensive, balanced approach to alleviate the pressures or risk factors that trigger violent conflict and an extended effort to resolve the underlying root causes of violence.[3] However, neither the commission generally nor the report articulated how this was to be done except to propose that prevention may be operational or structural in nature. Operational prevention is focused on addressing and responding to the immediacy of conflict, while structural prevention is aimed at identifying and responding to the underlying causes of conflict. Bellamy and Williams point out that structural and operational preventative initiatives currently exist more in theory than in practice.[4] A further significant challenge is that the nexus between protection and prevention is unclear. Are they the same? Is one dependent on the other? Should one have priority over the other? We aim to address these very difficult questions and posit that desperate efforts at protection (where it occurs at all) can only ever be a final response to deliberate and extreme human rights violations. Prevention and the need for prevention before protection in these cases has either been too little, too late, or non-existent in the first place.

Protection and Prevention

One important reason that strategic prevention is more theory than practice or actuality is because of the very complex nature and difficulty in identifying appropriate and effective preventative responses to potential conflict situations. Where preventative responses are not identified, or if they are identified but not effective, then direct intervention must remain as the final protection option to alleviate the immediate suffering of the victims of extreme violence. Humanitarian intervention may end up as a secondary prevention option to stop the violence from escalating further and wider out of control.

Until very recently, the prevention, reaction and rebuilding dimensions were considered primarily to be the responsibility of the sovereign state. Not only has this resulted in great harm to citizens by governments or regimes who deliberately brutalize their own people, but this approach has provided many in the international community a reason, if not an outright excuse, not to become involved in the affairs of another state regardless of even the most desperate humanitarian need to do so.

State sovereignty is intimately associated with human security in the sense that sovereignty is ultimately morally derived from the people. This means that, in the end, state security is dependent on human security. When states fail to provide human security this increasingly undermines the moral and legal legitimacy of the state itself. When states fail in this way, then intervention with the aim to protect and to prevent further atrocities must remain an option. We argue that if states deliberately violate this fundamental obligation, then there is a strong and legitimate case for the international community to firstly assume responsibility for the welfare of those people most at risk and secondly to act directly to stop extreme and deliberate brutalization of citizens by the state.

This position challenges and directly confronts the traditional norms of noninterference by outsiders into the affairs of a sovereign state. Yet the development of human security norms in international relations – security, moral, humanitarian and democracy norms – obliges the international community to act under these critical circumstances. Such intervention is also subject to a very wide range of factors including political will, domestic support and capacity to respond. R2P identifies the legal and moral obligations of states and the international community to protect civilians in harm's way. It emphasizes the primary responsibility of the state to uphold human security. If states are unable or unwilling to act, then the option for the international community to intervene remains.

We further argue that there is an urgent need for a reorientation of traditional international security norms from a focus that is primarily state-centric to one where human security has a much more prominent role in international relations. The hundreds of millions of killed, displaced and otherwise abused civilians require the international community to recognize the criticality of human security if we claim to live in an increasingly civil and moral world. More importantly, this requires substantive and direct action by states supported by the international community to ameliorate the suffering of those most in need. We acknowledge the extreme difficulty in trying to implement human security initiatives when states have either failed or are on the verge of failing, but we argue that R2P means much more than reacting to state dysfunctionality in this particular context. This also means that serious attention must be directed to prevention before these events occur and before the desperate need to protect arises.

Structure of the Text

We begin our work by engaging in a debate on the state security versus human security paradigm. This is done in an effort to contextualize then highlight some of the important differences between and within these concepts. The field of international relations has traditionally been dominated by a state-centric approach. This approach has focused on state security in terms of the sovereignty norm and the fundamental principle of nonintervention by external powers into the affairs of a sovereign state. The modern concept of state sovereignty is entrenched in customary international law derived from agreements between European states as part of the Treaty of Westphalia (1648) and then codified by the Montevideo Convention (1933). The Treaty of Westphalia recognized the supreme authority of the state within a system of equal and independent units as a way of establishing peace in Europe after thirty years of war. The sovereignty norm established the centralized authority of the state over its territories and citizens, reflecting the formality of evolving interstate relations.

Westphalian thinking is based on the principles of territory, autonomy, control and mutual recognition. These principles have developed into the primary analytical assumptions or constitutive norms to provide a benchmark for conceptualizing the theory and the reality of state sovereignty that has since passed into different instruments in law. Traditional ideas of realpolitik security were, and mostly still are, subsumed under the all-encompassing umbra of state self-survival, political influence and the extension of power. A range of international laws, conventions and protocols were developed to substantiate individual states' rights by a system of mutual responsibility between states. The Westphalian concept of sovereignty implies that each state is obliged to protect its citizens from harm, but throughout history the state frequently was the perpetrator of abuse against its own people. Many states were unwilling or unable to safeguard their citizens from fear and violence. The debates on genocide, torture, mass killing and systematic rape as strategic tools to defeat enemies of the state were portrayed as political events primarily within states rather than between states.

In the international relations of the twentieth century, the state sovereignty norm came to be institutionalized in the League of Nations and in the UN Charter (1945). Article 2(1) of the UN Charter affirms that 'the Organization is based on the principle of the sovereign equality of all its Members'. Article 2(7) consolidates the sovereignty norm in international relations by prohibiting external interference in a state's domestic matters. The state sovereignty norm and the principle of nonintervention guided the international community throughout the Cold War period. This helped to institutionalize international relations in an attempt to provide order and stability between states. The traditional assumption of the state sovereignty norm and the nonintervention principle has been that a community of sovereign states will organize international order in an anarchic setting in order to protect each state's national interest and to safeguard the citizens of the state. However, the post–Cold War period fundamentally changed the international order and led to a debate on the application of the different norms and principles in international relations, particularly in relation to how states engaged with their own citizens.

From the 1990s, research on international relations, war and peace and security studies identified the growing problem of failing or failed states. These states are increasingly unable to uphold the core duties that define the sovereignty norms, but more importantly they neglect or deliberately disregard many of the fundamental needs and wants of their citizens. The impact on the domestic setting is that states on the verge of collapse have led to negative spillover effects in a regional context.[5] During the twentieth century, more than 262 million people have been killed in intrastate wars, a number six times higher than the number of casualties from interstate wars perpetrated by foreign governments.[6]

Symptomatic of what has become known as the 'failed state syndrome' is an inability to maintain law and order and the application of draconian responses to internal unrest by security forces and the military. Serious questions are raised about the fundamental legitimacy of corrupt and incompetent governments. Social disunity and a lack of reliable access to even the most basic human services such as electricity and clean drinking water contribute to civil unrest and dissatisfaction with government policies. Governments that are still able to function under these conditions react in different but mostly predictable ways. Responses include increasingly brutal suppression of dissent, martial law and a clampdown on the media and the public voice. Often there is specific targeting of various ethnic or cultural groups deemed to be barriers to the ambitions of the government or the ruling elite.

The post–Cold War conflicts and the failed state syndrome have repeatedly shown that a myopic focus on the sovereignty norm is an assurance of neither human security nor state security. Previous research has identified the importance of human security in the form of prevention coupled with protection but the notion of prevention has not been well developed in the practical sense for a variety of reasons. This introductory chapter contextualizes state security, human security and the protection and prevention ethos. It introduces the central themes addressed throughout the book.

Chapter 2 focuses on the different yet conjoined nature of state security and human security thinking. The end of the Cold War, the many decades of globalization and interdependence and the diffusion and promotion of human security norms have led to the development of new perceptions on how the international order should look now and in the future. It is no longer considered to be the absolute right of any regime to abuse its people and misuse its power purely for its own ends. Belligerents cannot simply assume impunity for their actions and the international community has a responsibility and obligation to intervene when states are unwilling or unable to effectively respond to human security. We highlight the differences in function and form between the responsibilities of statehood and the requirements of human security. Both state and human security are important, but we argue that human security even at the most fundamental human level – freedom from fear and freedom from want – should be a priority if we claim to be striving towards a more civil and moral society.

Chapter 3 then addresses the evolution and development of R2P and the increasing need to be much more proactive by focusing not only on protection but also on what can be done regarding prevention. We argue that there is a need for a reorientation in thinking away from the traditional focus on state-centric security norms to one where human security and prevention initiatives have a much more prominent role in international relations. The 2001 articles on state responsibility, adopted by the International Law Commission (ILC) and supported overwhelmingly by the UN General Assembly, provide a formal agenda for dealing with states that breach their international obligations. For example, Article 12 on state responsibility declares, 'There is a breach of an international obligation by a State when an act of that State is not in conformity with what is required of it by that obligation, regardless of its origin or character.'[7] Such an act may include one or more actions or omissions or a combination of both.

All human rights – civil, political, economic, social and cultural – impose negative and positive obligations on states to respond to violations of such rights. This chapter further develops the notion of R2P with a focus on the 1999 international intervention led by the North Atlantic Treaty Organization (NATO) against the Federal Republic of Yugoslavia (FRY) in Kosovo. This intervention was significant not only because NATO's military action was undertaken without sanction by the UN and specifically against opposition by Russia and China, but also because the intervention was deemed, at least in some quarters, to be required to satisfy certain obligations by the international community to directly address gross and deliberate human rights abuses in the region. NATO's intervention in Kosovo resulted in a great deal of controversy about the principle to protect and who has the responsibility to protect. The legality or otherwise of forcible intervention remains a contentious matter to this day.

Chapter 4 presents the relationship between international law and human security. International law, particularly international human rights law, is not nearly as well developed as national or domestic law. Inevitably there is conflict between states' rights, the national interest and the evolving requirements and obligations of international law. This is particularly so when international law challenges the long held sanctity of state sovereignty. Despite the embryonic nature of international legal norms in this area they are critical guideposts for human security in an ordered, civil and moral international community. Such laws and conventions need to be respected and taken seriously because only under these conditions are they able to properly fulfil their intended function. Yet nonadherence and noncompliance does not necessarily invalidate law, nor does it nullify the spirit or the intent of law. Custom and convention are derived from values that evolve over time. Whether such conventions then evolve into substantive law depends on many factors, but in the end international law remains as humanity's best hope for collective action and for collective purpose.

The international community and individual states have legal responsibilities and obligations that are articulated either in substantive international law or according to formative customary law. Deliberations and rulings of international legal entities – such as the International Criminal Court (ICC), the UN-established ad hoc criminal tribunals in Yugoslavia and Rwanda, special courts in Sierra Leone, Lebanon, Cambodia and East Timor, and the International Court of Justice (ICJ) – reflect the development of international legal norms that place constraints on the behaviour of governments and government representatives. International legal norms are a critical component of a civil and moral society. The doctrine of universal jurisdiction also allows domestic courts to try cases of the gravest crimes against humanity, even if they are committed by government leaders of other states and even if such crimes are not committed in the national territory.

Human rights treaties and associated monitoring bodies such as international and regional human rights courts have developed and concretized the concept of positive obligations. This implies that there is an overarching obligation on all states' parties to secure the most basic and essential human rights for everyone. Whether or not such action actually takes place, how it takes place and the highly selective nature associated with this process are all highly contested areas, but this does not negate the requirement or the importance of authoritative international norms and conventions that are intended as more than just general guidelines for how a state behaves towards its citizens.

Chapter 5 then looks at various norms, particularly democracy norms, that support or contest the relationship between state behaviour and human security. Democracy norms and democracy promotion demand that attention is directed at increasing the way that citizens are able to meaningfully engage in the public politic. Democratic governance promotes R2P by embedding popular representation, peace and prosperity as foundational elements in the democratic process. The increasing number of democratic regimes in the world has led to an expanded zone of peaceful relations between democracies. This in turn has resulted in improvements in social development and economic trade and commerce. Without the fundamentals of democratic progression states frequently subjugate their citizen's attempts to participate in the public politic. This stymies societal development and results in high levels of political uncertainty. An essential conflict-prevention strategy is to support and enhance the democratization processes within nondemocratic societies. It is the lack of representation, peace and prosperity that have come to challenge failing and failed states and have continued to challenge human security worldwide. Democratic governments are better providers of human security and may, through democracy promotion, become strategic tools to further push for R2P.

Chapter 6 is a case study on how some areas of human security have been realized after the 20 October 2011 overthrow of Muammar Gaddafi's regime in Libya. This important event was a demonstration of the rise of people power in Libya and the engagement of the international community in the removal of a tyrannical regime that had been in power for 42 years. On 17 March 2011, the United Nations Security Council voted by 10 to 0 with 5 abstentions to enact Security Council Resolution 1973, which created a no-fly zone in Libya under Chapter VII of the UN Charter.[8] The resolution called for an immediate ceasefire and an end to all violence and abuses against civilians. It demanded that the Libyan authorities comply with their obligations under international law including international humanitarian law and that they ensure the rapid and unimpeded passage of humanitarian assistance. The 2011 conflict in Libya raised many security dilemmas: how to protect the human security of Libyan civilians, state and regime security, who should intervene, how to protect foreign nationals and how to deal with the flood of refugees in neighbouring states. International law and practice do not provide clear guidelines on such complex situations and responses are contingent on many factors.

How the international community deals with states that clearly violate humanitarian norms is sporadic and highly selective, but the requirement for human security is a constant. The human need to live free from fear and want is fundamental. The important nexus between state security and human security is that each relies on the other, but the historically predominate focus on state security and the protection ethos means that preventative strategies are either poorly implemented or, more commonly, ignored altogether.

Chapter 2

STATE VERSUS HUMAN SECURITY: THE GREAT DEBATE

This chapter introduces the major conceptual developments in the research on security. It addresses the conceptualization of both state and human security in relation to empirical, political changes in the international landscape from post–World War II to contemporary times. The discussion throughout focuses on state versus human security and the bulk of studies made on the content of and links between these two. The overall aim is to contextualize and introduce the discussion of protection and prevention responsibilities in Chapter 3. We begin with an outline of what state-centricity means as a security concept. Traditional views are presented followed by contemporary observations regarding state capacity relative to what has become known as weak, failing and failed states. Empirical data from the World Bank, the UK Department for International Development, *Foreign Policy*, the Fund for Peace and Transparency International is presented and analysed as to its relevance to state capacity and capability.

The Kosovo crisis and the Rwanda crisis of the 1990s and the current situation in Somalia, Chad and Sudan are critically analysed in this chapter to provide practical examples of what has come to be known as the failed state syndrome. According to the data mentioned above, Somalia, Chad and Sudan are failed states, with up to thirty other states under critical stress. Our intention is to not only demonstrate the multiple levels of failure within such states but also to show how the international community responds to such humanitarian disasters. All these events had, and still have, a significant impact on post–Cold War discourse regarding how the international community should or could act in future to enhance regional stability and what to do to protect people from rapidly escalating, manmade humanitarian disasters. Aiden Hehir, in *Humanitarian Intervention After Kosovo*, provides an insightful analysis into the dangers of unregulated humanitarian intervention. He presents intervention in East Timor, Afghanistan, Iraq and Darfur as examples of the selective nature of humanitarian intervention into the affairs of failing or failed sovereign states. He argues that the debate surrounding intervention has stagnated due to restrictive theoretical parameters. That is, the pro-intervention perspective, or the 'normative thesis' based on some sort of moral imperative, clashes with the dominant counter perspective articulated by realists who are highly sceptical that states will ever act without some self-interest.[1] The conflicts in Africa and Europe show that states can fail in developing and developed regions alike. This further highlights the many political and social challenges in finding a workable consensus about what to do and how to respond as events escalate out of control.

Security, Sovereignty and the State

The security of the state and the obligations of the state towards its citizens have a long history. Justinian, the sixth-century Christian emperor of the Roman Empire, published his codex of laws to establish a cohesive scheme of rights and duties between citizen and state. Christianity, Judaism, Buddhism, Hinduism, Islam and other great religions of the world all endeavoured to establish moral codes of conduct based on divine law. From the late sixteenth century, attention was increasingly being directed at a political agenda based on 'the rights of man' or 'natural rights'. The influence and teachings of philosophers such as Hugo Grotius, Thomas Hobbes and John Locke in the seventeenth century further developed the idea that the duties and privileges of statehood and citizenship were more than abstract theological debates. The right to political participation and freedom of religious belief and observance was fundamental to the 1640 English Revolution and the Glorious Revolution of 1688 against oppressive governments. These important events led to the English Bill of Rights in 1689. In the eighteenth century, John Locke argued that part of God's natural law was that no one may harm anybody else in their health, life, liberty or possessions. Natural law was seen to establish the right to do whatever was required to protect such rights. This view constrained the role of government. No one could be subjected to another's rule unless they consented and a government's responsibility was to protect natural rights. This limited what the state could legitimately do and it gave its citizens the right to defy and overthrow a government that overstepped its 'legitimate' authority. The Declaration of Independence by the American colonies (1776) and the French Revolution (1787–99) asserted that governments were established by the consent of the people and if the people were not assured of their basic requirements for human dignity and survival, then the security of the state itself may be subject to serious threat. The contest between the obligations of the state and the rights of citizens evolved into particular views about what the legitimacy of statehood was based upon. A state-centric approach prioritizes state security, whereas a human-centric approach prioritizes human security.

The state-centric approach may be described in terms of state sovereignty, state survival and state military capacity. Matters of national security have traditionally been focused on the centralization of command authority and the monopolization of power over territory, resources and people. The protection of state sovereignty has frequently been defined by the military capacity of the state to protect itself from external threats in an anarchic setting of state relations. As a consequence, 'war has shaped the evolution of states and states have shaped the evolution of war'.[2] However, the 1990s saw a broadening of perspectives on security and a new conceptualization of what security actually means, whose security is being referred to and how overall security may be enhanced. International politics has seen a potential for transformative change with the development of a human security perspective on state sovereignty.[3] In *Norms, Institutions, and UN Reform: The Responsibility to Protect,* Jutta Brunnée and Stephen Toope claim that although the UN member states cannot agree on a definition of terrorism, nor can they agree on a set of criteria for the authorization of military force by the Security Council, they have agreed in the UN 2005 Summit Outcome Document on one important normative innovation that has the potential for transformative impact in international law and politics. Brunnée and Toope argue that this normative innovation is the responsibility to protect and that, given the long history of debates around humanitarian intervention and the implications of the concept of a responsibility to protect, its inclusion into the Summit Outcome Document is astonishing.[4] The debate over security has increased as more and more human atrocities and mass killings are linked to events within failing or failed states.

Security has traditionally been referred to as an 'essentially contested concept'.[5] The contemporary notion of security is vigorously debated, although a common definition refers to security as the alleviation of threats to cherished values. What those cherished values are and who defines them are all subject to a great deal of debate. Paul Williams in *Security Studies: An Introduction* argues that if security is indeed inextricably linked to values, then security is unavoidably political. That is, it plays a vital role in deciding who gets what, when and how in world politics.[6] Traditionally, most discussions about security have been predominately state-centric, focusing on sovereignty, territorial claim and military capacity. Security threats in the post–Cold War era have shown how some states have challenged the traditional notions of security by opening the discussion to include a much wider perspective on what security is supposed to mean.

Scholarly debates on international politics have traditionally been dominated by a state-centric approach.[7] This is the traditional or narrow perspective of security and it is closely related to state survival and the ability to protect core national interests against external threats. These core interests were, and in many cases still are, about national security, military capacity, territorial integrity and the ability of a state to centralize power to secure its borders against external enemies. The state-centric approach to security in contemporary times is primarily a consequence of World War II and the Cold War(s), but the fundamental ethos of state security has a much longer history that may be traced back to the Treaty of Westphalia (1648).

The notion of state sovereignty and nonintervention in international politics developed from the Westphalia Treaty of 1648 and led to an international law derived from agreements between states.[8] These agreements related to the rights and obligations of states and were codified by the Montevideo Convention in 1933. The notion of sovereignty of each individual state in international relations was further articulated in the Covenant of the League of Nations (1920) and later by the Charter of the UN (1945). The charter stresses state security and the supreme sovereignty of states in international relations. Security of statehood concerns the legal and legitimate aspects of a sovereign state towards others and it requires a centralized supreme authority, a defined territory and a population. The charter emphasizes that the sovereign state is responsible to protect its territory and its population. Article 2 (1) emphasizes the norm of state sovereignty: 'The Organization is based on the principle of the sovereign equality of all its Members'. Article 2 (7) stresses that 'nothing in the Charter shall authorize the United Nations to intervene in matters within domestic jurisdiction.'[9] Article 2 (7) also mentions the sovereignty norm in international relations. The only exception to the sovereignty norm was a decision made by the UN Security Council and the UN General Assembly under Chapter VII of the charter. Chapter VII allows external military intervention in the affairs of a sovereign state if there is a major threat to international peace and security. The UN Charter is representative of the security interests of powerful states more than a principled emphasis on human rights. Despite efforts by nongovernmental organizations for stronger provisions on human rights, the UN Charter neither proclaimed specific rights nor created concrete institutions for their enforcement. Ultimately, the human rights language in the UN Charter was formulated in very general terms as an aspirational list of principles and values.

The overarching security concept was defined through the lens of state antagonism shaped by an international context of war and the threat of war. From the 1950s, studies on international politics focused on states as the core units of analysis, which placed state security at the centre of attention. States were considered to be the most important political entities and their relations with each other comprised the international system. Security studies focused primarily on the security interests of states and their different capabilities to survive in an anarchic setting. The immediate post–World War II era also generated increasing attention to a more human-centric approach when the international community responded to state behaviour. The Nuremberg trials, the Genocide Convention and various human rights treaties weakened the exclusive state focus of security issues.

The Cold War(s) were a competition between Soviet and American spheres of influence and reflected the primacy of state interests over all other interests. This was not only a military standoff between the two major powers, but a fierce rivalry between fundamental ideologies and global economic influence, both of which were deemed to be crucial to the security of the state. This contest included the European power struggle between West and East Germany, as well as low-intensity warfare between the Great Power proxies in Africa, East Asia and Latin America. These events promoted a significant amount of scholarly attention, particularly in the field of foreign policy analysis.

Security was perceived through the lenses of states' interests, strategies and capabilities in international politics. This led to numerous empirical studies of how foreign policy was conducted and why, what the main objectives of states were, and how foreign policy decision-making was implemented. Richard Merritt in *Foreign Policy Analysis* suggests that foreign policy making is essentially the task of devising strategies that utilize a nation-state's capabilities to achieve the goals its leaders set. He argues that what the nation-state's capacities are and how they are perceived, how decision makers mobilize these capabilities, who the individuals and groups that play significant roles are, what their patterns of interaction are, and what they perceive their valued goals to be are all sometimes intractable core concerns for foreign policy formulators and for foreign policy analysts.[10] Research also focused on how the foreign policy agenda was decided upon, what political entities (political, military and bureaucratic) influence foreign policy agendas, what kind of values should constitute national interests and what factors impact foreign policy making.[11] Another theme that engaged researchers, policy analysts and policy makers was how the traditional interactions between states in a global setting worked. Here the focus was on state relations and how a stable international order was idealized and maintained between and among unipolar, bipolar and multipolar entities.[12]

The bipolar Cold War order provided an uneasy peace, although such peace was at the point of a gun. The Cold War was about a balance of power between the United States and the Soviet Union. This was a negative peace in the sense that a lack of direct conflict was essentially based on a common strategy of mutually assured destruction (MAD) should one of the superpowers do more than merely point the gun. The end of the Cold War changed the international order dramatically.[13] It led to an uncertain era as the Soviet Union collapsed and the United States, now a militarily and economically strained hegemonic power, faced multiple challenges from the rise of competitor powers in China, India and elsewhere. Security analysts remained essentially focused on the continued importance of the state and adhered to familiar assumptions about the sovereignty norm.

Historically, states have claimed the right to conduct their own domestic politics without interference by external powers. International politics is to a large extent organized around the norms of state sovereignty and the principle of nonintervention in state affairs.[14] This aims to provide predictable responses and it legitimizes action taken by the state to protect itself in what is seen to be essential for the promotion of international order and stability generally.

The principle of nonintervention remained the glue that bound together much of the thinking in the security studies field. The sovereignty norm and the principle of nonintervention have traditionally been codified to reflect the superior power and rights of the state over all others. The principle of noninterference from external powers into the affairs of sovereign states was fundamental to how individual states saw their place in the world and how collectives of states in organizations such as the United Nations saw their role as protectors of state sovereignty.[15]

The state sovereignty norm may be defined by distinguishing its two components of internal sovereignty and external sovereignty.[16] Internal sovereignty is the state's authority over its territory, population and resources. Based on the state-centric model it is up to everyone to support the centralized power of the state in order to provide domestic security. An essential ingredient of internal sovereignty was, and remains, the monopolization of force. External sovereignty relates to the state's military capacity to protect its territorial borders and its capacity to engage in diplomatic relations. Diplomatic engagement includes the right to make treaties and to seek other forms of reciprocity designed to enhance the security of the state.

The end of the Cold War challenged many of the traditional assumptions regarding the role of the state and how international politics and intrastate relationships would be conducted in the future. The sudden collapse of the Soviet Union both as a military force and as an economical power surprised everyone. Equally unforeseen was the totality of the collapse and the speed at which it happened, but also that the disintegration of the Soviet empire occurred almost without a shot being fired.[17] These events demonstrate the fragility of the modern sovereign state when both internal and external pressures combine until a tipping point is reached, resulting in the collapse of the state. They also demonstrate a general lack of understanding regarding when or how such tipping points arise.

State and Human Security in Weak, Failing or Failed States

Many states have failed throughout history, but the collapse of the Soviet Union and the end of the Cold War raised a number of important questions for the contemporary world. The questions relate to the overall security of the state.[18] The international community has become increasingly preoccupied with the phenomenon usually dubbed the 'failed state syndrome'. The failed state syndrome implies a number of observable conditions and commonalities that indicate when a state is either well on the way to failing or perhaps already becoming a failed state.

Definitions and understanding of what this term means vary, but most researchers and commentators simplistically define such states to be in opposition to successful states. Successful states are deemed to have certain characteristics and capacities that failed states do not. Below we endeavour to present in detail the characteristics of weak, failing and failed states. The progression from weak, to failing, to failed state is not a clear-cut process, so the research has tended to concentrate on failed states in comparison to successful states. This is useful as a comparative process, but it also assumes that there is some sort of progression from state weakness to state failure. An alternate view is that many, if not most, failed states were never successful in the first place, so one must not only take care that success or failure is properly defined, but also that there is not an automatic transitional link from one condition to another.

Most research on state capacity has been based on the Weberian concept of what a successful state is supposed to be; that is, a centralized authority that has a legitimate monopoly to control and regulate geographical territory and population through established state institutions.[19] A functioning state has what may be termed a high level of state capacity. Francis Fukuyama refers to the ability of the state to support social services for its citizens and the capacity of the legislative, executive and judicial branches to perform, implement and uphold law and order.[20] The functionality of the state may be understood as the capability of the state to perform effectively within its territorial domains.

State capacity therefore relates to the willingness and capability of the state apparatus to carry out government policy and to respond to the needs and wants of its citizens.[21] Such a definition opens up a continuum from lower to higher levels of state capacity. Weak states have medium to low levels of state capacity, while failing states have low to very low levels of state capacity. Failed states have very little, if any, state capacity. The danger for weak states is that they may succumb to internal and external pressures where state capacity becomes so degraded that the state is in danger of failing or even totally collapsing.[22]

A decade after the end of the Cold War and the long-established bipolar order, many states faced both challenges from within and pressures from without on matters relating to state security. The proliferation of nuclear weapons, civil wars and other insurgencies, economic stress and decreasing access to essential resources all contributed to challenge the security of the state. Environmental degradation, concerns over climate change and mass population movements place increasing demands on states, resulting in a shift from traditional state-versus-state pressures to domestic, regional and global criticalitics.[23]

There are a number of commonalities regarding the geographical location of weak states, on why these states are failing and what the regional spillover effects may be as a result of these events.[24] Most weak or failing states are located in poorly developed, postcolonial regions, and while they have some state institutional and structural capacity these are often severely challenged by an underdeveloped economic base. They have minimal technological and resource development, public and private corruption is widespread and essential civil infrastructure is lacking. Weak states may uphold some of the basic institutions and duties of a sovereign state, yet there are significant challenges in providing the citizens of the state with their social and economic needs. There may also be the occurrence or reoccurrence of conflict between disparate groups and warring factions within the state.

The state capacity of failing states is more vulnerable than weak states because their governmental structures are on the verge of collapse and the government is increasingly incapable of supplying or responding to the basic needs of their citizens. Failing states can no longer guarantee the security of the state and they have limited capacity in the political, economic and security sectors. Often this is due to an armed opposition to the centralized authority, which challenges state capacity by actively trying to usurp governmental power. The failing state may be challenged by armed forces from abroad or by paramilitary groups from within, all of which undermines the state's territorial control and authority over its people. State institutions may still partially contribute to the economic profile of the state, provide some of the most basic social services and have a degree of political legitimacy; however the degree of societal engagement and the capacity to maintain the body politic is very limited. These states are frequently characterized by governmental corruption, widespread societal criminality, poverty and general political chaos.[25]

There are three core state functions that severely challenge failing states. One of the most essential of these functions is the provision of *socioeconomic services*, which are required to address economic growth and to support social development.[26] An inability to provide a reasonable level of living standard leads to a capacity gap that often promotes internal conflict where socioeconomic injustices are expressed unequally along ethnicity, clans, religious adherence or class divisions.[27] The lack of socioeconomic capacity amplifies social unrest by citizens against the state regime, which further undermines political unity.[28]

Another essential function of a state is to provide *security* by having the capacity to monopolize the legitimate use of force against external or internal threats. The absence of such a capacity leads to a security gap where armed domestic groups challenge state power or the state has great difficulty when directly confronted by external threats.[29] *Representation* is an important third function. State legitimacy is derived from the people and when states fail to protect political rights and civil liberties then a legitimacy gap develops that may threaten the overall security of the state. This in turn leads to the state resorting to the use of force, coercion and other forms of oppression in order to secure its political power base.[30] By comparison, strong states have more open representative, transparent and accountable governance and they tend to exhibit a level of political and social cohesion where citizens have some meaningful capacity to participate in their own governance.[31] An inability by the government to provide full capacity in one or more of these areas is due to weaknesses in institutional settings and an erosion of state capacity.[32]

Failed states are states that are no longer capable of fulfilling the basic functionality of a sovereign state and state capacity is severely or totally degraded. These states no longer control their geographical territory, nor do they have a monopoly over the legitimate use of force within the state. Centralized governmental authority and legitimacy is no longer present and the government is incapable of making collective decisions on behalf of the majority of its citizens. The state is considered to have failed when state structures have collapsed as a consequence of armed conflicts over authority and the armed opposition has been unable to replace the established regime. The consequence of such a failed state structure is an inability to deliver even the most basic of societal services, infrastructure development is non-existent and the state cannot provide a minimal level of human security for its citizens.[33]

After the Cold War, the major powers and the UN soon realized that the primary challenge to a peaceful international order no longer came from interstate disputes and that domestic conflict, civil wars and other internal insurgencies threatened local and regional stability.[34] The collapse of the Soviet Union resulted in the fragmentation of the Soviet empire and the establishment of fifteen new sovereign states. The security of these new states was immediately challenged by the internal demands and ambitions of many different ethnic and cultural groups. Russia remains extremely reluctant to fully recognize or respect the autonomy of many of these new states. The 1991 wars in the Caucasus between Armenia and Azerbaijan over

Nagorno-Karabakh were followed by the Russian invasion of Chechnya in 1994 and 1999.[35]

Elsewhere, the 1990s Balkan Wars and the subsequent breakup of Yugoslavia further came to symbolize a heightened level of insurgency, civil war and violent opposition to the established order that followed the death of Josip Tito in 1980. Secessionist movements in Slovenia and Croatia increased their demands for independence from Yugoslavia, resulting in widespread conflict and open warfare: Slovenia and Croatia in 1991, Bosnia in 1992, Kosovo in 1999 and increasing political tension in Macedonia throughout the late 1990s.[36] Two events in particular highlighted the international community's growing concern about regional instability resulting in social upheaval and humanitarian disasters of mammoth proportions. One of these events was the 1994 genocide in Rwanda and the other was the Balkan Wars resulting in the disintegration of Yugoslavia. The following discussion aims to present these two events as examples of the progression from a failing state to a failed state. This is followed by the examples of state failure in Somalia, Chad and Sudan.

Human Security During and After the Rwandan Genocide and the Balkan Wars

The history of Rwanda since independence from Belgium in 1962 is one of ongoing tribal tension between the minority Tutsis who had controlled power in Rwanda for centuries and the majority Hutus who had come to power during the civil wars of 1959–62.[37] In 1990, the Tutsi rebel group calling themselves the Rwandan Patriotic Front (RPF) supported by neighbouring Uganda launched sustained military attacks on northern Rwanda in an attempt to destabilize President Juvénal Habyarimana and the Hutu-led government. The civil war raged for three years until a ceasefire and peace treaty based on the Arusha Accords resulted in an uneasy power-sharing arrangement with a Transitional Broad-Based Government (TBBG) coalition between the Tutsis and Hutus.

The fragile peace very quickly collapsed after the displacement, imprisonment and killing of thousands of Hutus by Tutsis spurred on by the active military arm of the RPF. In the spring of 1994, the Habyarimana was assassinated, leading to a sustained outburst of violence in Rwanda. Over 1 million Tutsis and Tutsi sympathizers were stabbed, shot, clubbed, set alight or beaten to death by rampaging mobs of Hutus. Those directing the killings were supporters of the former single ruling party, the Republican National Movement for Democracy and Development known as the Mouvement Républicain National pour la Démocratie et le Développement (MRND). This organization's youth wing, known locally as the Interahamwe (they who attack together), was directly responsible for organizing and leading many of the Hutu mobs during the genocide.

Also directly responsible for the many organized massacres in Rwanda was the Coalition pour la Défense de la République (CDR). This was an exclusively Hutu political party with a youth wing known as the Impuzamugambi (they who have the same goal). The CDR and the Impuzamugambi orchestrated a violent campaign against any Hutus who supported the sharing of power with the Tutsi-dominated RPF. Supporters or sympathizers of the MRND and CDR in conjunction with members of the security forces carried out the massacres in Rwanda during 1994. The Presidential Guard, the Gendarmerie, the regular army and local government police were all involved in the genocide, with the aim of destroying any population groups viewed as potential supporters of the RPF and the multiethnic parties opposed to the MRND and CDR.

The small UN Assistance Mission to Rwanda (UNAMIR) led by General Roméo Dallaire was totally unprepared to deal with the explosion of violence or its aftermath.[38] Before the massacre, Dallaire warned the UN about the escalating violence taking place in April, May and June of 1994. However, the Security Council ignored the warnings and prepared to scale down and withdraw the 1,500 UNAMIR troops.[39] When it was clear that the genocide had started, the UN secretary-general proposed a small intervention force of 5,500 troops to be sent to Rwanda, but the US administration and President Clinton actively campaigned to dissuade the African countries that were prepared to participate from intervening. The administration still had fresh and very painful memories of the UN-sponsored December 1992 and May 1993 US peacekeeping intervention debacle in Somalia (Operation Restore Hope).[40] Touko Piiparinen argues that the key consideration by the UN was less the rescue of civilians than the decision over whether intervention in Rwanda would bestow credit or disgrace, success or failure on the organization.[41]

The failure to act in Rwanda was due to a variety of factors, including the reluctance of France as a colonial power in the region to become involved in stopping the conflict.[42] The major powers (the US and China among others) refused to recognize that the ongoing massacres in Rwanda were indeed genocide as this would have obliged the UN Security Council to act directly. The US was particularly reluctant to assume any such obligation based on its disastrous interventionist failures in Somalia in 1992, where the UN authorized the US to militarily intervene in order to stop the widespread killings and human rights abuses. The most important lesson to be taken from the US experience in Somalia is that a clear political objective is a necessary but insufficient precondition for any successful military operation. There was no clear political objective for external intervention in Rwanda. The 1994

Map 2.1 Rwanda, Burundi and neighbouring states

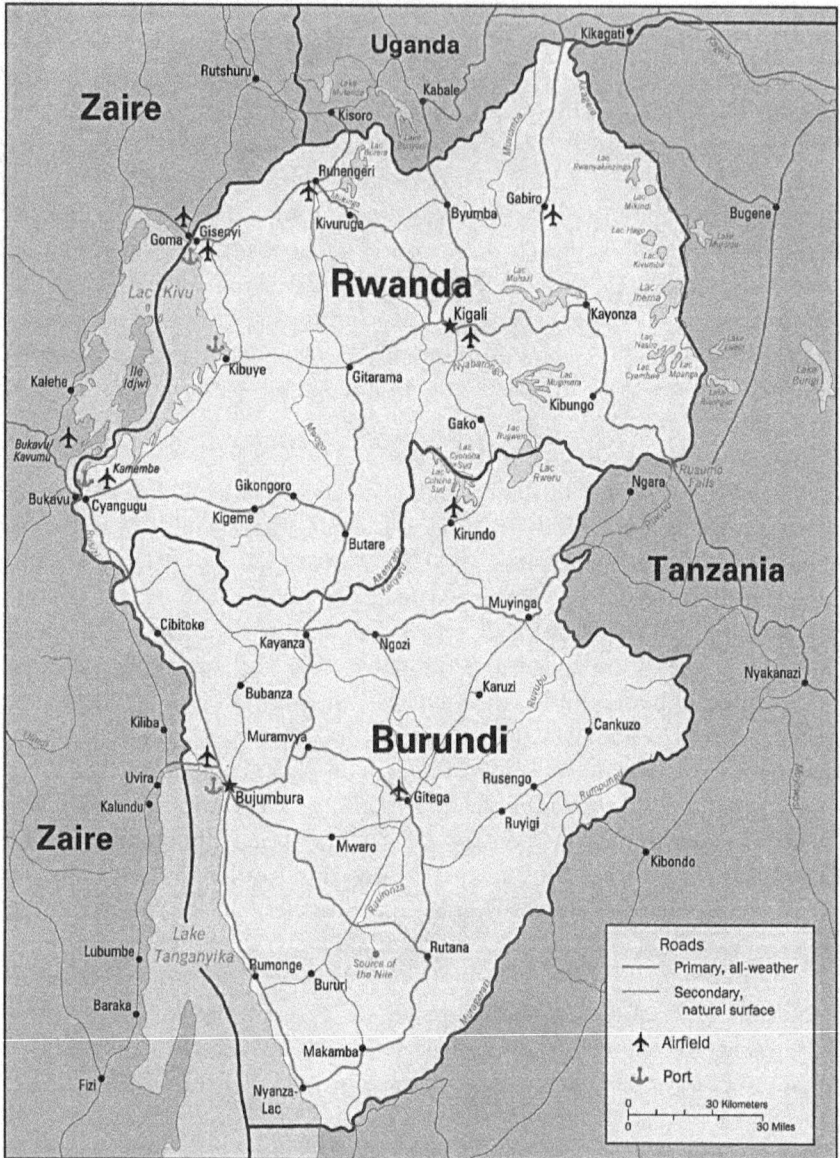

Rwanda genocide led to confusion and inactivity with no serious international effort to stop what was clearly developing into a humanitarian disaster.[43] The Rwandan war spilled over to Zaire, another failing state, which resulted in the overthrow of the Mobuto regime and escalated other regional and local wars.

The most troublesome and violent political event in Europe in the post–Cold War era was the collapse of the Socialist Federal Republic of Yugoslavia and the subsequent wars of secession in the provinces of Yugoslavia. The Federal Republic under the leadership of Josip Tito between 1945 and 1980 consisted of six republics (Serbia, Croatia, Slovenia, Bosnia–Herzegovina, Montenegro and Macedonia) and two largely autonomous provinces (Kosovo and Vojvodina). Map 2.2 shows Kosovo and the neighbouring states. The death of Tito in 1980 led to significant changes in Yugoslavia's political structure, where the constitution of 1974 had established a rotating presidential system that represented each of the provinces in the former Yugoslavia in turn. This cumbersome arrangement suited almost nobody and ultimately led to virulent nationalistic demonstrations and increasingly strident demands for independence.

In 1990, all six Yugoslav republics held popular elections where the dominant communist parties suddenly lost power everywhere except for Serbia and Montenegro. The leader of the Socialist Party of Serbia, Slobodan Milošević, retained power in these two provinces. Most of these elections triggered further nationalistic sentiments that paved the way for an increasing number of secessionist movements with the ultimate goal of breaking away from the Federal Republic. In December 1990, Slovenia voted for independence in a referendum quickly followed by declarations of independence from Bosnia–Herzegovina and Croatia. The UN Security Council passed Resolution 777 on 19 September 1992, which declared that the Socialist Federal Republic of Yugoslavia had ceased to exist and by implication that Croatia and Slovenia were now independent from the Federal Republic. This forced Belgrade to form the new Federal Republic of Yugoslavia (FRY), consisting of Bosnia–Herzegovina, Serbia, Montenegro, Kosovo and Vojvodina. This did not stop Bosnia–Herzegovina and Kosovo continuing their separatist ambitions, which resulted in increasingly brutal suppression by Serbia. The Serbs refused to recognize Bosnia–Herzegovina as an independent state and a breakaway from Kosovo – the historical and traditional heartland of the Serb people – was unthinkable.

The 1992–95 civil wars between the central power authorities in Serbia and the breakaway states throughout Yugoslavia already engulfed most of the Balkan region. This caused a great deal of concern in the EU about the mounting humanitarian disaster, but also that the conflagration could spread even further. By 1995, it was clear that the EU alone was incapable of sponsoring effective peacemaking efforts in the region. The negotiations in Bosnia had failed and the military presence of the United Nations Protection Force (UNPROFOR), whose troops were provided primarily by Britain and France, needed political and military backup from the US. The Dayton Peace

Agreement in 1995, overseen and consolidated by the UN, the International Monetary Fund (IMF), NATO, the EU and the Organisation for Security and Co-operation in Europe (OSCE), was a direct result of long and hard negotiation efforts by the US diplomat Richard Holbrooke.

The agreement forced Slobodan Milošević to retreat from Bosnia–Herzegovina after more than three years of open warfare and it imposed a general ceasefire throughout the Balkans.[44] The EU demanded full compliance with the Dayton Agreement; Bosnia, Croatia and Yugoslavia were closely monitored and any support given by external powers was to be linked to the implementation of the Peace Accords.[45] One reason among many for the effectiveness of the negotiations leading up to the Dayton Accords was the US decision to deal directly with Slobodan Milošević as the single spokesperson for the Serbian minorities in the former Yugoslavia and to exclude Kosovo from the agenda. This was a short-term tactical strategy to stop the long-running wars in Bosnia and Croatia, but this had long-term negative effects as the war in Kosovo developed in 1998–99 between secession movements in Kosovo and the Serbian authorities in Belgrade. These events and outcomes are further discussed in Chapter 3.

The Dayton Agreement halted the long-running Bosnia war, but the agreement bypassed Kosovo. The exclusion of talks on Kosovo at the Dayton meeting was one reason for the escalation of war in Kosovo in the late 1990s. This was partly due to the already tense situation in the region, which was too much for the overloaded international community to deal with. Negotiating with President Milošević to halt the ongoing atrocities in Bosnia and Croatia was seen to be the priority. President Milošević agreed to force the Bosnian Serbs to negotiate and comply with the conditions set out in the Dayton Agreement and was therefore perceived to be the strongest leader in the region – one who had to be involved and whose support of the agreement had to be ensured so that peace could be restored. Including the crisis in Kosovo in the negotiations would depict Milošević as the enemy and thus jeopardize the negotiations and the entire agreement.

The UN and the international community generally were divided on what to do about the escalating crisis in Kosovo after the disintegration of Yugoslavia in the late 1990s. In Kosovo, events reached a flashpoint during the summer of 1998 when Albanians, led by the Kosovo Liberation Army (KLA), mounted mass protests against Serbian rule. Serb police and army reinforcements were despatched to crush the uprising.[46] The first major massacre in Kosovo occurred in the spring of 1998 in the Drenica region, when 51 civilians were killed by Serb forces in retaliation for a KLA provocation. Open conflict between Serbian military and police forces and Kosovar Albanian forces in 1998 resulted in the deaths of over 1,500 Kosovar Albanians and forced

Map 2.2 Kosovo and neighbouring states

400,000 people from their homes. In January 1999, there were further massacres by Serb forces of Kosovo civilians in the village of Račak. By late 1998 and early 1999, events in Kosovo were rapidly escalating out of control with heavily armed Serb forces moving into the province.

The UN was incapable of deciding what to do about what was happening in Kosovo and NATO argued that the escalating violence in Kosovo warranted humanitarian intervention regardless of the internal disagreements within the UN Security Council. NATO declared its right to act under UN Resolution 1199, which had imposed the demand on Serbia for a general ceasefire. On 24 March 1999, NATO began its eleven-week air campaign against the FRY without explicit UN approval.[47] The former secretary-general of NATO Javier Solana stated at the Atlantic Council on 28 March 1999 that NATO's objective was to prevent more human suffering and more repression and violence against the civilian population of Kosovo.[48] The intervention by NATO resulted in the forced withdrawal of Serbian forces from Kosovo and the installation of an interim government by the UN in Kosovo.

The FRY changed its structure in 2003 to include Serbia and Montenegro after Montenegro's referendum in May 2006 that resulted in its declaration of independence from the federation.[49] In the case of Kosovo, the US, France and the UK argued for UN intervention to stop a potential genocide from occurring, but again the UN Security Council disagreed about what to do regarding the rapidly deteriorating situation in the region. By the beginning of April 1999, Serb activity in Kosovo had resulted in 226,000 refugees arriving in Albania, 125,000 in the former Yugoslav Republic of Macedonia and 33,000 in Montenegro.[50]

The international community was faced with the reality that the UN Security Council would veto any direct military action. After the Serbs' refusal to comply with the Rambouillet peace proposal (by now a peace ultimatum), the US and NATO waited for the withdrawal of the OSCE monitors and on 24 March 1999 started Operation Allied Force, the seventy-eight-day bombing campaign against Serbia, which swiftly resulted in an end to military hostilities in the region. The decision to launch a large-scale bombing campaign against Yugoslavia in defence of non-Serbs in Kosovo was a defining moment for NATO; it had acted not out of any threat to its collective defence, but ostensibly for wider humanitarian reasons.[51] A contentious issue relating to NATO's involvement in Kosovo is the mandate question. That is, under what authority or on which legal basis may NATO threaten or use military force other than for its own collective defence?

During the early 1990s, most NATO members believed that NATO should not act outside its own explicit mandate for collective self-defence without specific authorization from the UN, but today views differ sharply about the role, capability and authority of the UN and other organizations in legitimizing NATO action.[52] The Kosovo conflict brought to a head what had until very recently been a largely theoretical argument about when a state or collection of states may act unilaterally to address a humanitarian crisis. In Kosovo, NATO acted without a specific UN mandate to do so. In April 1999, at the NATO alliance's summit held in Washington, DC, the NATO members acknowledged that the UN Security Council has the primary responsibility for the general maintenance of international peace and security, but they were notably silent on specifically who, if anyone, can authorize NATO action in non–Article 5 situations.

The Kosovo crisis of 1998–99 and subsequent NATO action, justified on the basis of a humanitarian need to protect the Kosovo people, provoked new political, legal and scholarly debates on the subject of humanitarian interventions and the role of the state regarding its human security obligations.[53] Direct intervention by external powers into the affairs of a sovereign state has always been contentious, but increasingly such intervention has been justified on the grounds of national security after the 11 September terrorist attacks in the US.[54]

There is an increasing trend to invoke humanitarian reasons as well as national security reasons to justify intervention.[55] Traditionally, international peace operations had missed out on seriously addressing the problem of failing states or dealing with the associated humanitarian disasters as a result of these states being in various stages of collapse.[56] The UN was primarily involved in peacekeeping operations to oversee border disputes, supervise elections and act as a human barrier separating the warring factions. Most UN peacekeeping operations were based on the requirement for a formal agreement by the conflicting parties to allow peacekeeping activities to occur, and UN peacekeepers were only mandated to use violence in self-defence.

Over the last few decades, the UN has been faced by many new security challenges where UN peace operations have become much more complex in nature. Peacekeeping evolved into a combination of traditional peacekeeping with peacemaking and peace enforcement. This has resulted in UN involvement in local and regional disputes without the consent of the protagonists.[57] The evolving nature of peacekeeping has led to an increasing number of operations and interventions by the UN, resulting in a record number of peace enforcement missions from 1990 to 2000. These interventions were directly aimed at ending violent domestic conflicts and promoting peace in places such as Southeast Asia, sub-Sahara Africa, the Middle East and Southeast Europe. Numerous diplomatic initiatives were initiated by the US, the UK, the Organization of African Unity (OAU) – now called the African Union – and the EU in order to support peace enforcement, not just peacekeeping by invitation only in these regions.[58]

The post-conflict UN missions in East Timor (Timor-Leste) and Kosovo highlighted another development in extended peacekeeping that involved a harder-edged peace enforcement doctrine. Map 2.3 shows East Timor. These missions were mandated with a wide scope of responsibilities including a reiteration of the UN's capacity to assume trusteeship over territories once major conflict had ceased. The trusteeship system replaced the mandate system of the League of Nations. In 1999, a trusteeship and transitional authority over East Timor and Kosovo was announced by the UN.[59] UN Resolution 1272 established the United Nations Transitional Administration in East Timor (UNTAET) and UN Resolution 1244 established the United Nations Interim Administration Mission in Kosovo (UNMIK), empowering the UN in East Timor and Kosovo to be responsible for all branches of government.

The determination of UN trusteeship status of these two territories was unique in UN peacekeeping history for two reasons.[60] Firstly, this was a new step in UN legal practice, where the UN has formally assumed full responsibility as a territorial administrator with the intention that such administration be used as an instrument for conflict resolution. This has only occurred once before, with the 1996 United Nations Transitional Authority in Eastern Slovenia (UNTAES). Secondly, the request for trusteeship was not received from East Timor or Kosovo, as stipulated by the processes in Article 79, Chapter XII of the UN Charter, but directly from the UN Security Council.

The management of failing or failed states by the international community today remains a significant challenge. Not only are local and regional civil conflicts increasing in number and ferocity, but the question of whether or not external powers should become directly involved is fraught with legal and moral difficulties. Such difficulties include the need to confront the traditional sanctity of statehood and sovereignty issues and at the same time to address the appalling human rights violations when states are in various stages of dysfunctionality.

On the African continent, the Democratic Republic of the Congo, Nigeria, Rwanda, Somalia, Sierra Leone, Sudan and Uganda continue to face serious internal conflicts between authoritarian regimes and their opponents. Most recently, states in turmoil as a result of the Arab Spring uprisings include Tunisia, Libya and Egypt. Most of these states have for decades faced political upheaval and violent military clashes between different ethnic and tribal groups and there is little indication that long-standing animosities are being resolved. Map 2.4 shows the African states. Various international organizations have classified certain states to be either fragile states or failed states.

The World Bank has identified 30 states under critical stress, the UK Department for International Development considered that there were 46 fragile states, the CIA identified 20 failing states and the US-based Fund for Peace classified 60 states as being vulnerable to violent internal conflict.[61] Such classifications are based on a number of different and complex variables, not only within and between these organizations' data sets, but in the methodology and processes in accumulating the raw data in the first place.[62]

Transparency International provides an extensive data set that focuses on levels of corruption. The Corruption Perceptions Index (CPI) measures

Map 2.3 East Timor (Timor-Leste) and neighbouring states

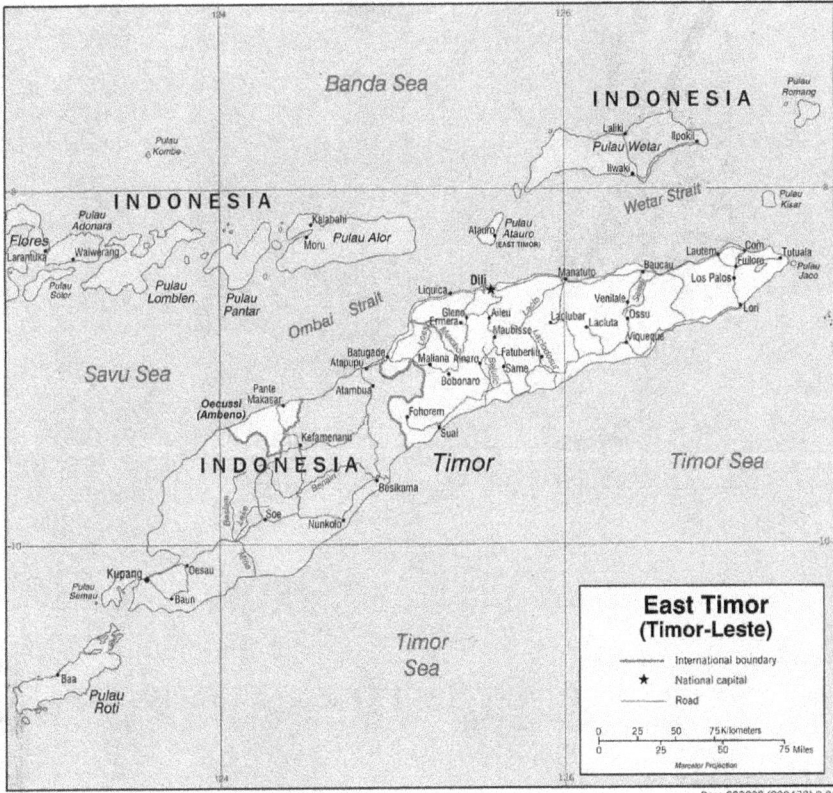

the perceived levels of public sector corruption in a given country and the result is presented as a composite index. The data is compiled from different expert and business surveys and the CPI scores 180 countries on a scale from 0 (highly corrupt) to 10 (highly clean). Global and regional data sets are also available from Transparency International.

The World Bank's Worldwide Governance Indicators (WGI) project covers over two hundred states, countries and territories. The WGI project attempts to measure aggregate and individual governance indicators derived from 35 data sources provided by 32 different private sector organizations plus responses from citizen and firm surveys. The project measures six dimensions of governance: voice and accountability, political stability and absence of violence/terrorism, government effectiveness, regulatory quality, rule of law and control of corruption. Performance in each of these areas is measured in units ranging from about −2.5 to 2.5, then the data is normalized into a 0–1 scale to develop distributed (aggregate) indicators.

Map 2.4 Africa

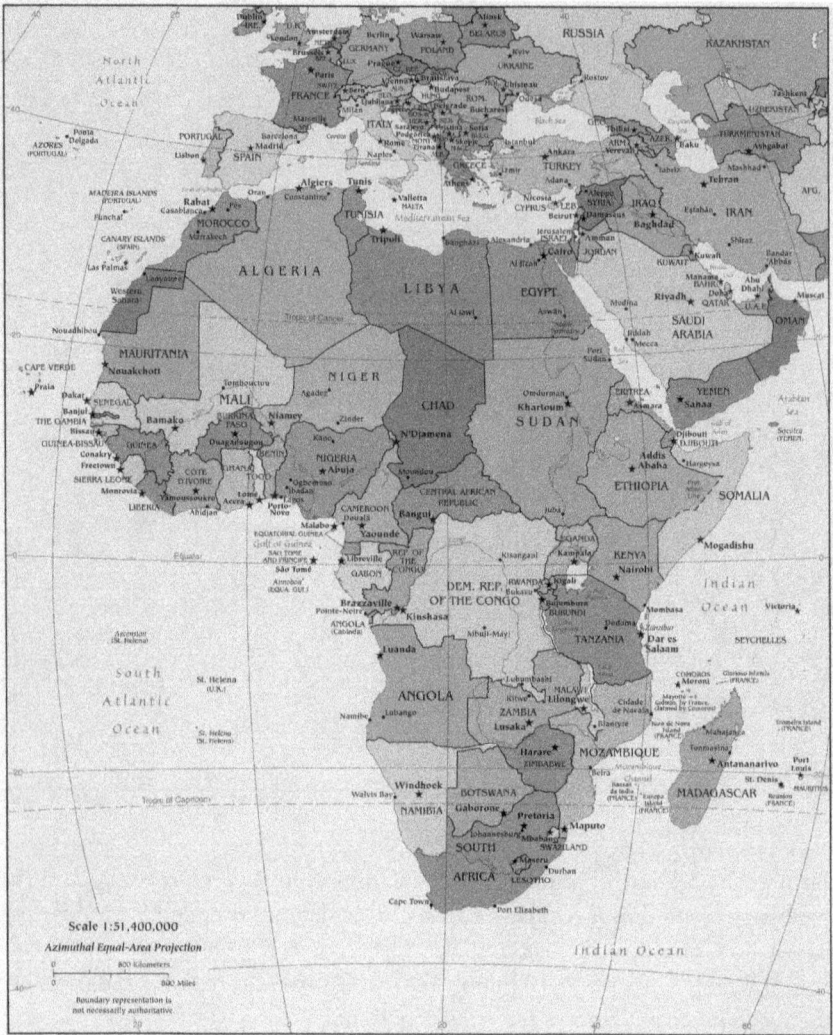

Voice and accountability measure the perceptions and reflections of citizens on the extent to which they are able to participate in selecting their governments, freedom of expression, freedom of association and a free media. The political stability and absence of violence/terrorism category measures the likelihood that the government would be destabilized or overthrown by violent, unconstitutional means. Government effectiveness measures perceptions of the quality of public and civil services, the degree of their independence from political pressures, the quality of government policy and the credibility of the government's commitment to such policies. Regulatory quality is a measure of the ability of the government to permit and promote private sector development. This measure aims to reflect the soundness of government policies that support these initiatives. The likelihood of crime and violence, the quality of law and order initiatives and the effectiveness of an independent judiciary are measured under the rule of law category. Control of corruption measures the extent to which public power is exercised for private gain and corruption.

Foreign Policy, together with the Fund for Peace, annually publish their Failed States Index. This index attempts to measure the condition of a state based on 12 indicators that are grouped into 3 dimensions: social, economic and political. Social indicators consist of increasing demographic pressures, significant movement of refugees or internally displaced persons and the legacy of vengeance-seeking group grievances or group paranoia. Economic indicators include uneven economic development along group lines and sharp and/or severe economic decline. Political indicators in this index attempt to measure the criminalization and/or delegitimization of the state, the progressive deterioration of public services and the suspension or arbitrary application of the rule of law. They also measure widespread violation of human rights, a security apparatus operating as a state within a state, the rise of factionalized elites and the intervention of other states or external political actors.

Together these 12 indicators try to provide a measurement of the social, economic and political status of 177 states. The 2012 eighth edition of the Failed States Index identified Somalia as the number one failed state according to the index rankings. Somalia, the Democratic Republic of the Congo, Sudan, Chad, Zimbabwe, Afghanistan, Haiti, Yemen, Iraq and the Central African Republic were ranked as the ten most vulnerable states.[63] Somalia, the Democratic Republic of the Congo and Sudan were ranked sequentially as the top three failed states in the index.

Prior to 1960, Somalia was governed under a complicated power-sharing arrangement between British Somaliland, Italian Somaliland and French Somaliland (now Djibouti). Somalia achieved independence in 1960 but has been confronted with very high levels of political tension and civil warfare ever since. Oppressive, corrupt governments and vicious interclan rivalries have resulted in extreme levels of human rights abuses against many Somali citizens. In 1992, the UN authorized the US to militarily intervene in Somalia in order to stop the widespread killings and human rights abuses. The mandate by the United Nations Operation in Somalia (UNOSOM) was to disarm all the factions in Somalia and to secure the delivery of aid to the Somali people. However, Somali warlords that had previously fought against each other then formed an alliance and turned their weapons against the 38,000 UN peacekeepers.

By the mid-1990s, this had resulted in over 250,000 Somali deaths and more than 250,000 people being forced from their homes by the Sudanese government and related paramilitary groups. Disarming the warring Somali factions failed and very little of the much-needed aid was delivered to the Somali people. Powerful Somali clans controlled the distribution of resources and the majority of the aid ended up in the hands of Somali warlords. New internal factional wars erupted immediately after the failure of the peacekeeping mission, resulting in a further displacement of over 1 million people and forced more than 10 per cent of the population to flee the country.

The ongoing UN failures in Somalia raised many serious questions about how the international community should or even can respond to failing states that brutalize their own people. Early in 2000 and again in 2004, several attempts were made by various factions and clans within Somalia to set up a transitional government, but these attempts also failed in part due to external pressures from Ethiopia and Eritrea, who supported opposing clans and different ethnic groups. Internal violence and civil war continued with the Republic of Somaliland and Puntland claiming autonomy from Somalia in 1991. Map 2.5 shows Somalia.

Somalia has lacked a central sovereign government for almost two decades. In 2009, Sheikh Sharif Ahmed became president, but he was – and still is – president in name only. His attempts to set up a centralized, working governmental structure have so far been unsuccessful in dealing with the violence between the clans and warlords. The ongoing civil wars have resulted in the almost complete destruction of the social fabric and the collapse of the Somali economy. Somalia has a young and growing population, but the socioeconomic conditions are very poor, with a high infant mortality rate, low levels of literacy, widespread health problems resulting in epidemics and a large number of displaced persons. Somalia is not a functioning or viable state according to any reasonable interpretation of the baseline criteria for statehood.[64]

Chad is ranked second as a failed state according to the index. Map 2.6 shows Chad and neighbouring states. Chad gained its independence from France in 1960, but ever since has faced political and ethnic-based violence between the Christian south and the Arab Muslim–dominated north. In 1969, the country erupted into full-scale civil war and Chad's first president François Tombalbaye was assassinated in 1975. France was Chad's most important foreign donor and patron throughout this period. In 1981, France limited its military involvement in Chad due to concerns over a possible confrontation with neighbouring Libya; however, this changed during the late 1980s when France increased its military involvement in order to reinforce Hissène Habré's prime ministership in Chad.

Both the United States and France supported Habré's brutal regime in Chad because he was seen as a bulwark against Muammar Gaddafi in Libya. Despite the influence of these external powers, a new government was formed in Chad led by President Idriss Déby Itno and supported by Libya. Déby immediately consolidated his power by suspending the constitution, dissolving the legislative branch and then manipulating the 1996, 2001 and 2005 elections in order to be re-elected. He also revoked the restrictions on presidential term limits, which allowed him to stay in power after the 2006 elections.

The strictly authoritarian regimes in Chad have been supported for decades by various external powers and influences, resulting in one humanitarian crisis after another. Mass movements of people, particularly from Sudan and the Central African Republic, fleeing internal and provincial civil wars, have added to widespread and extreme levels of human misery throughout the region. Open warfare between Chad and Sudan erupted in 2005 and again in 2007 when Chad blamed Sudan for an attack against the Chadian city of Adré. This escalation of violence in the Darfur region of Sudan led to over 250,000 refugees and 180,000 internally displaced persons in Chad.

The deprivations and violence continued in Chad despite mediation efforts by the EU and the UN and the signing of a number of peace treaties. Rebel factions in Chad unified into the Union of Resistance Forces and in early 2009, supported by Sudan, increased the political divisions and challenged the regimes in Chad and Sudan. The citizens of Chad today continue to face serious risks of disease, poverty and starvation and they are subject to constant human rights abuses by their own government. International aid frequently fails to reach those most in need and international investment that would help to rebuild the state's social fabric and economic infrastructure is practically non-existent. Rebellions that persistently flare up into open civil war greatly contribute to the failure of Chad as a viable and functioning state.[65]

Sudan's ranking as the third failed state in the index is a result of the wide disparity between the functioning of its central government in Khartoum and the many local and regional power centres that continually challenge state security. In 1954, Sudan's transitional government was established after an agreement between Sudan, Great Britain and Egypt. In 1956, Sudan achieved full independence under a new constitution. The constitution did not address whether the governmental structure was to be a federal or unitary-based arrangement, nor did it address the Islamic or secular character of the new state. 17 years of civil war between the southern, mostly Christian

Map 2.5 Somalia and neighbouring states

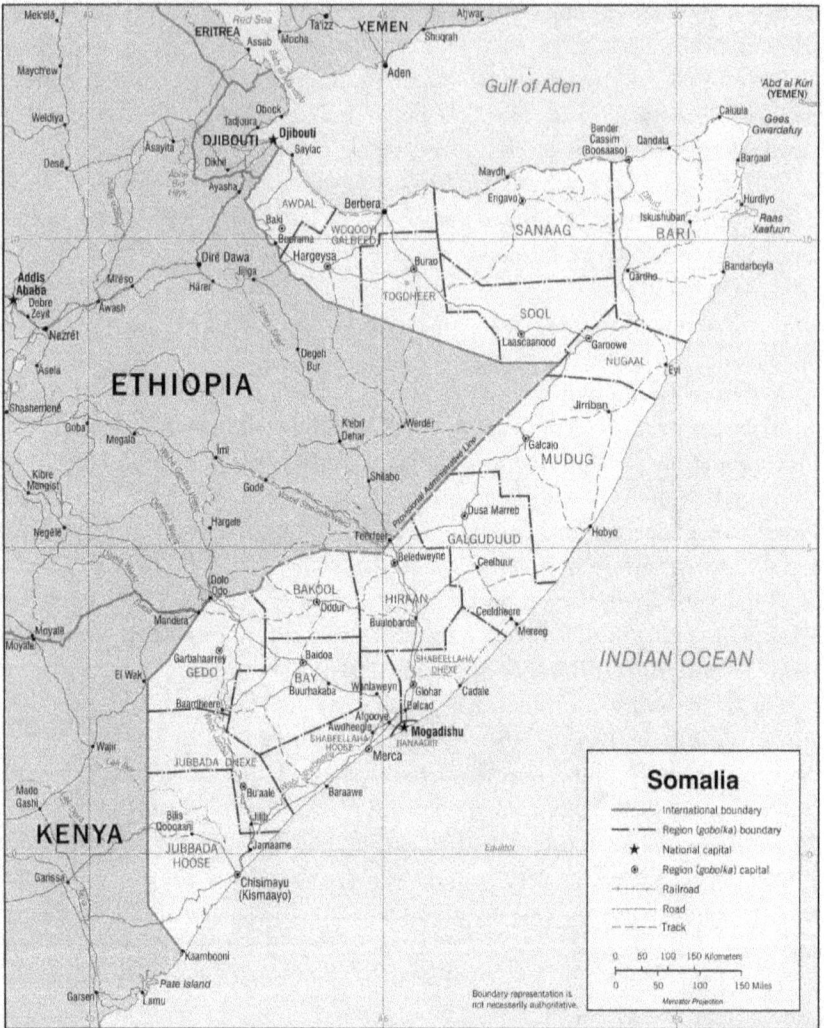

Sudanese and the Arab-led Khartoum government followed independence due to the government's failure to keep its promise to establish a federal system of government that recognized certain levels of regional autonomy. In 2003, conflict escalated to widespread, open warfare throughout the western region of Sudan between Arab paramilitary groups and non-Arabs. The war in Darfur in particular has led to a humanitarian catastrophe with over 200,000 people killed and more than 2 million people displaced.

Map 2.6 Chad and neighbouring states

Western governments have declared the many human atrocities by the Arab paramilitary groups against non-Arabs to be genocide, and the president of Sudan, Omar al-Bashir, was charged with war crimes and crimes against humanity in March 2009 and three counts of genocide in July 2010 by the International Criminal Court (ICC). The Comprehensive Peace Agreement of 2005 eased the tension between north and south Sudan and, following a successful referendum in 2011, Southern Sudan became independent in 2011.

Local and regional warfare in Darfur and throughout Sudan has created a humanitarian disaster of epic proportions, particularly for non-Muslims, but

Map 2.7 Sudan and neighbouring states

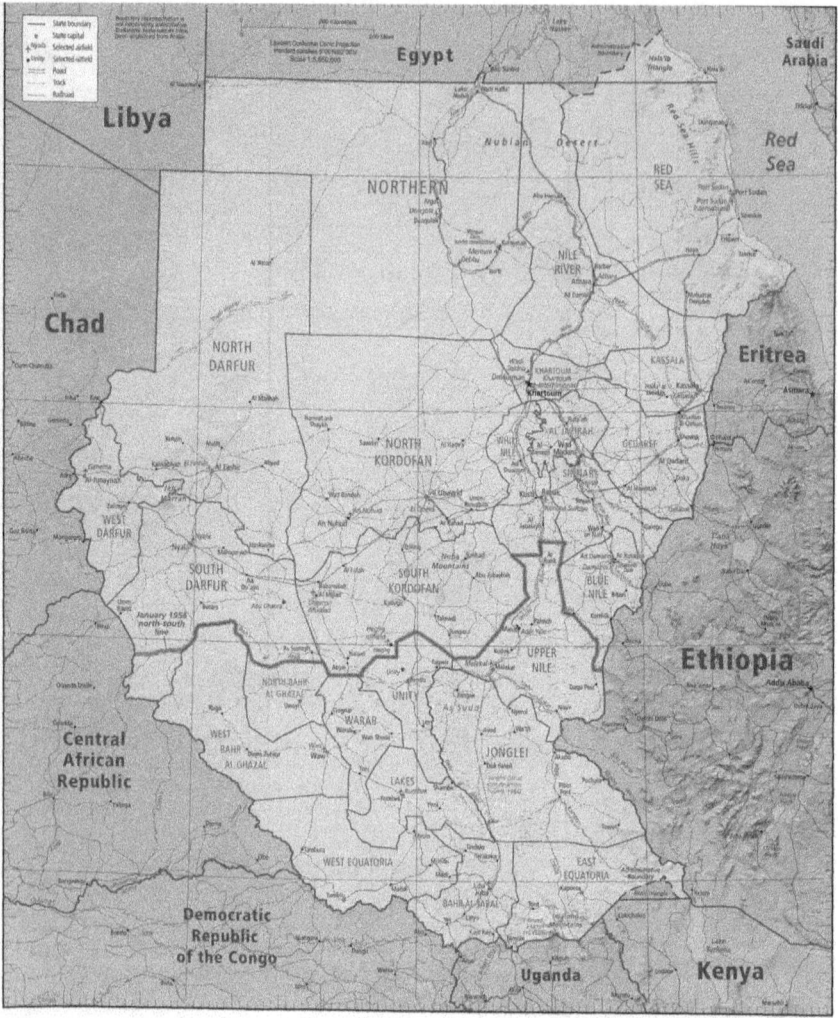

also for Arab Sudanese caught up in the fighting. As well as inequality and high unemployment rates, many Sudanese are faced with disease, poverty and starvation as a result of decades of civil war.

Sudan has extensive oil reserves, but open warfare and corruption by the government in Khartoum has resulted in almost none of this rich resource potential being realized. Foreign humanitarian aid for the people of Sudan and for Darfur in particular has been diverted by the various regional warlords and by the Arab paramilitaries for their own use, resulting in widespread starvation and deprivation. Up to 5 million people have been displaced in and around the Darfur region, adding to the misery, poverty and high death rates of the Sudanese.

In 2009, more than 230,000 people were displaced due to the ongoing atrocities in Sudan. This is a direct consequence of the failure to implement the 2005 peace treaty. Although the central Sudanese government has now been restructured as an alliance between the Government of National Unity (GNU), the National Congress Party (NCP) and the Sudan People's Liberation Movement (SPLM), its legitimacy is weak, with military forces being divided between the Sudanese People's Armed Forces and the rebellions in the Sudanese People's Liberation Army in the south.[66]

The failed states described in this chapter symbolize a great challenge in international politics. Failed states not only jeopardize state security, but also cause spillover conflict and fighting in regional areas. In addition, the failure to provide a minimal level of state security has a significant negative impact on human security. When states fail in their basic functions, civilians, including women and children, experience the most suffering and pain. The Failed State Index is representative of the many indexes and think tanks that have come to focus on failing states in international politics. Both in academia and international politics, the syndrome of failing and failed states has received increasing attention.

The Need for a Human-centric Approach

Pivotal to state security is the evolving notion of human security. So far we have outlined some of the many challenges faced by weak, failing and failed states; and in all of the examples that we have presented the failure of the state to respond to the basic needs of their citizens has resulted in extreme levels of human deprivation and misery. State security and human security have a complementary relationship. Neither can do well without the other. The idea of human security has been reconceptualized in many different ways, but one of its most distinctive features is a reorientation away from the primary focus on the traditional state-centric, state security approach to one where the focus is more human-centric.[67]

Human security means protecting and enhancing the fundamental freedoms and capacities that are the essence of life. Freedom from discrimination, poverty, violence and disease, the capacity to engage peacefully with one another, to have access to education and health and to inhabit an environment that is not injurious to health and wellbeing are essential requirements for a good life. People and communities need to feel safe and to be safe within their own state borders, not merely to be secure against external aggression.

Human security thinking emerged from the development sector and not from the security policy realm. The concept of human security arose from a growing dissatisfaction with the dominant notions of development and security during the 1960s, 1970s and 1980s. The discontent arose from what was seen as a serious deficiency in a post–Cold War world where malnutrition, poverty, the increasing disparity between rich and poor, environmental erosion, mass refugee movements and racial and ethnic conflicts were increasing in scope and severity.[68] Threats of a world war and transnational wars had decreased, but intranational wars had increased.

Throughout the 1970s and 1980s, there were discussions on nonmilitary aspects of security, such as environmental security and food security, but these discussions remained at the periphery of mainstream security thinking, which was mostly dominated by Cold War geostrategic issues. From the 1970s, the literature on alternatives to the state-centric paradigms began to complement the social and political sciences, with contributions from a wide and disparate range of international commissions, researchers and scholars. The state-centric approach to international politics was questioned by peace researchers analysing the security conditions for states and people, with a particular emphasis on third world developments.

The Club of Rome Group and the multinational World Order Models Project (WOMP) both postulated that there were alternative ways to conceptualize development within a complex global system in order to address the basic human needs of individuals.[69] They stimulated and popularized some of the fundamental dynamics behind human security thinking in international and public policy. In the 1980s, the Independent Commission on International Development Issues (ICIDI), chaired by Willy Brandt, and the Independent Commission on Disarmament and Security Issues (ICDSI), chaired by Olof Palme, also contributed to a change in thinking regarding the ideas of development and security.

In the ICIDI *North-South* report, Brandt referred to the 'necessity of the will to overcome dangerous tensions and to produce significant and useful results for nations and regions – but, first and foremost, for human beings – in all parts of the world'.[70] The 1982 report of the ICDSI, *Common Security*, similarly pressed for alternate ways of thinking about security by arguing, 'Common security requires that people live in dignity and peace, that they have enough to eat and are able to find work and live in a world without poverty and destitution.'[71]

The development of human security thinking increased with the power shift in global politics as a result of the end of the Cold War with the collapse of the USSR and the fall of the Berlin Wall in 1989. The prospect of large-scale interstate warfare was no longer the primary concern of the international community and attention shifted to the prevention of abuses to civilian populations within states and to the protection of people when preventative efforts failed.

Increasingly it was argued that the state-centric approach to international relations too narrowly defined security relative to state interests by excluding important security preconditions. Barry Buzan published his seminal work *People, States and Fear* in 1983, which argued that the entire approach to the security question needed to address not only state functionalities regarding military and political security, but also that much more attention must be directed at societal, (socio)economic and environmental matters if security overall was to be realized.[72]

The international community has increasingly endeavoured to shift the traditional focus of state responsibility from sovereignty protection to a wider range of internal and external issues such as humanitarian intervention, environmental degradation, extremism, global health, forced displacement and access to the basics of life: food, water and shelter. This has required a shift from a state-centric to a more human-centred approach that regards the individual as the ultimate beneficiary and contributor to the security of the state. States are recognized by international law as trustees for the people committed to their care and, as such, they are not the bearers of ultimate value – human individuals are.[73]

In 1991, Buzan expanded his ideas on security by once again advocating that the classical notion of security, defined as state security and military capability, was an overly narrow perspective on security and that the post–Cold War era implied new international relations with security issues far beyond the scope of analysis provided by the traditional state-centric approach.[74] Such security debates have led to a reconceptualization of what security is supposed to mean and from where security threats may develop. The reconceptualization of the relationship between state and human security has broadened the discussion to involve consideration for a spectrum of security actors beyond state security and state survival issues and the myopic focus on the national interest. This also intensified debate on what human security itself means. One approach addressed human security in terms of universal rights and freedoms. Another focused on humanitarian interventions and the jurisdictional right to halt atrocities and genocide and to ameliorate the plight of people subject to conflict and war. Both are narrowly focused on freedom from fear and human security in terms of the threat of violence from a state or other political entity. Another approach is an even wider perspective of human security to encompass human development issues that include freedom from want and not only freedom from fear.[75]

Governmental leaders are deemed to be directly responsible for the protection not only of their own citizens, but also that they have a significant measure of responsibility toward all people regardless of where they are located. In the UN Charter of 1945, the fundamental rights and liberties of the individual were emphasized and embedded in the sovereignty norm. It was the political and practical reality of the Cold War that undermined the humanitarian dimension to influence international relations rather than an inherited legal aspect of the UN Charter that prioritized the state sovereignty norm.

Since the 1990s, the secretaries-general of the UN – Javier Pérez de Cuéllar (1982–91), Boutros Boutros-Ghali (1992–96), Kofi A. Annan (1997–2006) and Ban Ki-moon (2007–present) – have encouraged a change from the UN's traditional focus on state security and the sovereignty norm to much more attention being directed towards human security issues. This new direction was articulated forcefully in the 1994 *Human Development Report* and in the United Nations Development Programme (UNDP), which identified seven areas that were critical to the welfare of all people.[76]

The report argued that a much greater emphasis was required by the international community for economic, food, health, environmental, personal, community and political security. The UNDP report stimulated wide discussion within the UN and the international community in general. It encouraged a greater focus on development issues associated with human security. Javier Peres de Cuellar, Boutros Boutros-Ghali and Kofi Annan stressed the responsibility of each state to protect its people and to stand by those human rights emphasized in the UN Charter.

All three leaders proclaimed that the international order faced a shift from the sovereignty norm towards human rights, democracy promotion and other human security imperatives.[77] Questions about the legality and legitimacy of humanitarian intervention during the Balkan conflicts prompted intense debates among OSCE, the NATO members, the five-nation Contact Group (US, Britain, France, Germany, Italy and Russia) and in the UN. Kofi Annan stressed the importance of the relationship between human rights and the responsibilities of state sovereignty:

> The state is now widely understood to be the servant of its people, and not vice versa. At the same time, individual sovereignty – and by this I mean the human rights and fundamental freedoms of each and every individual as enshrined in our Charter – has been enhanced by a renewed consciousness of the right of every individual to control his or her own destiny.[78]

It is not the political legacy of sovereignty that provides legitimacy to the state; rather, it is the state's ability to act in the interests of its people.[79]

In 1991, the Stockholm Initiative on Global Security and Governance issued a report entitled *Common Responsibility in the 1990s*, which referred to 'challenges to security other than political rivalry and armaments' and to 'a wider concept of security.'[80] This wider concept of security was described as human security in the 1994 UN Human Development Report, which listed four essential characteristics of human security: 1) universality, relevant to people everywhere; 2) interdependence and interconnectedness; 3) prevention rather than intervention after the fact; and 4) people-centred not state-centred.[81] The report was the first international document that clearly and explicitly articulated human security as a concept for future vision and an agenda for action.

In 1994, Mahbub ul Haq, former Pakistan finance minister and consultant of the UN Development Programme, presented his paper 'New Imperatives of Human Security', which provided a theoretical model and explanation of the human security ethos.[82] In 1995, the new concept of human security was presented in cosmopolitan terms by the Commission on Global Governance report, 'Our Global Neighbourhood'.

The UNDP published a further report in 1999 that stressed the need to broaden the security discourse to include and prioritize the overall importance of human security.[83] The report stressed that support for human security required a multifaceted approach in order to address economic, food, health, environmental, personal, community and political security. Human security focuses on the challenges and threats that exist for people in their daily lives. Often these challenges are the consequence of poorly developed governmental structures. Constant conflict and other internal dissent between opposing factions are important reasons why a society becomes dysfunctional. When health pandemics, poverty, resource depletion and environmental degradation are added to the internal strife within a state, societies edge closer to complete collapse.

The progression and overall development of the analysis of human security by researchers and policy makers has identified a number of inconsistencies in conceptualizing what human security actually means, what the primary drivers of human security are and how to deal with them, but an understanding is developing about the critical linkages between state security and human security. There is no doubt that political and military security aspects often correlate with human development indicators but what is much less understood is how to address the very complex issues raised by prioritising human security in this way.

The Independent Commission on Human Security, co-chaired by Sadako Ogata and Amartya Sen, stated in its 2003 report that 'attention must now shift from the security of the state to the security of the people'.[84] A number of governments, led by Canada, Norway and Japan, embraced the concept of human security through their foreign policy frameworks. Canada in particular has in the past contributed significantly to the field of human security policy development, with Lloyd Axworthy – a key supporter of Canada's human security focus – reporting that Canada's Security Council used the language and concept of human security regularly.[85]

Canada has developed its foreign policy with a firm foundation on peace, development and human security, and the Canadian conception of security fundamentally revolves around a focus on conflict prevention, public safety and peace building operations. The Department of Foreign Affairs and International Trade Canada (DFAIT) has collaborated with international partners to improve the legal and physical protection of civilian populations, with particular attention to conflict prevention. In May 1998, the Lysøen Declaration calling for joint action in the human security area was presented by the Canadian and Norwegian foreign ministers, Lloyd Axworthy and Knut Vollebaek.

This declaration, with its emphasis on the concept of human security – emphasizing threats to individuals rather than state security – appeared for the first time in an official bilateral agreement negotiated by Canada.[86] Axworthy's aim was to use the Lysøen Declaration as a foundation for further engagement with other countries and to create a standing group, a 'Humanitarian Eight', of like-minded states that would rally around a human security agenda.[87] Switzerland, Austria, Ireland and Thailand all expressed enthusiasm in joining such a group. Within a year the bilateral Canadian–Norwegian initiative evolved into the multilateral Human Security Network (HSN) and today the HSN has 12 member states including Austria, Chile, Costa Rica, Greece, Ireland, Jordan, Mali, Slovenia, Switzerland and Thailand, with South Africa as an observer.[88] However HSN is no longer a major diplomatic reference point for Ottawa and, as it enters its second decade, the new Conservative government under the leadership of Prime Minister Stephen Harper has reorientated its major foreign policy directions elsewhere.[89]

In 2008, the president of the United Nations General Assembly, Srgjan Kerim, called for a new paradigm: 'This new paradigm must not be built around another illusory "world order" and what is needed "is to go beyond refined notions of the state and sovereignty."'[90] He proposed a new culture of international relations based on human-centred security. The endorsement of the responsibility to prevent and to protect was an important step in the progression of a new global norm and new legal instruments for the support of human security.

Although state security is important for people's security, the latter also determines state security. At the same time as the security from external threats is essential for human security within a state, absence of such external threats does not necessarily mean domestic human security. State sovereignty could in fact jeopardize human security when state authority and power is misused against its own people, shielded by the state sovereignty norm and the nonintervention principle. In sum, proponents of the human security approach challenge the state-centric perspective by arguing that in an increasingly globalized world the emphasis on force, particularly with the proliferation of weapons of mass destruction (WMDs), is not only counterproductive but dangerous.

The human security approach proposes that the increasing lethality of WMDs is not the only threat to states. There are a range of other serious concerns such as environmental degradation, economic pressures, cultural and religious flashpoints and access to diminishing resources. The problem with the state-orientated thinking is that it does not address the many challenges and threats to security that defy state boundaries today. Such threats cannot be solved by one state alone or even by a few states working together. Strong states may be able to resist some of the pressures of these challenges, but weak states cannot. State-centric paradigms that focus mostly – in many cases entirely – on state capability are not able to respond to the overall dynamics of international security.

The lynchpin of all human security readings is that the primary focus on state security is at the expense of the well-being and security of individuals. Systems theory focuses on the structures of the international system as created by states, but overlooks the domestic, regional and international drivers, such as nongovernmental organizations (NGOs), multinational corporations, international cartels and the UN, that are increasingly influencing state behaviour. Individual states often have little control over these matters. Environmental issues, access to resources, the global financial crisis and, if there is indeed a global war on terrorism, the activities of insurgents and extremists are not bound to a state or to a region. Human security proponents attempt not only to deepen the referent object debate, with the referent object being the individual and the collective, but also to broaden the perception of threat.

Conclusion

The numerous failing states and international crises, due to the misuse of state power within states, has shown that human insecurity is most often subject to the threat of insurgency and civil war rather than external military threats by other states. This has resulted in a debate on the need for a complementarity relationship between state security and human security. This debate has, to a large extent, been prompted by the events in Rwanda and the Balkans, where the international community had failed to effectively respond to genocide and mass human deprivation. It has also been promoted by the increasing number of UN operations that use preventive diplomacy and engage in peace-enforcing missions. While the state-centric approach to security continues to focus on security threats to the state, human-centric approaches to security have focused on individual and collective security issues that are required to complement the security of the state.

There is a requirement for a broadened perspective on security to encompass three critical sectors: economic, societal and environmental. The economic sector includes welfare issues and access to resources; the societal sector is about sustainability of cultural traits such as religious adherence, ethnical identity, language and societal cohesiveness; and the environmental sector refers to pollution, global warming and sustainable development issues. Human security advocates have acknowledged that focusing on the security of the state is important, but they argue strongly that this does not necessarily lead to human security. Neglecting human security challenges the fundamental security of the state and this may result in the failure of a state itself.

Chapter 3

RESPONSIBILITY: PROTECTION AND PREVENTION

This chapter outlines the development of the R2P ethos from a concept to a principle to what supporters now call a protection and responsibility norm. In September 2000, the Canadian government announced at the UN General Assembly the launch of the International Commission on Intervention and State Sovereignty (ICISS). The ICISS's main goal was to promote ideas about the right of humanitarian intervention and to endeavour to seek an international consensus on how to deal with failing states in future crises. This chapter explores the proposals made by the commission and analyses the international debate within the United Nations and other forums on how to approach what is often perceived as the state versus human security dichotomy. We present the different perspectives that have been played out within the United Nations in part as a reaction to the ICISS report presented in 2001.

The report stressed that each sovereign state has the responsibility to protect its people from harm and that the ultimate sovereignty of the state is derived from its people. If a state fails to uphold law and order and to protect its people, then the international community must react and assume that responsibility.[1] We also attempt to answer the question: what is a responsibility to prevent (R2Prevent)? This is one of the most difficult questions to address; if protection itself is so difficult to pin down, then what hope is there of determining a coherent concept that engages the preventative ethos.

The problem is not the theory of prevention – everyone agrees that prevention is the best cure – rather the problem is regarding how, when and by whom should preventative strategies be implemented. We argue that the most effective way, perhaps the only way, to address this question is to be very context specific. Preventative, proactive strategies are possible, but it depends on a specific place, time and context. We conclude this chapter with a discussion on the reaction of the international community to the Kosovo war and the 1999 military intervention in the region.

Responsibility to Protect (R2P)

The events in Rwanda and in Kosovo, as briefly outlined in the previous chapter, prompted the UN to proclaim that governments were obliged to protect their citizens and if governments failed in their basic obligations then the international community as a whole should respond to prevent serious and deliberate human rights abuses. Yet, there were at least two significant challenges to the UN's position. Firstly, general expressions of outrage were never going to be enough for the international community to act collectively. As a result, neither the UN nor the wider international community have been able keep the promise of 'never again' after the Rwandan genocide.[2] Secondly, the outrage expressed immediately after the humanitarian disaster in Rwanda did not result in any formal, collective agreement regarding what to do when future Rwandas eventuated.

The importance of R2P is that since 2005 there has been a formal, collective agreement between all states that there are limits to acceptable human behaviour, particularly in relation to how states treat their citizens. It is now more likely than not that violations of the R2P protection norm may promote a direct and active response by the international community or by a coalition of concerned states. Our case study of direct intervention in Libya is an example of such a response. Of course, many difficult challenges remain. Was intervention in Libya by the coalition of concerned states a fluke? Where is the international community's direct action in Syria? When, how and what type of response is needed or even possible in and around the many global flashpoints? Where and how does the idea of prevention fit with protection? Throughout our book we attempt to directly confront many of these difficult, practical issues. Our focus is on what can be done rather than what cannot; a step forward is preferable to no steps at all. We argue that one positive step forward is the formal development of the protection norm.

In 2001, the *Responsibility to Protect* report was presented by the ICISS.[3] The main objective of the report was to address what most state leaders saw as a clash of norms in international relations with regard to state sovereignty and human rights. The commission based its arguments on observations regarding the tragic events in Rwanda and Kosovo. The genocide in Rwanda resulted in minimal if any international engagement before or during this humanitarian disaster and the international response to ending the war in Kosovo resulted in direct military intervention. Both events triggered much criticism. The international response to the situation in Rwanda was too little and much too late, and in Kosovo direct military intervention, particularly without a UN mandate, was condemned by many. The commission sought a new consensus on intervention and on how to try to prevent future Rwandas and Kosovos from happening again.[4]

In 2005, the UN General Assembly World Summit in New York endorsed the principle of R2P and acknowledged the obligations of sovereign states to protect their people. However, debates on the ICISS report and the subsequent UN proposals have continued, particularly about what the new principles of responsibility actually mean to the 193 member states. While many states expressed support for the overall principle of responsibility, as conceptualized by the ICISS and the UN, many powerful and influential states remain sceptical about such commitments, raising concerns over the diminution of the sovereignty norm.[5]

The history of interference into the internal affairs of other states by external powers using military intervention based on proclamations of urgent humanitarian need has a poor record. There are very few such interventions that have been successful. Interventions in the East Timor conflict and in Kosovo are perhaps the exceptions, but intervention is much more than the just use of direct military force. Intervention by external parties in the affairs of a state may take the form of robust diplomacy, the delivery of food and other essential aid, economic and investment assistance, cultural exchanges and so on. These types of interventions are directly aimed at improving and supporting human security, and while they may not have the public profile of military intervention, they are critical to the overall well-being of all citizens. If military intervention is being considered, then important prevention-based initiatives have either been poorly implemented or not implemented at all.

A narrow interpretation of R2P comes into play where external parties attempt to at least separate the warring factions and to provide some protection for innocent people caught up in situations where the state is either unable or unwilling to do so. We argue that a wider interpretation of R2P is needed that encompasses the idea that protection must start much earlier and that it must occur before states and regions become embroiled in outright conflict. This requires a reorientation of the narrow to the broad perspective of what R2P actually means.

The 2010 CRS report to Congress declared Darfur to be a major humanitarian disaster with an estimated 2.7 million people displaced, more than 240,000 people forced into neighbouring Chad and an estimated 450,000 people killed since 2003.[6] In mid-2007 the UN Security Council passed Resolution 1769 (2009), authorizing the deployment of 26,000 peacekeepers (currently 22,000 in country) from the African Union to Darfur.[7] According to Trevor Salmon, the presence of these under-resourced and ill-prepared peacekeepers has not brought peace or even managed to limit the violence in Darfur.[8] One may even infer that the 'never again' promise itself means waiting until genocide has happened or is about to happen before the protection response eventuates.

Chester Crocker takes a more optimistic view by arguing that regardless of selectivity, egregious mistakes and continuing controversies, the very fact that the protection and prevention debate is taking place at all over the legitimacy of humanitarian intervention marks a change that has endorsed the norm of an international responsibility to protect civilians from large-scale violence when states cannot or will not protect their own. R2P is often referred to as a concept or a principle.[9] A principle implies a certain, heightened level of shared understanding that allows it to function as a foundation for action, whereas a concept is a notion very much in the formative state.[10]

Advocates of R2P claim that R2P has evolved, or at least is very rapidly evolving, from a principle to a formative – perhaps even substantive – norm, yet there remains a great deal of scepticism about the use of the term in this way. Critics such as Barry Buzan point out that there is very little about R2P that reflects a heightened level of understanding and that functionality for action is anything but assured.[11] In the words of Ban Ki-moon, 'Today, the Responsibility to Protect is a concept, not yet a policy; an aspiration, not yet a reality.'[12]

The responsibility to protect people from belligerents who deliberately engage in extreme, deliberate and repeated actions that threaten the fundamental and essential human security of others revolves around the notion of what it means as a collective to live in a civil and moral society. Yet questions about belligerence, the meaning of human security and human protection (whether a principle, a concept, an idea or something else), and the ultimate question about who has some form of responsibility to respond to gross violations of human rights, are all subject to a great deal of debate. These types of issues are problematic not only because there is no real consensus about any of them, but also because they challenge how we live in an increasingly populated and globalized world.

The response by the international community to the protection thesis under the interventionist umbrella has been either to respond selectively as some sort of patchy collective, perhaps under the auspices of international organizations such as the UN or by various individual states or coalitions of states reacting to local or regional events by going it alone without a UN mandate. R2P is important, but we need to see a reorientation of the primacy of protection to prevention as such reorientation is not only needed for human security in order to save lives, but it is also legally founded.

The notion of human security includes certain assumptions, such as: that human values are important, that how humans treat each other is important and that some types of human behaviour are deemed to be appropriate while others are not. The ramifications of direct intervention by external agencies into the affairs of a sovereign state have direct relevance to those on the receiving end of such intervention, but also to the wider human community. It is difficult to dispute that if we believe we live in a civil and moral society, then we have some sort of obligation to support the concept of human security for all. Many realists will challenge all of these assumptions. As for the claims about a civil and moral society and the international community, realists will reject such notions as idealized and fanciful. On a practical level, the costs, logistics and technicalities of trying to help the suffering millions around the world today are simply overwhelming.

Intervention and Protection

Central to the humanitarian protection principle is the question of external intervention into the affairs of a sovereign state. States that have chosen to respond forcibly have assumed a mantle of responsibility, mostly due to their own internal cultural or religious imperatives, political requirements, protection of a national interest, or in the form of pre-emptive action to stop a real or imagined dangerous situation from becoming worse. Direct pre-emptive action that aims to address serious humanitarian issues is rare compared to pre-emptive action to defend the home front, support the national interest and secure access to essential resources.

Intervention with the intent of alleviating human misery is significantly more problematic than attempting to intervene for nonhumanitarian purposes. For example, should a state engage in aggressive action against its neighbours for the purpose of conquest or access to resources, then violation of state sovereignty demands a response, often involving the use of force. Such a reaction has a great deal of historical precedence. Sovereignty and protection of the state as an inherent right has been a cornerstone of international relations for up to four hundred years by the formal codification of state sovereignty in various legal instruments and conventions.

Despite the principle of noninterventionism being both implicit and explicit in any basic understanding of sovereignty, this has not stopped states and powers from regularly meddling in the affairs of other states or deliberately violating the sovereignty norm. The debate is ongoing regarding the ethics, the legitimacy, the legality and the overall rationality of forcible humanitarian intervention in order to protect populations from the excesses of governments. In recent times, humanitarian reasons were presented or assumed as part of the rationale for intervention by India into East Pakistan (now Bangladesh) in 1971, Vietnam's entry into Kampuchea (now Cambodia) in 1979, Tanzania into Uganda in 1979 and French support for the coup to overthrow the Central African Empire in 1979.[13] The 1990s saw forcible interventions with the claim of humanitarian necessity in Liberia (1990–97), Somalia (1992–93), the Bosnian war (1992–95), Eastern Zaire (1994–96), Haiti (1994–97), Sierra Leone (1997–present) and East Timor (1999–present).[14]

Gareth Evans considers that the international community has handled none of these cases well or confidently: 'With Somalia, Bosnia and Rwanda, such interventions as did occur were too little too late, misconceived, poorly resourced, poorly executed, or all of the above.'[15] Most of these interventions were also quickly condemned by those who regard such actions to be illegal, self-serving and a clear violation of the norms of nonintervention as set out in Article 2 (4) of the UN Charter.[16] From the early 1990s there has been a growing argument in the UN, in academia, between policy makers and among sectors of the legal fraternity that in instances where there are severe violations of human rights occurring, the use of force may be the only viable option. Under these dire circumstances, the concept of noninterference must, at times, yield to the international responsibility to protect populations at severe risk.[17] Despite a heightened awareness of the responsibility to protect, the international community, and the UN in particular, seem incapable of acting swiftly or decisively when the need arises. The UN was unable to stop the Rwandan genocide of over 900,000 people in 1994, or to respond effectively to the war in Slovenia (1991) or the Croatian war of independence (1991–95).

Developments in R2P

In September 1999 the UN secretary-general Kofi Annan addressed the UN General Assembly, where he appealed for a consensus regarding the fundamental role of the state with its citizens. The notion of state sovereignty, he argued, was fundamentally being redefined at its most basic level from a traditional position of primacy over the citizen to an understanding that not only does statehood carry inherent rights, but that 'states are now widely understood to be instruments at the service of their peoples and not vice versa.'[18] He did not devalue the traditional role or the importance of the state, rather he appealed for a new consensus by the international community that the wellbeing of citizens enhanced the legitimacy of the state itself. The question of state legitimacy is an important one because Annan's message to the world community was that if states deliberately violated the well-being of their citizens, then external pressure and other more direct forms of intervention may be justifiable.

Annan's statements were primarily a response to the international community and particularly the UN's failure to act before or during the genocide in Rwanda, and to the Security Council's open disagreements about what to do regarding the war in Kosovo after the end of the war in Bosnia. His approach was to reiterate support for the fundamental principle of protecting human security within states, but also that this support required the direct engagement and involvement (meaning forcible intervention if required) from the wider international community. The notion of direct support involving the intervention by external states or parties into the affairs of a sovereign state remains hugely problematic as a normative response to manmade humanitarian disasters.

Lloyd Axworthy, Canada's foreign minister (1996–2000), and the Canadian government responded to Annan's statements after the Kosovo crisis by establishing the ICISS in September 2000. The intention of establishing the commission was to investigate how the international community might achieve a consensus between the role of the state, the obligations of the state, and how a range of protection principles for the citizens of a state may be practically realized. The ICISS sought a new formative framework for the international community in order to avoid two common failings of the UN. For example, in the Kosovo disaster the UN was divided on how to respond, so a collective of states acted without explicit UN Security Council authorization; in Rwanda the UN was united in its outrage regarding the genocide, but ineffective in its response.

The ICISS report *The Responsibility to Protect*, published in December 2001, proposed that the historical debate of sovereignty versus intervention should be reframed in terms of the responsibility to protect and that there was an emerging norm of a collective international responsibility to protect.[19] The primary responsibility to protect the security of citizens was entrusted to the state, but if states fail to exercise this responsibility then 'the principle of non-intervention yields to the international responsibility to protect'.[20]

The ICISS also outlined criteria based on just war theory, and these criteria were reiterated by Kofi Annan in his 2005 report, *Larger Freedom: Towards Development, Security and Human Rights for All*. That is, six principles have to be satisfied in order to justify military intervention: the just cause threshold, four precautionary principles (right intention, last resort, proportional means and reasonable prospects for success) and the requirement of right authority. The previous 2000 *Kosovo Report* declared the threshold principles to be the direct protection of a victimized population, reasonable prospects for success and that there were two valid triggers for humanitarian intervention.

The first is severe violations of international human rights or humanitarian law on a sustained basis. The second is the subjection of a civilian society to great suffering and risk due to the 'failure' of their state, which entails the breakdown of governance at the level of the territorial sovereignty.[21] However, there is no guarantee that states will agree that the just cause threshold or any other particular threshold has been crossed, that the precautionary principles have been satisfied, or that the right authority is identifiable and is able to be agreed upon.[22]

Important questions remain unanswered: who has the right to wage war – individual states, a coalition of states, the UN? And how can this right be justified? Annan's 2005 report set out a blueprint for UN reform of the operation and function of the Security Council, however this was removed during the negotiations in New York prior to the UN World Summit. An important, if contentious, proposal by Annan and the ICISS was that in order to improve the effectiveness of the Security Council, the permanent members should agree not to exercise their veto powers if there was majority support for a resolution authorizing the use of force for humanitarian reasons. This was removed as a discussion point during the UN World Summit in 2005. Despite these and many other challenges, Juan Garrigues argues that R2P implies a significant empirical and normative progression, and that this has existed since 2001 when the ICISS presented its report and created the term.[23]

The responsibility to protect all individuals lies at the fault line between the international system's commitment to state autonomy and integrity, respect for human dignity and the protection of human rights. R2P as a norm reasserts the responsibility or the obligation of states to protect their citizens, both within and beyond their national borders, under the umbrella concept of the common heritage of mankind in international law. Teresa Chataway and Chris Abbott propose that the concept of R2P is a distinct development in the history of human rights since the adoption of the Universal Declaration of Human Rights and that it comprises of the following three key elements: 1) responsibility to prevent aims to address both the root and direct causes of internal conflict and other man-made crises that place populations at risk; 2) responsibility to react aims to respond to situations of compelling human need with appropriate measures, which may include coercive measures like sanctions or international prosecution and in extreme cases military intervention; 3) responsibility to rebuild aims to provide, particularly after military intervention, full assistance with recovery, reconstruction and reconciliation and to address the causes of the harm the intervention was designed to halt or avert.[24]

The 11 September 2001 terrorist attacks in the US and the subsequent invasion of Iraq and Afghanistan by coalition forces prompted the UN secretary-general on 3 November 2003 to appoint a High-Level Panel on Threats, Challenges and Change. The aim of the panel was to develop a collective security strategy that included not only how the UN should respond to aggression, but also to generate new ideas about the types of policies and institutions required for the UN to be effective in the twenty-first century. Kofi Annan argued that a threat to one was a threat to all, and that the threat or the actuality of a major terrorist attack anywhere in the industrial world would have devastating global consequences. The panel published its report *A More Secure World: Our Shared Responsibility* in December 2004:

> Whatever perceptions may have prevailed when the Westphalian system first gave rise to the notion of State sovereignty, today it clearly carries with it the obligation of a State to protect the welfare of its own peoples and meet its obligations to the wider international community.[25]

The report argued for a new security consensus and identified state violence (including civil wars, large-scale human rights abuses and genocide) as a particular concern that the UN and the world must be prepared to address in the future. A central theme of the report was the responsibility to protect civilians from large-scale violence and incorporated the responsibility to protect as a fundamental principle.[26] Kofi Annan stressed that there were a number of wide ranging but particularly important findings of the report: development and security were inextricably linked because extreme poverty provides a fertile breeding ground for civil conflict; the threat of inadequate biological security challenges not only the global public health system but raises the spectre of bioterrorism; sanctions and mediation are important tools for prevention, and prevention must be the UN's principle aim; and, when all else fails, it may be necessary and legitimate to use force. He argued that the report 'makes a crucial contribution to the search for common criteria, by which to decide when the use of force is justified.'[27]

Ultimately, the ICISS, the High-Level Panel and the 2005 World Summit failed to substantiate the legitimacy of humanitarian intervention as a substantive and practical norm because world events after 11 September 2001 and the invasion of Iraq and Afghanistan by the coalition forces had overtaken efforts to qualify the principle of a responsibility to protect. The primary concern was that the criteria, principles and concepts behind legitimizing the use of force for humanitarian reasons would be misused most pointedly by the US and its allies, as the Iraq invasion based on a requirement for regime change testifies.[28] The US was and remains opposed to the outcomes of the UN World Summit. The US rejects any guidelines that could constrain its capacity to engage in the use of force generally.[29]

There are at least three fundamental limitations on the principles of responsibility to protect. Firstly, there is the problem of political will generally. If there is no general consensus between political entities about when or if they need to act to protect populations at risk, then the question over who has the responsibility to act does not even rate on the agenda. Unless this vexing problem is addressed, the issue of obligation or responsibility will not be confronted. The very selective nature of past interventions and the myriad issues that they have raised, coupled with the aggressive posture and behaviour of the West in places such as Iraq and Afghanistan, do not bode well for a more coherent substantiation of the glacially evolving protection norm. Even in Kosovo the Security Council made no reference to the protection needs of the Serbian and minority populations, nor did it address the problem of how to promote the peaceful coexistence of Kosovo's ethnic communities as a preventative approach. The issue of protection was, in mid-June 1999, seen to be a critical and immediate issue only with regard to the Kosovo Albanian population.[30]

The second major problem is what to do if the Security Council cannot or will not agree on a response to address serious humanitarian issues. One option is for a state or a collective of states to act unilaterally or collectively, but this may create even further problems with perceptions (real or otherwise) of other agendas, self-interest or imperial expansionism. A third issue is that if the world's most powerful military superpower, the United States, rejects the fundamental concept of any limitations to its capacity and capability to use its military power whenever and wherever it chooses then this is a serious constraint on the progression of the overall protection thesis.

Finally, the fundamental notion of prevention was essentially sidelined by the many difficult and still unresolved questions relating to protection. Even the role of the UN Peace Building Commission, established in December 2005 by General Assembly Resolution A/RES/60/180 (2005), is expressly limited to postconflict situations.[31] Steven Toope et al. argue that the Peace Building Commission has no mandate for early warning or intervention: 'How then will the preventative aspect of the Responsibility to Prevent play itself out?'[32] The overall difficulty is that states may sign up to the principle of the R2P, but disagree over its application in particular cases or even generally.

The need to prevent violence has been preached and argued by many, but the serious application of societal, operational and structural strategies that effectively deal with the everyday basic human needs of citizens in potential or actual conflict zones has been very selective, where and when it has occurred at all. The notion of R2P has developed as a contemporary response by the wider international community in an attempt to deal with individual, collective and state responsibilities regarding immediate human security issues, but R2P is essentially an after-the-fact response. By this we mean responding to human crises when they reach such an extreme level of concern regarding the behaviour of some governments against their people that forcible intervention seems to be the only remaining option. In these cases, to do nothing would have a high probability of events resulting in genocide and other crimes against humanity.

R2P has evolved since the 1990s, when proponents such as Kofi Annan, the ICISS and the UN High-Level Panel on Threats, Challenges and Change first attempted to articulate R2P as a formative concept, with the idea that it should develop into a new type of responsive norm regarding how the international community should react to serious human rights violations. The majority of the lengthy discussions, meetings, reports and press releases about the development of R2P focused on proposing 'a new direction' in the sovereignty norm. This new direction placed much more emphasis and responsibility on the state and on the international community generally to deal with serious human security issues. It attempted to qualify many complex and difficult questions about the legitimacy of external intervention into the affairs of a state that violates its fundamental obligations to its citizens. These discussions culminated in the UN *Summit Report* after the 2005 UN World Summit.

The World Summit and the subsequent report did not address some of the more contentious proposals raised previously in various forums, such as what to do if the UN Security Council could not or would not authorize forcible humanitarian intervention. Most importantly, the report did not qualify any particulars about prevention. Despite all these limitations, the progression of R2P as a formative norm remains an important milestone for the human security ethos. Toope et al. propose that

> given the history of debates around humanitarian intervention, and the possible implications of the concept of responsibility to protect for sovereignty, non-intervention and so-called 'friendly relations', its inclusion in the Summit Outcome document is astonishing. The norm of responsibility to protect has now been articulated, and at least formally endorsed.[33]

Anne-Marie Slaughter also claims that a redefinition of sovereignty was 'a tectonic shift, reinterpreting the very act of signing the Charter in ways that will create a new legal and diplomatic discourse about member states' obligations to their own people and to one another.'[34] R2P presents itself with intellectual clarity and political usefulness, and it is now a norm that is part and parcel of a new vision of human security.[35] Carsten Stahn proposes that the articulation of the concept of R2P is a remarkable achievement and that 'the inclusion of the concept in the Outcome Document not only marks one of the most important results of the 2005 World Summit, but is testimony to a broader systemic shift in international law, namely, a growing tendency to recognize that the principle of state sovereignty finds its limits in the protection of "human security"'.[36]

Despite such optimistic views, the implementation of R2P from a theory and evolving norm at the development stage into actual practice remains hugely problematic. Such a transition requires consensus, political will and a great deal of leadership, none of which are evident today in the ongoing crisis in Iraq, Afghanistan, the Sudan, Syria and many other places. There are two fundamental reasons for this. Firstly, there is the critical impasse in the conversation about the interpretation, or perhaps the ongoing reinterpretation, of R2P. That is, who is responsible, what does protection mean, how do we go about practically responding to human crisis and how does the prevention thesis fit into the picture? How should we deal with human security issues before they develop into human catastrophes that may invoke the protection paradigm? The second major problem is that R2P tends to focus on the reaction pillar and in particular the application of forcible intervention.[37]

The threshold for military intervention is very high and includes war crimes, ethnic cleansing and crimes against humanity, but what is needed is a much more pre-emptive, preventative approach in dealing with human security issues long before they reach a stage of criticality. That is, emphasis must be placed on strengthening and promoting the prevention ambit, which includes a commitment to promoting good governance: democratization fostered by appropriate diplomatic, humanitarian and other peaceful means. The R2P thesis was successfully applied by the international community during the Arab Spring uprising in Libya in 2011–12. The application of R2P, the international response, and critical developments in Libya before and during international intervention are analysed and discussed in Chapter 6. Despite the success of humanitarian intervention in Libya under the formal banner of R2P, the question remains whether this was a one-off success story or if these events heralded a much more robust protection ethos by the international community. There are various ways of considering this question. One view may be that the protection ethos need not be strictly linked or limited to R2P. That is, there have been other successes of humanitarian intervention, such as the 1999 UN peacekeeping missions in East Timor and the effective (albeit belated) NATO intervention in Kosovo. The selective nature of how, when and even if the international community directly responds to extreme human rights violations remains a contentious issue with successful outcomes, however measured, few and far between.

Another view could be to limit the discussion regarding the effectiveness or otherwise of R2P to after its formal endorsement by the UN World Summit in 2005. From this perspective there are immediate challenges to those who claim that R2P is now well on the way to becoming, or already is, a normative response to unacceptable state behaviour. Firstly, the direct application of R2P since 2005 has been very limited and highly selective. The UN formally endorsed R2P for the first time in 2006 by authorizing

UNMIS to send peacekeepers to Darfur, but it suffered from poor planning, lack of resources and poorly trained peacekeepers. The 2010 CRS report to Congress declared Darfur to be a major humanitarian disaster. The second direct application of R2P was during the 2011–12 Libyan crises and was in this case successful, removing the Gaddafi regime and protecting the Libyan people. However, there is no suggestion that the international community is prepared to formally apply R2P in many other places that are also currently subject to humanitarian disasters, such as Iran, North Korea, Somalia, Chad, Sierra Leone, Zimbabwe, the Democratic Republic of the Congo, Syria or anywhere else.

The current humanitarian disaster in Syria is only one example where the principles and the theory of R2P come up against practical realities. There was clear evidence from mid-March 2011 that the civil war in Syria resulted in a humanitarian crisis of mammoth proportions. The UN Human Rights Council (HRC) held a Special Session on 29 April 2011 on the human rights situation in Syria in response to many allegations that the government of Syria was committing grave human rights violations against prodemocracy protesters. Kyung-wha Kang, the UN deputy high commissioner for human rights, condemned the Syrian government and stated that the 'preponderance of information' that had emerged from Syria depicted 'a widespread, persistent, and gross disregard for basic human rights by the Syrian military and security forces.'[38] The UN General Assembly Resolution A/HRC/RES/S-16/1 of 29 April 2011 authorized the UN Office of the High Commissioner for Human Rights to dispatch a fact-finding mission to Syria to investigate all alleged violations of human rights law.[39]

The Syrian government refused official requests for the fact-finding mission to enter Syria, so the team was limited to gathering information from outside the country. In August 2011, the HRC held another Special Session on Syria that found the Syrian authorities' actions in Syria could constitute crimes against humanity. Subsequent to the HRC's A/HRC/18/53 report of September 2011, the UN General Assembly passed Resolution A/HRC/RES/21/26, which expressed 'profound concern' and 'strongly condemned the continued grave and systematic human rights violations by the Syrian authorities'.[40] The HRC's report noted that

States unanimously agreed at the 2005 summit that each individual State has the responsibility to protect its population from crimes against humanity and other international crimes. […] When a State is manifestly failing to protect its population from serious international crimes, the international community has the responsibility to step in by taking protective action in a collective, timely and decisive manner.[41]

An Independent International Commission of Inquiry was formed to investigate all alleged violations of international human rights law since March 2011 in Syria. The commission was charged 'to identify those responsible with a view to ensuring that perpetrators of violations, including those that may constitute crimes against humanity, are held accountable.'[42] The commission's 16 October 2012 report stated that

> the Commission had recorded accounts of murder, arbitrary detention, sexual violence and torture, committed by both parties to the conflict – the Syrian Government forces and the Free Syrian Army. However, gross violations of human rights and international humanitarian law were more prevalent on the part of the Government.[43]

There is currently no indication of the possibility of any direct and forceful intervention by external parties into Syria. In the Security Council, China and Russia continue to veto even the threat of UN sanctions.[44] Most in the international community continue to express outrage at the events unfolding in Syria, but the practical application of R2P is unlikely in this case. The events in Syria throughout 2011–12 and the international community's response show once again that well-meaning principles and the ideals fundamental to the R2P thesis have a long way to go before they are able to overcome the on-the-ground realities of what to do about states that brutalize their citizens. This does not mean that R2P is fundamentally flawed. It means that high aspirations and fine principles will continue to be severely challenged by the realities of realpolitik.

Intervention, Protection and the War in Kosovo

Forcible intervention by NATO against the Federal Republic of Yugoslavia (FRY) in Kosovo was especially significant in the development of R2P because it established a potential norm of resort to force without authorization by the UN Security Council. Maps 3.1 and 3.2 show Bosnia–Herzegovina and the former Yugoslavia. The *Fourth Report of the 1999–2000 Session* of the UK Foreign Affairs Committee (23 May 2000) concluded that 'NATO's military action, if of dubious legality in the current state of international law, was justified on moral grounds.'[45] The 1995 Dayton Peace Agreement halted the Bosnian war after UN-sanctioned NATO airstrikes (Operation Deliberate Force) against Serb-held command and control systems in Bosnia–Herzegovina, but the agreement bypassed Kosovo, Bosnia–Herzegovina and neighbouring states.

In 1998, UN Security Council Resolution 1199 (1998) demanded that all parties, groups and individuals immediately cease hostilities and maintain

Map 3.1 Bosnia–Herzegovina and neighbouring states

a ceasefire in Kosovo. The resolution insisted that the FRY implement immediately the measures towards achieving a political solution to the situation in Kosovo as contained in the six-nation Contact Group (US, UK, France, Germany, Italy and Russia) statement of 12 June 1998.[46] Both resolutions and all demands were ignored by the warring parties.

Operation Deliberate Force was used as a model for US policy makers and for NATO Command in its approach to dealing with the escalating conflict in Kosovo.[47] The strategy was to threaten Yugoslavia with direct military action, but at the same time present peace proposals in September 1998, then again at Rambouillet in France during February and March 1999. However, throughout the 1990s, the humanitarian situation in Kosovo quickly deteriorated. The clandestine Kosovo Liberation Army (KLA) formed by Kosovo Albanian radicals carried out a series of attacks in rural areas,

Map 3.2 Former Yugoslavia and neighbouring states

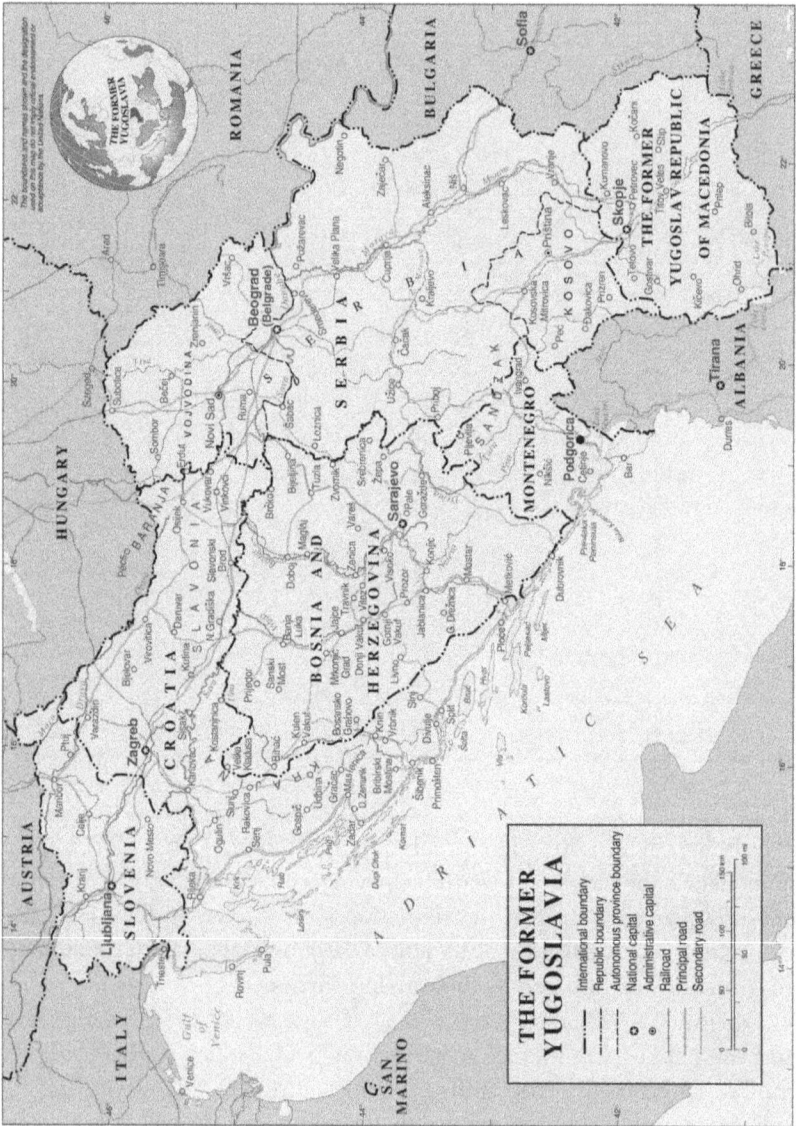

resulting in heavy retaliation by Serbian security forces. The fighting escalated throughout Kosovo. Between March and June 1998, 800,000 Kosovo Albanians – almost half of Kosovo's Albanian population – were driven out of Kosovo into Albania, Macedonia and Montenegro by the Serbs.[48]

Serb forces carried out mass looting, rape and murder, and tens of thousands of homes and mosques were destroyed, leaving 300,000 Albanians homeless by October 1998. Repeated pleas by the international community and threats by the UN to all the belligerents to stop the human carnage were having little if any effect on the events unfolding in Kosovo. Images of Serb tanks belching black smoke and smashing into farmhouses were broadcast into the living rooms of the global community, which resulted in increasing international concern that the war in Kosovo would evolve into even more of a bloodbath than it already was.

The Contact Group summoned both sides to talks in Rambouillet and proposed that the conflicting parties sign the Interim Agreement for Peace and Self-Government in Kosovo, drafted by the Contact Group, Organization for Security and Co-operation in Europe (OSCE) and NATO partners. The proposal required autonomy for Kosovo and for NATO's Kosovo Force (KFOR) to replace Serbian forces, and for the Serb forces to be withdrawn or demilitarized.[49] Belgrade rejected the agreement on the basis that matters relating to Kosovo's autonomy went much further than what the Serb/Yugoslav government saw as reasonable.

The agreement proposed that Kosovars could take part in Serbian elections with a guaranteed number of seats in the Serbian parliament. Kosovo would have its own constitutional court and independent judicial system, and a number of seats on the Serbian supreme court.[50] Appendix B, Chapter Seven of the Rambouillet proposal gave NATO free and unrestricted military access throughout the FRY.[51] Initially the Kosovo Albanians rejected any part of the proposal for Kosovo to remain part of Serbia and for the KLA to be disarmed three months after the signing of the agreement. The Serbs also found that the implementation of the proposed agreement and the mechanism for final settlement for Kosovo to be unacceptable. In particular, the Belgrade delegation rejected the Kosovo delegate's demand for a binding referendum on independence from Yugoslavia. The delegation also rejected the presence of a NATO ground force in the FRY for at least three years after the agreement was signed.[52]

The Kosovo Albanian delegation signed the agreement on 18 March 1999 after assurances regarding the ongoing presence of NATO forces in the FRY, changes to the initial agreement calling for a referendum on independence from Yugoslavia after three years, and after assurances by the United States that if the Kosovo Albanians signed but the Serbs did not, NATO bombing would commence immediately.[53] The FRY/Serb delegates refused to sign and dismissed the text as a nonagreement and Western diktat.[54] On 24 March 1999, NATO began Operation Deliberate Force, an eleven-week air campaign against the FRY when the Serbs failed to sign up to the Rambouillet agreement. After 78 days, Milošević capitulated and agreed to admit KFOR into Kosovo and to withdraw Serb forces from Kosovo, resulting in tens of thousands of Serbs fleeing Kosovo due to fears of reprisals by the returning Kosovars and Albanians.

The events in Kosovo leading up to the NATO air campaign through to the capitulation of Slobodan Milošević and the Serbian military forces were pivotal to the evolving debate regarding the use of force for the protection of populations at risk. UK foreign secretary Robin Cook argued that President Milošević would not have committed himself to full compliance with Security Council Resolution 1199 (1998) if the diplomatic efforts backed by the contact group had not also been backed by the credible threat of military action by NATO.[55] However, Resolution 1199 (1998) did not give explicit authorization for the use of force: 'Should the concrete measures demanded in this resolution and resolution 1160 (1998) not be taken, [the Security Council decides] to consider further action and additional measures to maintain or restore peace and stability in the region'.[56]

NATO secretary-general Javier Solana questioned whether UN authorization was needed in the first place to deal with the escalating violence in Kosovo: 'There may be a moment in which it is necessary to act for humanitarian reasons, when a UN Security Council Resolution will not be necessary or will not be even appropriate because the UN Charter does not contemplate humanitarian acts.'[57]

Russia and China did not support external military intervention in order to deal with the Kosovo situation. In late September 1998, Russia repeatedly denounced any intention to use force in Yugoslavia. On 22 September, the Russian foreign minister, Igor Ivanov, warned, 'The use of levers of power to resolve the Kosovo conflict might lead to a big war with unpredictable consequences for the Balkan Region and Europe at large.' The defence minister, Igor Sergeyev, stated that alliance air strikes could mark a return to the Cold War and jeopardize the already much-delayed ratification of the START II arms reduction treaty by the Russian parliament.[58] In March 1999, Russian prime minister Yevgeny Primakov announced on Russian public television that Russia was categorically against the use of force in Yugoslavia, and that such intervention would destabilize Kosovo, Yugoslavia and Europe in general and would have global ramifications.[59] On 12 October 1998, Chinese foreign minister Tang Jiaxuan also formally denounced forcible intervention in Kosovo:

> The Chinese Government resolutely opposes the use of force or the threat to use force in international relations, and hopes that the Kosovo crisis will be resolved

peacefully at an early date. Some countries are now threatening to use force against Yugoslavia. This is disturbing.[60]

Russia and China were also concerned about the ramifications of UN authorizations for intervention in Kosovo because they believed that this would set a dangerous precedent for the international community's response to separatist and independence movements (meaning support for insurgencies and possible intervention against established regimes) in places such as Chechnya, Taiwan and Tibet.[61]

The UK prime minister Tony Blair's Chicago speech 'Doctrine of the International Community' on 24 April 1999 outlined what he saw as a new paradigm in international affairs regarding the need to recognize and respond to implications of growing global interdependence for security and to protect populations at extreme risk. He set out arguments to justify humanitarian intervention; however, his speech was particularly vague about any details regarding implementation, broadly generalizing about the need to deal with dictators and the need to spread the values of liberty.

Chris Abbott argues that not only were Blair's criteria for intervention too weak to separate humanitarianism from imperialist intention and application, but his version of intervention seemed to emphasize military intervention and then only as a reactive measure.[62] That is, military intervention after, for example, genocide had already begun. Very little attention was paid to preventing these crises in the first place, and it looked like intervention would only be exercised by the strong against the weak.

In relation to Kosovo, Blair claimed, 'No one in the West who has seen what is happening in Kosovo can doubt that NATO's military action is justified.'[63] He outlined five objectives: a verifiable cessation of all combat activities and killings; the withdrawal of Serb forces from Kosovo; the deployment of an international military force; the return of all refugees and unimpeded access for humanitarian aid; and a political framework for Kosovo building on the Rambouillet accords. 'We will not negotiate on these aims', stated Blair. 'Milošević must accept them.'[64] He declared that there were three possible reasons for the use of interventionist force in Kosovo: 1) primarily to avert what would otherwise be a humanitarian disaster, 2) instability and civil war in one part of the Balkans would inevitably spill over into the whole of it, and 3) following the 'promise' that the brutal suppression of the civilian population would not be tolerated, to walk away would not merely destroy NATO's credibility, but more importantly it would be a breach of faith with thousands of innocent civilians.[65]

NATO presented two justifications for forcible intervention in Kosovo. Firstly, that the use of force was within the mandates as outlined in the

UN Security Council resolutions. Secondly, NATO referred to the concept of humanitarian intervention for the protection of peoples at great risk of significant harm.[66] However, while Resolution 1160 (1998) and Resolution 1199 (1998) both stated that the situation in Kosovo was a threat to peace, neither gave explicit authorization to use force.[67] At the 3989th Security Council meeting on 26 March 1999, the Slovene delegate Danilo Türk stated that he would have preferred Security Council authorization, even though it was not possible at the time.[68]

The meeting was convened to address a letter dated 24 March 1999 from the permanent representative of the Russian Federation to the United Nations president of the Security Council. The meeting aimed to resolve a draft Resolution 328 (1999) by Belarus, India and the Russian Federation, which stated deep concern about NATO's use of military force against the FRY without authorization by the Security Council. The draft resolution affirmed that such unilateral use of force constitutes a flagrant violation of the UN Charter, in particular Articles 2 (4), 24 and 53.[69]

The three states reaffirmed their commitment to the sovereignty and territorial integrity of the FRY and that the use of force by NATO constituted a threat to international peace and security. They demanded an immediate cessation of the use of force and an urgent resumption of negotiations. After intense and lengthy discussion, the draft proposal was put to the vote.[70] The proposal was supported by China, Namibia and the Russian Federation, but it was rejected by Argentina, Bahrain, Brazil, Canada, France, Gabon, Gambia, Malaysia, Netherlands, Slovenia, Great Britain and the United States. The majority of the discussion by those who rejected the draft resolution centred on the primary need for protection, with many claims and assertions about the humanitarian disaster occurring in Kosovo.

Even those who drafted the proposal repeatedly stated their strong support to protect the citizens of Kosovo, but that in the end the action proposed by the UN and NATO would cause an even greater humanitarian disaster, with likely ramifications for all of Yugoslavia and throughout the region. As the Security Council rejected the Belarus, India and Russian Federation proposal and continued the NATO air raids, it could be argued that the use of force was implicitly authorized by default and subject to Resolutions 1199 (1998) and 1203 (1998), which affirmed that the situation in Kosovo was a threat to peace.

NATO's 1999 intervention in Kosovo resulted in a great deal of controversy about the principle to protect, and who has the responsibility to protect. The Security Council was divided about the legal justification and the moral justification (the stronger of the two justifications argued) for forcible intervention. The NATO air war was roundly criticized as being strategically inept for not also including a substantial ground campaign.[71] Albrecht Schnabel and Ramesh Thakur argue that fundamental policy differences between the NATO allies led to a lowest-common-denominator approach, and the air strikes did not prevent widespread atrocities against civilians on the ground in Kosovo or the mass exodus of refugees into neighbouring countries.[72]

In the 2000 report *Conflict, International Response, Lessons Learned*, the Independent International Commission on Kosovo (IICK) made the following observations regarding the conflict: 1) it did not so much create a precedent for intervention elsewhere as raise critical questions about the legitimacy and practicability of the use of military force to protect and defend human rights; 2) it exposed the limitations of the current international law on the balance between the rights of citizens and the rights of states; 3) it demonstrated the difficulties that ensue when even the most sophisticated and professional military forces are deployed to achieve humanitarian goals; and 4) it showed, in the UN administration's difficulties in Kosovo, the immense obstacles that lie in the path of creating multiethnic co-operation in societies torn apart by ethnic war.[73]

What the report did not do was canvas preventative strategies that may have avoided the need for intervention in the first place, subsequent to the relentless path to war in Kosovo. The report follows the traditional 'lessons learned' approach after conflict and, as is the case with most of these types of reports, these are very narrowly defined. The primary lesson that should be, but is rarely, learned is that states should assume a responsibility to prevent in order to avoid the ultimate need for rear-guard, after-the-fact protection.

What is a Responsibility to Prevent (R2Prevent)?

Embracing the notion of R2Prevent requires a conceptual reorientation in thinking about state and human security. Acknowledging R2P is an important step in the development of a civil society, but when protection ends up as a desperate response to some calamity, as it so often does, then prevention has either largely failed or it has not been effective in the first place. Both R2Prevent and R2P are context specific. They may involve diplomatic pressures or incentives, economic inducements or sanctions, or coercive action – or a combination of these. The possibility of indictment of individual leaders by the ICC, targeted economic penalties on leaders and their close associates, and support for embargoes are some of the more punitive tools of prevention and protection strategies.

Legal inducements include adherence requirements to treaties and the development of compliance measures by international judicial institutions that may adjudicate on disputes between states, groups or individuals. Where punitive options are not appropriate, and there are many situations where they are not, then economic alternatives such as assistance from international financial institutions, bilateral or multilateral trade arrangements, and trade incentives may be appropriate inducements to facilitate prevention and protection endeavours.

Whatever mix or primacy aspect of the two is applied in one place may not be effective elsewhere. Neither R2Prevent nor R2P are a guarantee for peace or security. What is certain is that without serious attention to prevention and protection, human security will continue to be severely challenged. The foundational elements of R2P involve the responsibility to prevent, the responsibility to react and the responsibility to rebuild. Prevention is the single most important dimension of the responsibility to protect and it is high time for the international community to be doing more to close the gap between rhetorical support for prevention and tangible commitment.[74]

UN secretary-general Ban Ki-moon's report *Implementing the Responsibility to Protect* outlines a three-pillar strategy for advancing the agenda of R2P: the protection responsibilities of the state; international engagement, assistance and capacity building; and a timely and effective response. There are two important stages in the preventative thesis. The first stage is precrisis or structural prevention. This is where attention may be directed, for example, at democracy promotion initiatives, supporting institutional reforms that reduce corruption and nepotism, education to reduce intolerance and to increase reform capacity, support for human rights, and fostering economic development. Supporting the development of all aspects of civil society is a crucial part of the structural preventative approach. The second stage is direct or operational prevention where the focus is on trying to prevent the escalation of violence before events spiral totally out of control. In this case, the potential for such violence is extreme, real and imminent. Strategies may include active diplomacy, aid conditionality, embargoes against arms transfers, working directly with institutions and organizations that support peaceful resolutions to conflict, responding to the needs of Internally Displaced Persons (IDPs) and refugees, and encouraging negotiation and cross-table talks between conflicting parties.

Once events on the ground have spiralled out of control, then much more direct preventative strategies need to be implemented. These strategies include peacekeeping missions, direct monitoring of flashpoints followed by interventionist responses to stop killing and abuse, and setting up and actively protecting safe havens for those fleeing the conflict zones. The direct imposition of military intervention must be considered where there is potential for the violence to escalate to such a level that genocide and other crimes against humanity are a real possibility. All of these stages require the co-operation and engagement of the international community, firstly to try to prevent the potential for violence, but when serious conflict erupts, regardless of efforts to dissuade belligerents, then direct intervention must be considered to address the suffering of innocent civilians.

Deborah Mayersen provides a useful outline of the various stages of the preventative thesis in *The Responsibility to Prevent: Opportunities, Challenges and Strategies for Operationalization*.[75] She argues that any particular strategy will have both advantages and disadvantages that need to be considered carefully before implementation. The most likely effective approach will be multifaceted and tailored to a specific context. This is a critical point. There is no single approach or even a combined approach that will suit all circumstances because the complexities are many and varied regarding how different states behave towards their own citizens and how societies may respond to outside intervention. External intervention has its own difficulties because potential interventionists need to be motivated to respond to the looming disasters developing in failing or failed states. The potential that direct intervention may exacerbate the risk for all parties is high. This is why 'last-ditch prevention' to stop an already disastrous situation from becoming even worse is usually too little, too late.

Structural preventative strategies are important, but as always the issue that overarches them all is how they are to be implemented. This is where critics of the preventative approach lose interest in talking about medium- to long-term prevention. They do not argue that these strategies are unimportant, but their concern revolves around how they can possibly work, particularly when states are so intransigent that they simply ignore most or even all efforts by the international community to engage with them. They further challenge the idea that the international community is willing and able to engage with such states in the first place. To counter some of these views, Mayersen provides detailed discussion and useful practical examples regarding how each of these strategies may be practically addressed and implemented, but again, context and careful consideration for different circumstances and how the international community may contribute to the prevention thesis is the key. Ban Ki-moon declared 2012 to be 'the year of prevention'. However, 'prevention does not mean looking the other way in times of crisis, vainly hoping that things will get better. We have done that too often. Nor can it be just a brief pause while Chapter VII "enforcement measures" are being prepared.' Instead, 'prevention means proactive, decisive and early action to stop violence before it begins'.[76]

Jennifer Welsh and Serena Sharma present a useful discussion in their study *Operationalizing the Responsibility to Prevent* regarding the relationship between prevention and protection, a clarification of the aim of prevention and systematizing preventive tools. They argue that there is still very little scholarly analysis of how to approach the prevention of mass atrocities, or empirical research on what tools, coercive and noncoercive, are most effective in preventing R2P crimes.[77] In addition, they say, the tendency to conflate the prevention of mass atrocities with the more general prevention of armed conflict has contributed to conceptual confusion over the appropriate scope and aim of the preventive dimension of R2P. Their approach is to constrain the discussion of prevention to R2P where the aim is to prevent an already serious situation from escalating to genocide and other mass killings.

> In sum, preventive strategies associated with R2P should be aimed at attacks directed at any population, committed in a widespread or systematic manner, in furtherance of a state or organizational policy, irrespective of the existence of discriminatory intent or an armed conflict. These crimes against humanity encompass genocide, ethnic cleansing, and that sub-set of war crimes which is widespread and aimed at civilian populations. In addition, they can be committed by individuals associated with a state or state-like entity, or individuals associated with a non-state organization or rebel group.[78]

It is true, as the authors claim, that framing prevention and R2P closely together in this way has brought a greater degree of precision and clarity to the principle, and encouraged both analysts and policy makers to draw on international legal standards, but by the time events have escalated to trying to stop mass killings that in reality have most likely already begun, the broader application of the R2Prevent thesis has essentially failed.

Prevention as a duty or a procedure deals with the phase prior to the situation where significant harm or damage has actually occurred. Desmond Tutu, Anglican archbishop emeritus of Cape Town, South Africa succinctly stated that, 'It is by preventing, rather than reacting, that we can truly fulfil our shared responsibility to end the worst forms of human rights abuses.'[79] Prevention must be contextualized to a people, a state or a region, and different preventive strategies are appropriate to different places, different times and different situations. There is no singular or universal solution, but this does not mean that there are no solutions at all. There are a number of viable and practical preventative approaches that make an endgame need for protection much less likely.

R2P and protection in general provide a more tangible understanding than the prevention thesis of events and reaction by the international community or by a coalition of states. When Kuwait was attacked by Iraq in the early 1990s, the protection response was based on violation of state sovereignty. When coalition forces invaded Iraq after 11 September 2001, the protection response was a reaction to concerns over weapons of mass destruction

(WMDs) falling into the hands of terrorists. The international community may argue about the validity or otherwise of the protection response, but they usually can understand the simple rationale behind the need for protection.

Prevention and preventative action is much less tangible and very difficult to implement. Emma Rothschild argues that 'one of the distinctive characteristics of prevention is that it takes place under conditions of imperfect information. [...] Without good information, anticipatory actions are always likely to be too late. [...] One does not know that one cares about something, or reflect on what one has it in one's power to do, until one knows about some particular injustice or crisis.'[80]

Therefore, the prevention thesis is much more complicated because it relies on the international community being proactive. What does this mean? Prevention means strong states showing practical and moral leadership by not supporting despotic regimes, not selling vast quantities of military equipment particularly to states that have little or no interest in their citizen's human security needs and not providing diplomatic or political support to states that abuse their own citizens. For example, the regime in Iraq was directly and indirectly supported by many Western powers for decades prior to the Gulf War in 1991, despite its dreadful human rights record and its aggressive actions in the region. The rapid militarization of Iraq and the lack of international response to the violent activities of the Iraqi regime contributed to the Iraqi invasion of Kuwait, until the selective 'protection' of Kuwait by a UN-sponsored coalition force seemed to be the only option.

Strong states in particular have a special obligation to act responsibly in their behaviour towards others. If powerful states only pay lip service or ignore vital international humanitarian conventions, then there is little point in hectoring weaker states to change their behaviour. Leadership and compassion in this area is seriously lacking, as is an understanding of what prevention actually means. Alex Bellamy points to at least three factors that have contributed to the relative neglect of the responsibility to prevent: the inherent difficulty in translating a commitment to prevention into coherent policy, the impact of the place of prevention in the war on terrorism and the question of authority and agency.[81]

For prevention to be effective the following criticalities must be addressed: first, a reorientation from traditional state security paradigms to grass roots human security embracing preventative strategies – in the end, and in the beginning, the best protection is prevention; second, the international community has a moral and legal responsibility to prevent the escalation of extreme violence and serious human deprivations – this responsibility must be embraced early and directly to ameliorate human suffering; third, serious attention to the notion of prevention before the need for protection has a greater chance of success in the reduction of serious wants and in the reduction of fear for citizens and states at risk; fourth, the sheer waste of precious lives and the scarce resources of would-be interventionists and citizens at risk alike are the usual outcomes when protection becomes a priority in desperation. A focus on prevention is future-orientated and it does not rely on pyrrhic diplomatic or military outcomes that ultimately fail to even protect those most at risk.

The prevention of conflict begins and ends with the promotion of human security and human development.[82] However, when policy makers, researchers and norm entrepreneurs talk about prevention, they usually frame the discussion through the lens of protection as the primary point of reference. Today, prevention is generally seen to be subset under the broader spectrum and primacy of protection.[83] The problem is that conceptualizing prevention in this way is extremely limiting. To do very little or nothing at all to ameliorate the condition of populations at risk, and then to aim to instigate preventative measures in order to protect such populations when events spiral out of control, does not address the wider potentiality of what prevention could and should mean.

The fundamental idea of the R2Prevent approach is that human security issues must be addressed pre-emptively and, most importantly, before an overwhelming need for immediate protection presents itself. Both R2Prevent and R2P are about timing, practical application and, as particularly is the case with the R2Prevent thesis, dealing with grassroots human needs. The R2Prevent approach is to directly prioritize prevention in order to alleviate the need for protection, and the focus must be on potential flashpoints. Some of these flashpoints today are the steadily deteriorating relationship between North Korea and the international community, and the unstable situation in Iraq after the withdrawal of substantial numbers of coalition troops. Others include Iran's nuclear ambitions, the never-ending problems between Israel and Palestine, and the escalating violence and unrest in Egypt after the Arab Spring revolutions.

All of these flashpoints have the potential to develop into enormous humanitarian disasters. State responsibility in the area of human security and protection remains key, but in an increasingly violent and complex world surely prevention must come first. The international community may occasionally directly intervene in an effort to protect those already subject to widespread and extreme levels of violence, but when a situation has deteriorated to such a level, then prevention efforts, if they have occurred at all, have mostly been too little and too late.[84]

A general criticism against the human security approach, particularly in the area of prevention, is that these themes are to many people basically incomprehensible in a meaningful and practical sense. That is, what does human security really mean, why and how is prevention different to protection (if at all) and is the idea about prevention and all the talk about grass-roots human security just fine words and a lot of theorizing? The problem of context is a serious one and it affects both R2P and R2Prevent. What may or may not work in one area or circumstance may or may not work in another. For example, when critics of the prevention thesis ask how one can seriously talk about prevention in Afghanistan when people need immediate and direct protection from extreme violence, they are asking a valid question, but the context is wrong.

This is a protection question, and all protection can do in this context is to prevent a disastrous situation from becoming even worse. The prevention question to have asked long before an invasion and the beginning of the ten-year war in Afghanistan should have been: how can we prevent such conflict from happening in the first place? Ramesh Thakur argues that despite prevention being described as the single most important dimension of protection, the responsibility to prevent has been relatively neglected.[85]

Protection and Prevention: Where to Now?

The problems and anxieties of the twenty first century present some new and some very different challenges from those faced by individual states and the international community since the fall of the Berlin Wall and the end of the Cold War. Today we are engaged in what many believe to be a global war on terror precipitated by the attacks against America by a small group of extremists on 11 September 2001. The ramifications of the response by the international community and in particular by the US and its coalition partners to the 11 September attacks have been global.

The results have been ever more draconian, antiterrorism laws being introduced by powerful and not-so-powerful states alike. Basic civil and political rights continue to be dishonoured, if not ignored outright. The trillions of dollars spent on the wars in Iraq and Afghanistan have contributed to the global financial crisis and the world's wealthiest nations are staggering under the cost. The impact of the diversion of funds away from essential infrastructure and other desperately needed development work in poor countries has yet to be fully realized by the international community, but, of course, poor countries are counting and experiencing the cost every day. Millions of lives have been disrupted, hundreds of thousands of people killed and injured and essential public infrastructures destroyed in the zones of conflict.

The wars in Iraq and Afghanistan have escalated the ambitions of many separatist or insurgency groups to further their own causes at the local or regional level. However, this does not mean that there is a global terrorist network. Individual extremists and various extremist groups may have some affiliations and perhaps general sympathy with the goals of al-Qaeda, but this does not make a global terrorist conspiracy a reality. Many extremist groups have in common a hatred for established authority unless it is their own, and they are driven by ideological and religious motives that outsiders find difficult, if not impossible, to understand. There is fear, confusion and misunderstanding on all sides. The vast majority of Muslims are not extremists, but when they see how the West has responded since the events of 11 September 2001, they question the fundamental agenda of non-Muslims with fears of a global holy war and other conspiracies of their own.

The invasions of Iraq and Afghanistan have been a disaster for Iraqis and Afghans. By 2008, up to 5 million Iraqis had been forced to flee their homes, with a further 3 million Afghans fleeing to Pakistan and 915,000 to the Islamic Republic of Iran. In 2011, the UN High Commissioner for Refugees (UNHCR) reported that there were at least 1.5 million IDPs in Iraq and that the inability of Iraq to form a government following the March 2010 elections would further exacerbate the situation.[86] Death estimates in the Iraqi zones of conflict alone range from 43,000 to over 655,000 depending on who one believes.[87] The UK *Guardian* reported in October 2010 that the WikiLeaks data suggests a grim picture regarding Iraqi death tolls during the six years between 2004 and 2009.[88] The database records the following death counts: 66,081 civilians, 23,984 insurgents and 15,196 Iraqi security forces. 34,814 people were recorded as murdered in 24,840 incidents and there were 65,439 improvised explosive device (IED) explosions over the period with 31,780 deaths recorded. 3,771 coalition troops have been killed and total wounded (civilian and combatant) was 176,382.

In 2010, Iraqi Body Count (IBC) claimed a further 4,023 civilian deaths from estimates derived from 8,250 distinct reports collected from 143 sources, covering 1,620 incidents. IBC has updated its estimates based on the WikiLeaks data set for total war deaths up to 2010 as 156,719.[89] IBC statisticians have stated that, 'taken as a whole and seen in the context of immediately preceding years, the 2010 data suggest a persistent low-level conflict in Iraq that will continue to kill civilians at a similar rate for years to come'.[90] Jacob Shapiro points out some of the major issues regarding all these statistics.

Firstly, he says that not every death – or anything close to it – was recorded because there was no coalition or Iraqi unit around to record the deaths, or else the coalition and Iraqi units in the area were engaged in such high levels of combat that they did not have time to track down every casualty on all sides. Secondly, the reporting standards varied over time between units in the field and behind the lines of combat. He stated that, 'although the data paints a grim picture, the facts are likely to be much, much worse, because of underreporting'.[91] The facts that Shapiro is referring to only relate to war deaths and not injury or deprivation as a direct result of the ongoing conflict.

If the IBC statisticians are correct, then civilian war-related injuries range from three injuries per death using a mean calculation to five injuries per death using a median calculation.[92]

It is not possible to accurately determine war-related deaths and injuries in Iraq. Civilian injuries were not tallied at the outset, and as Azhar Rafiq and Ronald Merrell note, the widely disparate figures may say more about the political bias of those attempting to collect or interpret the data than anything resembling the truth: 'However, it is beyond doubt that there have been hundreds of thousands of injuries in the violence in Iraq since 2006.'[93] The aggressive, militarily interventionist posture by the coalition has not resulted in the prevention of violence and deprivation for the Iraqi people. The fragile Iraqi government seems incapable of dealing with its own factional divisions, never mind dealing with sectarian violence or preventing further conflict.

Conclusion

The response to the terrible attacks in America on 11 September 2001 have been a catalyst for the rise in ethnic, racial and religious intolerance with inferred or explicit claims that certain states or even entire populations are part of some sort of evil empire.[94] Such claims resonate with the anticommunism hysteria of the 1960s. A myopic focus on the state-centric protection paradigm is much too limiting in our increasingly globalized world. The need for homeland protection is not in contention regarding national security matters, nor is the need to prevent extremists from planning or carrying out their dreadful acts against civilians and noncombatants. We all accept the necessity for this type of protection and prevention.

The problem is that limiting protection and prevention in this way is not making us safer nor is it reducing the levels of fear in many parts of the world today. We appear to be surrounded by major flashpoints everywhere. North Korea and Iran's nuclear ambitions terrify their neighbours near and far, and the ongoing humanitarian disaster in Darfur continues while we pontificate whether it really is a genuine genocide. Coalition forces have withdrawn from Iraq where the public infrastructures and civil society are a long way from recovering, and the war in Afghanistan continues unabated.

The idea that individual states and the international community could have prevented the crisis we now face, and that we have a responsibility to rectify the current state of play in world events, is contentious. Many will say that our capacity to respond in different or new ways to the rise of intolerance and extremism is limited due to the aggressive posture of the superpowers and the ineffectiveness of organizations such as the United Nations. The claim that many of these world events, especially the wars in Iraq and Afghanistan and the global war on terrorism, are largely of our own making is equally contentious. Had we taken a different path post–11 September, with prevention and overall human security uppermost in mind regarding the so-called war on terrorism, the world would most likely be a very different place today. That is, prevention in the context of avoiding the conflagration of religious and ethnic hatred that is directed against some of the major world powers.

The self-interest protection ethos, with its myopic focus on state security to the cost of nearly everything else, is just not working. If we take 'working' to mean a reduction in tension and a reduction in the fear of further widespread attacks against coalition states, then it has not worked in Iraq and it is not working in Afghanistan. The on-the-ground security situation for Iraqi and Afghan people is extremely tense and is in many places outright hostile. Proclamations by the senior partners of the coalition that 'things are improving' in Iraq and Afghanistan after ten years of war challenge reality and what is actually happening to the citizens within these states and surrounding regions.[95] The evidence is clear to see on the news, in the research, by the ceaseless and desperate work of humanitarian organizations and NGOs, and at selected high-level political gatherings and think tanks where honesty and truth have a measure of relevance.

The UN had a very important role to play post–11 September regarding how the international community and how the US in particular should react to these attacks. Unfortunately, the politics of fear both within and without the UN and the instinctive need to lash out against an elusive enemy carried the day, resulting in the invasion of Iraq (without UN approval) and the war in Afghanistan (with UN approval). The pre-emptive wars against these states were intended to *protect* big, soft Western targets and to *prevent* further extremist attacks, but little if any consideration was directed to the severe consequences of using military force in this way and for this reason.

Conventional warfare has a very poor record in dealing with insurgency and extremism. It is particularly unsuccessful in dealing with ideological or religious and ethnic-based conflicts. Prevention and protection need to be considered as long-term, pre-emptive strategies, with the specific intention of reducing fear and reducing want for all people who do not harm others. The only way to address serious ideological, ethnic and religious differences is by paying attention to winning the hearts and minds of potential protagonists. This requires some serious rewiring in our thinking about how we go about the complex business of protecting and preventing. Prevention must come first. By the time we are in the protection phase then prevention has failed or at most we can only hope to prevent an absolute catastrophe from finally occurring.

Chapter 4

STATE RESPONSIBILITY, HUMAN SECURITY AND INTERNATIONAL LAW

The relationship between international law and human security is an important one because legal norms, however derived, are the cornerstones of an ordered, civil and moral society. This chapter provides a discussion on international law and its relevance and relationship to state responsibility. The international community and individual states have obligations and responsibilities according to both formative and substantive law, reflected in the deliberations and rulings of international institutions such as the International Court of Justice (ICJ), the International Criminal Court (ICC), the International Monetary Fund (IMF), the World Bank and others. Despite the modern progression of international law, some legal positivists will argue that international law is not real law, but they have few answers as to why most in the international community of states actually recognize and abide by such law. We provide some discussion on this point because a common criticism of international law is that it frequently fails to hold states accountable for their behaviour, and therefore is not real law.

The work by the UN International Law Commission (ILC) was pivotal in bridging the gap between international law and substantive international legal norms that attempt to articulate the role of the state and its responsibilities regarding international humanitarian law (IHL) and international human rights law (IHRL). We argue in this chapter that all these areas of law consist of important and complimentary legal instruments that help to define state responsibility, particularly in the realm of human security. IHL and IHRL are two separate areas of law that have historically evolved quite differently. The notion of human rights originated as a matter of constitutional and national law with the aim of codifying state responsibilities and obligations regarding how the state treats its citizens. We propose that this has now progressed to encompass certain human security obligations that are not just incumbent upon individual states but on all states.

The Relevance of International Law to State Behaviour

International law, sometimes also referred to as the law of nations, may be considered in a number of ways. One approach is to conceptualize international law as consisting of layers.[1] The first layer consists of laws that codify and regulate state responsibility and mutual obligation between states. These are the traditional laws and conventions that are primarily state focused and state orientated. The early work of the ILC on state responsibilities and obligations falls into this area. The second, more recent component, often referred to as IHL, is the law of the international community. IHL developed as an adjunct to traditional international law, which dealt primarily with state-to-state issues. International law has two basic components: customary international law (CIL) and treaty law.[2]

International law is binding on all states with a branch consisting of the law of treaties. Such treaties are either contractual or they have a law-making character by which states lay down new rules of international law. Community law may be developed as a result of a treaty, for example the 1957 Treaty Establishing the European Community (EC Treaty). Such communities have an international legal personality. This in turn creates a dependency of community law on international law.[3] International law also has both a public and a private component.[4] The public side reflects laws governing relations between states whereas the private component of international law, in this case more precisely defined as transnational law, is involved with transactions between individuals and entities of different states.

Traditionally, the positivist school of thought, which sees legal norms as commands being issued by a superior authority, has been uncomfortable with the idea that some forms of international law could be rooted in then somehow evolve from custom, communal relationships or some sort of social contract between states or institutions.[5] Proponents will claim that law itself is essentially juridical, and because international law has no supreme authority, it does not have procedural commonality and it has little if any enforcement capacity. Dispute settlements, when and where they exist at all, are arbitrary therefore international law cannot even be considered to be real law. National security discourses, particularly post–11 September 2001, have frequently depicted public international law as being naive, advisory only (and therefore mostly irrelevant) or quaint and obsolete. The fundamental criticism is that it is incapable of carrying out its declared function as an arbiter of state behaviour.[6]

There are at least two responses to these views and they need to be presented if one is going to argue that international law does have relevance as a constraint on state behaviour. Firstly, law is not only juridical; it has at the same time political, social and psychological aspects that cannot be simply ignored.

It is true that international law is dependent on the development of juridical process, but as with all positive systems of law it requires certain political and social conditions to be fulfilled.[7] These include a desire for justice, good faith, co-operation and mutual respect. For example, the Vienna Law of Treaties involves four distinct iterations: negotiation, signature, ratification and entry into force.[8]

These processes rely upon and ultimately impose corresponding obligations on state participants to negotiate in good faith, to avoid actions that defeat the treaty's purpose and function, and to comply in good faith with the terms of the treaty.[9] R2Prevent encapsulates the preventative and protective outcomes of these inclusions. Law that is without these important elements is fundamentally deficient as a reflection of the wider needs and wants of a society.

The precepts of international law depend on these fundamental elements, but to ignore them as critical components in the development of law relegates the development of law to rules that simply appear via legislatures or in legal chambers. This may be the case in autocratic regimes, but not in states that value democracy and actively pursue the democratic process as an important social and legal construct. Convention, custom, politics and many other aspects of the public and the private voice all influence the formation of substantive legal norms.

Legal positivists will argue that the presentation of convention and custom as the supposed drivers behind the validation of legal norms is only really done to rationalize and further the interests of the powerful, or it is done to try to substantiate idealized aspirations for world peace, saving the planet and human rights, again mostly in the interests of the powerful. Yet, this misses the fundamental point that regardless of the intent or the influence of convention, customs and protocols, the progression and development of all law remains dependent on these fundamental building blocks.

Secondly, the overarching view that if a law cannot make violators (state or otherwise) comply with the letter – or even the spirit – of the law, then it is not a real law is problematic. This particular view reflects a great deal of scholarship and legal attention that has traditionally been focused on the notion of compliance in regard to CIL.[10] It is true to say that international law is reliant on reciprocity, self-interest and decentralized sanctions for enforcement and compliance. However, one must look more closely at what the notion of compliance actually means. In the case of state censure by some sort of international legal entity, compliance may involve the enforcement of sanctions, diplomatic censure, or particular punitive measures that attempt to force a state to adhere to a law, convention or custom. Yet it may also mean the capacity to foster co-operative behaviours by the process of inclusion or exclusion, and it may mean moral leverage and the 'mobilization of shame'.[11]

The World Bank, IMF, International Labour Organization (ILO) and the International Civil Aviation Organization (ICAO) are all examples of organizations that utilize inclusion or exclusion as a legal tool for state compliance. States materially advance their interests through these organizations, but if they fail to meet the prescribed standards of co-operative behaviour, then they may face the penalty of nonparticipation and lose the benefits of co-operation.[12]

Robert Drinan defines the mobilization of shame as 'the moral power which, more than laws or economic sanctions, will induce nations to follow the less followed road that leads to democracy and equality'.[13] This, he claims, involves the activities of fact-finding bodies, watchdog groups and internationally sanctioned commissions raising questions about the human rights practices of specific nations and offering suggestions for improvement. At least one important goal of this process is to 'induce [violating] governments to regret their conduct and feel ashamed.'[14] Adherence to treaties is another form of compliance requirement in law. Yet states rarely obey rules simply because they are threatened by sanctions or because they have sanctions forced upon them.

Harvard law professor Abram Chayes, former legal adviser to the US State Department, says that states obey international law because of the persuasive dynamic created by the treaty regimes to which they belong. The fundamental legal instrument for maintaining compliance with treaties is 'an iterative process of discourse among parties, the treaty organization, and the wider public.'[15]

The compliance or otherwise of states to international law (we argue that international law is real law) is an important factor when considering state responsibility and human security. Too often states have abrogated their responsibility to protect their citizens and others by noncompliance with international laws, conventions or customs, or even adherence to their own national laws. Basic civil rights are regularly circumvented and sometimes totally ignored, even by states that otherwise have democratic processes and institutions in place, but this does not mean that important international laws are irrelevant. For example, domestic laws against murder are not irrelevant despite murder being committed by individuals within states.

No one would suggest that the legal prohibition against unlawful killing is irrelevant and the same rationale may be applied to international law. The reasons why states behave in the way that they do are many and varied, but in an increasingly populated and globalized world adherence to the basic tenets of international law are increasingly coming under external scrutiny from other states, international forums and organizations.

Some will also challenge the legal relevance of another contentious legal area and term; customary international law. Traditionally, customary law is based upon some sort of tacit, formal or informal agreement between states or other parties. This construction has found expression in the idea that a custom founded in recognized general practice may be followed *ex opinione juris* in order to qualify as a binding rule in law. Article 38 of the ICJ recognizes the qualification of customary law as 'evidence of a general practice accepted as law'.[16]

There are two factors to consider here: One is the so-called objective nature of state practice, the other is the subjective factor known as *opinio juris sive necessitatis*, or the belief that a particular practice is accepted as law based on the principles of custom. Custom is generally considered to have evolved from state practice and *opinio juris*, where state practice is followed out of a belief of legal obligation.[17] State practice is not always seen as being objective:

> When inferring rules of customary law from the conduct of States, it is necessary to examine not only what States do, but also why they do it. In other words, there is a psychological element in the formation of customary law. State practice alone does not suffice; it must be shown that it is accompanied by the conviction that it reflects a legal obligation.[18]

So, conceptualizing what state practice means or identifying what a state believes is challenging. Does it mean the physical activity of states, statements by states, or is it some combination of the two that over a period of time has coalesced into some sort of internally and/or externally recognized convention or custom that may eventually transpose into a form of substantive law? The validity of law based on this type of progression has always been hotly contested, but this has not stopped the process of adjudication and legal judgements being made on this matter in international courts. For example, the ICJ has made a number of determinations regarding the existence or otherwise of the application of customary law during the 1950 *Columbia v. Peru Asylum* case, the 1969 North Sea Continental Shelf cases (*Federal Republic Of Germany v. Denmark, Federal Republic of Germany v. Netherlands*) and the 1974 Fisheries Jurisdiction Case (*United Kingdom v. Iceland*).[19]

One particular challenge facing the notion of CIL is that there is no agreement on what constitutes state practice, nor is there agreement on how widespread a custom must be or how long a custom must be in place in order to satisfy the state practice requirement.[20] Yet challenges such as these are not necessarily a disadvantage. Theodor Meron suggests that

> when customary law *is* applied today [it] relies principally on loosely defined *opinion juris* and/or inference from the widespread ratification of treaties or

support for resolutions and other 'soft law' instruments: thus, it is more flexible
and open to relatively rapid acceptance of new norms.[21]

This has resulted in alternative ways of developing a modern international
legal order that is no longer slavishly linked to treaty making, and CIL is an
important contributor to this process.[22]

International Humanitarian Laws: Progression and Promises

In this chapter we have argued that international law is real law and that it
has a positive role as a means of securing human security. The development
of IHL and IHRL is consistent with the fundamental rationale of the human-
security approach. There are many challenges that have yet to be addressed
if the basic aspirations of human security are to be realized. The role of IHL
and IHLR as substantive legal instruments still has a very long way to go, but
the establishment of international criminal tribunals, especially the ICC, are
indicators of positive progress. The complementarity between prevention and
protection underpins the discussion of the development of the human security
ethos, and it is relevant to an investigation into the validity of international
law and state responsibility. The punitive outcome of the application of law is
not an end in itself. What is also important is the ameliorative, restorative and
preventive nature of the law.

   IHL and IHRL are two distinct areas of law that have historically evolved
quite differently. The notion of human rights originated as a matter of
constitutional and national law that aimed to curb the power of the state in
relation to its dealings with its citizens. Essentially the aim was to codify by
convention and practice state responsibilities in order to prevent some of the
more egregious behaviours of states and to assist in the protection of citizens.
This remained the case until after World War II when human rights became to
be seen as more than simply a reflection of the levels of engagement between
governments and their people. They became part of substantive international
law beginning with the adoption of the 1948 Universal Declaration of Human
Rights (UDHR). Humanitarian law has developed over more than a century
and as a legal instrument of positive law has been far more accepted by the
international community than human rights law.[23]

   IHL is derived from four sources: 1) treaties and agreements; 2) customary
law; 3) general principles of law common to major legal systems; and 4) judicial
decisions and scholarly teachings.[24] These sources are listed in Article 38 of the
Permanent Court of International Justice (PCIJ, the predecessor to the ICJ) Statute.
The First Assembly of the League of Nations adopted Article 38 unanimously
in 1920. William Slomanson points out that this PCIJ source list evolved from

the common practice of local or regional tribunals that had used these same sources for investigating the substantive content of international law. The so-called 'Permanent Court' employed these sources for seeking the details about the actual content of International Law.[25]

The motivation behind humanitarian law is, as its name suggests, primarily humanitarian, not a principle of rights.[26] It is also not just about protection, because in order to protect there must also be a strong preventative element. Humanitarian law evolved from the idea of civilized and chivalrous behaviour between two parties at war, so military strategy, reciprocity and mutual expectations played a significant part in its historical development.[27] Evidence of formal rules that attempted to place at least some constraints on human behaviour during times of war may be traced as far back as 1386 in the Ordinance for the Government of the Army, when King Richard of England prohibited acts of violence against women and unarmed priests.

Oliver Cromwell's *Laws and Ordinances of Warre, Established for the Better Conduct of the Army* (1643) states, 'None shall kill an Enemy who yeelds, and throws down his Armes.'[28] The 1863 Lieber Code, or *Instructions for the Government of Armies of the United States in the Field*, was one of the first attempts to codify the laws of war and they were the origin of the Project of an International Declaration Concerning the Laws and Customs of War, presented to the 1874 Brussels Conference.[29] The Lieber Code was intended primarily as rules for conduct during the American Civil War, but its development stimulated the adoption of the 1899 and 1907 Hague Conventions on land warfare.

The first Geneva Convention of 1864 for the Amelioration of the Condition of the Wounded in Armies in the Field defines 'the basis on which rest the rules of international law for the protection of the victims of armed conflicts.'[30] The 1864 convention was originally signed only by Switzerland, Baden, Belgium, Denmark, France, Hesse, Holland, Italy, Portugal, Prussia, Spain and Württemberg but over time nearly all states have signed the treaty. The 1906 Geneva Convention was signed by 35 states and further updated in 1929 and 1949 with an expansion of the original 10 articles to the current 64 articles. Attempts to regulate the methods and means of warfare in treaty law go back to the 1868 St Petersburg Declaration, the 1925 Geneva Gas Protocol, the 1972 Biological Weapons Convention, the 1977 Additional Protocols, the 1980 Convention on Certain Conventional Weapons, the 1993 Chemical Weapons Convention and the 1997 Ottawa Convention on the Prohibition of Anti-Personnel Landmines.[31]

In 1993, the International Conference for the Protection of War Victims convened in Geneva to discuss particular ways to address violations of international humanitarian law, but it did not propose the adoption of new treaty provisions. Jean-Marie Henckaerts said that the conference reaffirmed the necessity to make the implementation of humanitarian law more effective and called on the Swiss government to convene a panel of experts to study practical ways of promoting compliance with IHL. The Intergovernmental Group of Experts for the Protection of War Victims met in Geneva in 1995 and adopted a series of recommendations aimed at enhancing respect for IHL. The recommendations were specifically aimed at preventive measures to assist the effective implementation of the law.[32]

Theodore Meron claims that IHRL has mostly deferred to IHL where there has been a conflict of legal primacy between the two. He argues that the International Covenant on Civil and Political Rights is an example of where the legal primacy between the two bodies of law is evident in the wording of the covenant, which states that, 'to the extent that in present international law "lawful acts of war" are recognized, such lawful acts are deemed not to be prohibited by Article 6 [...] if they do not violate internationally recognized laws and customs of war.'[33] He suggests that the 1996 judgement by the Nuclear Weapons Advisory Opinion of the ICJ was not reflective of the primacy of the humanitarian ethos inherent within IHRL:

> The right to life and international environmental protections did not render the use of nuclear weapons unlawful. Rather, these rights and protections constituted factors in the calculus of proportionality and discrimination under the law of war. The Court stated that the use of nuclear weapons would 'generally' be contrary to the law of armed conflict but declined to rule on its legality in the extreme circumstances of self-defense the right to life.[34]

Yet conventions and legal rulings are often interpreted very differently and the conjunction, or even the difference, between IHL and IHRL is open to a great deal of debate. Judith Gardam, for example, presents a counterview to Meron regarding, for example, the significance of the Nuclear Weapons Advisory Opinion. She claims that

> the only instance in which IHL played a central role in the issues before the Court, will be considered in retrospect to represent a lost opportunity. What the Court failed to do, as Judge Higgins points out in her Dissenting Opinion, was to explain, elaborate and apply the key elements of humanitarian law.[35]

The evolution of the broader concept of humanitarian law has a long history. The development of modern IHL has in effect paralleled the important work of the ILC, particularly from the 1960s. The current gap between the idea of state responsibility, IHL and humanitarian law in general is unfortunate, but this gap is narrowing as states are increasingly confronted with the many humanitarian issues they are facing today.

The International Law Commission and State Responsibility

Prior to the late 1940s, public international law conceived state responsibility and state security to be primarily about the responsibility of the state regarding its treatment of nonstate citizens or aliens, with particular reference to the injury of persons and property.[36] The ILC initially approached this mammoth task during the 1950s from the historical perspective of attempting to quantify and qualify state responsibilities regarding how states should deal with noncitizens. From the early 1960s, the direction and emphasis of the ILC's work changed, culminating in the focus toward state responsibility and human rights generally.

This resulted in near universal acceptance by all states of the ILC articles during the October 2002 Sixth Committee at the 56th session of the UN General Assembly, and in the adoption of the General Assembly's Resolution 56/83 (2002), 'Responsibility of States for Internationally Wrongful Acts'. The resolution makes particular reference to state responsibilities regarding the protection of fundamental human rights and state obligations under the peremptory norms of general international law. The topic constituted one of the fundamental pillars of the international legal order and one of the main normative elements of the rule of law in international relations.

Throughout history, mass population movements by people fleeing wars or natural catastrophes resulted in the development of international laws and conventions that attempted to codify how states should deal with floods of migrant interlopers. This was seen to be the primary threat to the peace and security of the state; today, however, the international realm is a much more complicated place. The relentless march of globalization has resulted in the international community fragmenting and integrating both at the same time.

Globalization has brought many benefits such as increased economic, social and political engagement between communities and states in the Global North, but it has also resulted in a wide and complex range of serious challenges for everyone. Poor states and regions in the Global South in particular are faced with environmental concerns, reduced access to resources, mass population movements, food shortages, frequent civil wars and other internal strife. Many of these developments and challenges were not envisaged by early lawmakers and by those who limited their conceptualization of state responsibility primarily to how a state should treat noncitizens.

The responsibility of states, legal or otherwise, has always been a highly contentious issue. The codification of state responsibilities into legal form developed to substantiate the sovereign rights of states, but history shows us that the actual protection of the sovereign rights of states has often been extremely tenuous or at times even totally ignored by the rapacious expansionism of powerful states. After major wars, victorious powers meet to divide the spoils of war where state lines are redrawn and regions remapped to reflect new power distributions. This process has a very long history. For example, the Congress of Vienna (1814–15) was convened by all of the European countries and states, with the exception of Turkey, at the end of the Napoleonic Wars in order to redraw the territorial landscape of Europe for the next hundred years. Europe was divided and partitioned into zones and a new state of nations was determined by the major powers, represented by the French foreign minister Talleyrand, the British foreign minister Lord Castlereagh, the Austrian chancellor Prince Metternich and Russia's Tsar Alexander.[37]

Yet the formal gathering of victorious powers after such tumultuous events does reflect the desire of states to mutually formalize and codify new territorial landscapes. The Congress of Vienna determinations were not just limited to the redrawing of territorial boundaries. A wide range of other legal issues were also addressed, such as the free navigation of international rivers, the abolition of the slave trade and the rank of diplomatic agents, and these provisions were then adopted by the signatory powers of the Treaty of Paris in 1814.[38] Over one hundred international conferences and congresses were convened between 1864 and 1914 resulting in more than two hundred and fifty international instruments of substantive law that were based upon the restatement of principles of existing law and by the formulation of new law.[39]

By the early twentieth century, laws had evolved that prohibited certain methods of warfare by the state and imposed constraining responsibilities on military conduct, on enemy civilians and on soldiers no longer engaged in battle. These laws were codified in the 1899 and 1907 Hague Conventions and 1929 Geneva Convention on the Wounded and Sick in Armies in the Field. Yet these so-called laws of war lacked any real mandates outlining specific consequences for individuals who violated such laws. The ILC throughout most of its history had very little to say about individual accountability. This began to change after World War I and particularly after World War II, where the sheer scale of death, injury and destruction prompted the international community and lawmakers to directly consider sanctions and constraints, not only against states, but also against individuals who engaged in what was deemed to be unacceptable conduct during war. The Nuremberg and Tokyo tribunals after World War II were a watershed in international law, particularly regarding the relatively new branch of IHL.

These events marked an increasing trend in the ILC to prescribe at least some individual criminal conduct to be a violation of the laws of war and to mandate limits on the behaviour of governments in relation to how they deal with their own citizens. The Genocide Convention in 1948 and the Geneva Conventions on Armed Conflict in 1949 reflect this ongoing trend in the development of international law.

The ILC had its genesis in these early intergovernmental efforts to deal with the development and codification of international law. The work of the ILC was focused on the responsibility of states and it developed in two broad phases from 1955–96, then from 1998–2001. In 1953, the UN General Assembly requested the commission to undertake the codification of state responsibility, and in 1956, the ILC appointed F. V. García-Amador of Cuba as special rapporteur.

García-Amador attempted to address this issue by a return to the traditional focus on state responsibility for injury to aliens and the narrower topic of diplomatic protection. Robert Rosenstock points out some of the many challenges of attempting to address state responsibility and linking such responsibility to individuals:

> As defined by the positivist school that dominated the field from the late eighteenth century, it governed principally relations between states (and between their sovereigns), with individuals usually at best third-party beneficiaries. The notion that the law would even govern behaviour of governments *vis-à-vis* their own government was anathema to the entire exercise. [...] The only areas of international law that systematically addressed violations of individual rights by states concerned actions by governments against citizens of *other* states – acts deemed an affront to those states and thus within the ambit of international law.[40]

García-Amador argued that the topic of state responsibility was itself so complex and so vast, with an 'infinite variety of situations which arise in practice', that any successful attempt at codification of state responsibility in international law must be based on previous extensive work already carried out in these areas.[41] He envisaged that this was the way forward and that this approach would eventually lead to the integration of substantive rules for the protection of aliens with emerging human rights law.

García-Amador submitted six reports between 1956–61, but his approach to the codification of state responsibility by attempting to link the protection of aliens and diplomatic protection with human rights law was divisive and none of his proposals were discussed in detail either by the commission itself or by the General Assembly. His work was abandoned by the ILC in 1961 when his role as the special rapporteur ended. The ILC appointed Roberto Ago of Italy as chair of a subcommittee to investigate what to do next and how to proceed in addressing the vexing issue of substantiating state responsibility, with increasing attention being directed towards human rights law.

Ago chose to change the direction and the focus of the ILC's work from the specific primary rules (such as for injury to aliens), which if breached would give rise to state responsibility to the general rules of state responsibility. Ago's view was supported by the commission and he was appointed special rapporteur in 1964. His fundamental approach has served as the basis for the ILC's work ever since.

For the next ten years, Ago worked on the origin of state responsibility, and in particular the commission focused on the basic question of what the legal ramifications are or should be if a state violates its international responsibilities. Willem Riphagen of the Netherlands (1980–86) and Gaetano Arangio-Ruiz of Italy (1988–96) were appointed as special rapporteurs of the ILC, followed by James Crawford of Australia (1997–2001). The commission adopted its Draft Articles on the Responsibility of States for Internationally Wrongful Acts in August 2001, thereby finalizing one of the ILC's longest and most controversial studies. The General Assembly adopted Resolution 56/83 (2001) in December 2001, which commended the articles 'to the attention of Governments without prejudice to the question of their future adoption or other appropriate action.'[42]

Daniel Bodansky and John Crook describe the work of the ILC from August 2001 as dealing with the more general secondary rules of responsibility and remedies for breaches of a primary rule, rather than attempting to define particular primary rules of conduct.[43] In particular they identify some of the important issues that the ILC was now mandated to address, including: what is an internationally wrongful act, when does a breach of an international obligation occur, when can a state be held responsible for acts (or omissions) of nonstate actors or of another state, what circumstances justify otherwise wrongful conduct, and what must a state do to remedy an internationally wrongful act?

At least one significant result of the ILC's efforts in attempting to clarify the international responsibilities of states is that it has influenced the deliberations of the ICJ (perhaps in some part as a result of Ago's election to the ICJ as a judge in 1980) and other international tribunals, either directly by the commission's many articles and reports, or indirectly by government comments and statements relating to the work of the ILC. James Crawford suggests that this provided an outcome that

> formed part of a process of feedback that paralleled and indeed overshadowed the less direct and more subtle 'feedback loop' with the International Court of Justice. Such opinions cannot simply be manipulated. The fact that government comments were carefully taken into account may well have played a role in the

relatively benign reception of the articles by the Sixth Committee at the fifty-sixth session of the UN General Assembly in October 2002, and in the rapid adoption of the Assembly's Resolution 56/83. Of more than fifty governments that expressed views in the debate, only two (Mexico and Guatemala) made criticisms of such a kind as to imply rejection of the ILC's proposals – and they did so in terms of a preference for an immediate diplomatic conference rather than outright rejection of the text.[44]

Alain Pellet argues, 'If the ILC did not exist, we should invent it or some kind of similar mechanism. Indeed, one of its main functions is to facilitate and encourage a uniform international law, responding to the needs of international society as a whole, its constant and everlasting needs for uniform transversal rules.'[45] An important challenge that the ILC has yet to satisfactorily address is the influence of nonstate actors and what the responsibility of states is in dealing with individuals or groups such as terrorists and insurgency movements. Edith Brown Weiss argues that these legal relationships largely remain outside of the scope of the ILC's study of international responsibility, which generally adopts the traditional state-to-state approach.[46]

Conclusion

International law is an important adjunct to human security that is reflective not only of normative frameworks, but it must be responsive to universal human needs and wants. Freedom from fear and freedom from want transcend cultural boundaries. The state-centric system developed in the seventeenth century that justified and reiterated state power is subject to serious challenges in the much more complex and interlinked, globalized world of the twenty-first century. We live in a world of transnational pressures and growing interdependence, yet we are responding with the centuries-old interpretation of individual state responsibility that is focused primarily on protecting the sovereignty of the state.

Those that argue that international law is not real law essentially base their views on the issue of compliance to law and the requirement for a clear and authoritative command from a superior authority, procedural commonality and the capacity for enforcement of the law. Yet the apparent prerequisites for these elements do not explain why international law is respected and adhered to in the majority of cases, albeit in varying degrees. Nor does it explain the development of international tribunals such as the ICJ, the ICC and the ad hoc criminal courts in places such as Rwanda and the former Yugoslavia that are set up specifically to adjudicate and to make legal judgements on state and individual responsibilities.

The development of international law post–World War II has seen a shift in attention from matters relating primarily to state security to an increasing focus being directed towards prevention and protection in the area of human security. The recognition of the relevance and the importance of CIL in the development of substantive legal instruments has been subject to a great deal of conjecture, but it is difficult to argue that social customs and norms have no relationship to evolving legal norms.

The important work by the ICL reflects efforts by the international community to deal directly with responsibilities of the state in the modern world. The development of the Vienna Law of Treaties (1969), Geneva Conventions on the Law of the Sea (1958), the Vienna Conventions on Diplomatic Relations (1961) and the Law of Consular Relations (1963) are among the important achievements of the ILC.[47] The ILC is generally considered to be one of the success stories of the UN and its work in codifying general international law is well known and widely acknowledged.[48] The commission has been and will continue to be judged not only on its processes, but more importantly on its outcomes.

Chapter 5

PROMOTING DEMOCRATIC NORMS FOR PROTECTION AND PREVENTION

The gradual shift of norms in international politics has seen an increase in the number of democracies. This is a positive trend for human security and it opens the way for an active strategy among democracies to encourage political change within dictatorial regimes by the promotion of democratic ideals. Such encouragement includes the need to show leadership by example in the development and support for democratic ideals. Chapter 4 set out the legal grounds for R2P and the state obligations to protect and support human security. This chapter deals with international norms in general and democracy norms in particular. We argue that there has been a gradual shift away from the traditional state sovereignty norm in favour of democracy norms that are more supportive of the human security ethos.

The development of democracy norms embeds a moral duty for the state to represent its people and to promote political and socioeconomic welfare. The notion of moral duty also extends to affluent states that have the capacity to actively promote the political and socioeconomic welfare of the less fortunate, wherever they may be. Notions of state responsibility and state obligation are always contentious, but if one claims that democracy promotion is important and that a civil and moral society exists, then there is a clear moral imperative to act. There are many practical examples of individual states and the international community acting to provide assistance and support to those in need, particularly in the aftermath of natural disasters. The selectivity and extent of moral duty is the divisive issue, rather than whether it exists at all. Democratic governance challenges the polarization of power, and when a democratic state fails to meet the expectations of its citizens, democratic institutions and processes have the capacity for a self-correction. Dictatorial and autocratic regimes have few such constraints. Their priority is focused on state security and on the retention of personal power. When such states fail the result is usually a human catastrophe. Democratic states have an inherent responsibility to the welfare of their own citizens, but in an increasingly globalized world they also have a responsibility to address human security issues for people everywhere.

Emerging Democracy Norms

International norms reflect forms of behaviour based on custom, convention and practice. Norms identify fundamental values that are deemed to be important and therefore need to be protected. Newly emerging international norms are a response to an increasing commonality of values among new and old democracies alike. Such normative development responds to increasing functional interdependence between states, with most aspects of international relations now being regulated and constrained by norms of conduct. Norms protecting the sovereignty of states dominate, but the protection of individuals' rights and the wider requirements of human security are causing change in traditional balance-of-power arrangements. The sanctity of state sovereignty as an international norm is increasingly being eroded, and new international norms that aim to protect and foster the fundamentals of human security have gained strength.

The increasing number of democracies in the world has resulted in an expanded zone of like-minded states. The international community at large has come to endorse democratic norms in a far more intensified way than ever before in history. This is a direct result of growing state compliance to democratic norms within an increasing number of policy areas. Many states have committed themselves to act in accordance with particular standards of behaviour deemed essential for democratic development.[1] Pivotal events that have prompted the attention for greater democratic freedoms include the June 1989 demonstrations at Tiananmen Square in China, the deconstruction of the Berlin Wall and later unification of East and West Germany, and finally the collapse of the Soviet Union in 1989–90.

The spread of democratic norms may be traced further back to the wave of democratization that began in Southern Europe during the 1970s and culminated in Eastern Europe in the 1990s. At least 30 states engaged in regime change from nondemocratic to democratic governance, resulting in a fundamental reorganization of political landscapes throughout Africa, Asia and Latin America. Autocratic civil and military regimes were overthrown in Latin America.[2]

In Asia, new democratic governments were established in Indonesia, the Philippines, South Korea and Taiwan. Almost half of the African states established new democratic regimes or made significant progression in political liberalization. While authoritarian regimes were predominant in the 1970s, the move towards democratic promotion had made important inroads in the 1990s. The global wave of democratization left only two areas essentially untouched: North Africa and the Middle East.[3] These regions continued to experience severe democratic deficiencies. Today a new wave of democratic reforms is sweeping through both regions, where decades-long dictatorial regimes are toppling or are under significant stress from populations no longer willing to adhere to the dictates of their long-term autocratic masters.

Egypt, Libya, Tunisia, Yemen, Saudi Arabia and Qatar are all experiencing political unrest, resulting in a move towards important democratic transformations. More recently, Syria and Bahrain are undergoing substantial political and social turmoil. What at first seemed to be limited requests for some basic democratic reforms in the December 2010 Jasmine Revolution in Tunisia soon spilled over to become a major political crisis for many authoritarian regimes. The overthrow of dictatorial regimes in Egypt, Libya, Yemen and Tunisia sparked a democratic revolution in up to ten other regionally located states.

The increasing number of democracies worldwide marks a shift away from the traditional state-security paradigm towards a greater focus for human security and development. The dramatic progression of democratic reforms from the end of the Cold War to the recent events in North Africa and the Middle East marks a turning point in the process of democracy promotion and international politics. The Cold War symbolized a political battle over the guiding ideological platform for international politics, while the end of the Cold War marked a decisive step in favour of democratic norms.

As a growing number of states have turned to democratic governance, the international realm has seen an expanding normative structure to show states how politics could and should be conducted. Such democratic normative structures set out the standards of behaviour within states as well as between states, thereby creating a normative structure that has a significant impact on how politics is conducted domestically and internationally. We argue that there is an increasing international understanding of the merits of the fundamentals of the democracy ideal, which reflects the promotion of the democracy norm at the national level to support political legitimacy. Such understanding has progressed despite the lack of clarity or affirmation in some areas of international law and despite the familiar semantic arguments about the interpretation of various human rights instruments such as the UN Charter.

The collective identity of the Western community is based on a liberal view of human rights regarding individual freedoms, political rights and civil liberties. These rights form an important part of the Western identity. The idea of democratic governance within states and between states developed side by side with the evolution of the modern state and the modern international system of states, yet its roots may be traced back much further in time. In the seventeenth and eighteenth centuries, European liberals supported the revolutionary provocations in America, England and France, where increasing attention was being directed to individual rights, popular elections and economic and social rights. By the mid-nineteenth century, liberals, socialists and conservatives approached the idea of greater democratic freedom from different perspectives, but at the core was the desire for common people to have more say in how their societies and political systems functioned.

The notion of common humanity is intimately linked with the idea of universal rights and universal responsibilities to safeguard rights and liberties for all humankind. These rights and responsibilities were argued to be fundamental natural rights intrinsic to the human experience. The birth of the Westphalian order implicitly endorsed the idea of universal rights and responsibilities. The Treaty of Westphalia not only institutionalized and formalized the international system of sovereign states, but was complimented by the notion of *natural rights* and the *rights of man*. Such rights are the historical linkage to contemporary human rights thinking, which has as its foundations in democracy progression and support for human security. This is now an international, cross-cultural and normative approach that goes well beyond the traditional state-centric security approach.[4] Throughout the twentieth century, fascism, Nazism and communism challenged democratic ideals and crafted alternative political visions. This led to crucial turning points in 1919, 1945 and 1989, where democracies were tested but also promoted.[5]

Western leaders led the rhetoric in democracy promotion. President Woodrow Wilson (1913–21) stressed that the US engagement in World War I was a way of safeguarding democracy. US foreign policy in the 1920s and 1930s proclaimed that interventions in Central America were a way of promoting democracy. US president Franklin Roosevelt (1933–45) and the UK's prime minister Winston Churchill (1940–45, 1951–55) advocated in the Atlantic Charter the right of all peoples to choose the type of government that they believed would lead to a more peaceful and secure world.[6] The Truman Doctrine, a policy set forth by US president Harry S. Truman in a speech on 12 March 1947, expressed democratic principles as a strategy against communist expansion. Such principles were institutionalized in the NATO Treaty of 1949, where member states committed to safeguard democracy, liberty and the rule of law.[7]

Presidents John F. Kennedy and Jimmy Carter further declared a commitment to democratic ideals and human rights in the 1960s and the 1970s to guide future US foreign policy. The Ronald Reagan, George H. W. Bush and Bill Clinton administrations contributed to democracy promotion in foreign aid policies, such as the National Endowment for Democracy initiated in the early 1980s that aimed to coordinate US efforts on democracy promotion.[8]

Despite these and other declarations regarding the importance of democratic ideals and the intention to actively promote democracy worldwide, successes were overshadowed by a number of failures. These failures were due to a variety of factors, including the practical difficulties of implementing democratic principles and the pragmatic prioritization of the national interest over democracy promotion.[9] US foreign policy toward Latin America and the Middle East during the Cold War resulted in the US proclaiming democracy promotion, but being much more concerned with maintaining regional stability and state security. In regions where US power could not subordinate local regimes the US sought stability and predictability. Where US power could directly influence local events such power was used to remove any threat to US interests. US and European allies within NATO were also concerned about the spread of communism in Europe. This resulted in NATO being much more interested in preserving the status quo with existing anticommunist, right-wing dictatorial states, rather than introducing fragile and uncertain democracies.

The events of 11 September 2001 also led to new foreign policies by the US administration, where President George W. Bush proclaimed that the promotion of democratic norms would become a priority objective in US foreign policy. However, the coalition's intervention led by the US in Iraq once again opened a critical political debate on how democracy promotion was supposed to be implemented. The war against terrorism included the widespread abuse of democratic rights and liberties by regional regimes that were supported by coalition forces in Afghanistan, Iraq and Pakistan. Illegal imprisonments, the practice of rendition where suspected terrorists were transferred to states that had no prohibitions against torture, and the notorious treatment of prisoners in Abu Ghraib and Guantanamo Bay were all examples of fundamental failures in the support for basic human rights. These practices severely challenged democracy promotion and the democracy norm. At the same time, the US administration publically lectured the dictatorial regimes in Pakistan, Saudi Arabia and Egypt about their human rights record and lack of democratic progression.[10]

Relations between states remains the defining feature of international politics, but encounters and interactions between regime types, as well as external interventions into the domestic affairs of states, are reflective of new directions in the development and progression of international norms.[11] One of these new directions includes the notion of community or collective norm development. Community norms support the idea that an international society exists, providing not only important levels of functionality, but also a measure of shared identify between multiples of states. Communal norms regulate state behaviour in specific policy areas, which reinforces standardized patterns of behaviour that in turn strengthen the community norms.[12]

The end of the Cold War led to a predominate, although not exclusive, Western view that openly argued for the continuation of the diffusion of democracy and democracy promotion throughout the world, with the majority of attention being focused on Europe and the former Soviet territory.[13] The debate on democracy norms symbolized the powerful role of normative development in international politics.

Democracy Promotion and Human Security

Although democratic regimes may consist of different structural designs, democracies develop norms in two dimensions: institutional and value-based. The institutional dimension is where political infrastructures and processes promote the engagement of citizens with the public politic. One such engagement is the citizen's capacity to have a voice in state affairs through the electoral process. The institutionalization of free and fair elections enables political elites to compete for the support of citizens and for the subsequent orderly transfer of political power between winners and losers.[14] In this sense, democracy norms have consisted of a procedural method for choosing political leaders that are accountable to their voters. Free and fair election procedures are a cornerstone of the democratic process.[15]

The value-based dimension consists of substantial rights and liberties to be protected and supported to ensure participation and contestation, but also to foster the development of democratic norms beyond the limitations of political institutionalism. Such democratic norms have embedded political rights and civil liberties such as freedom of speech, freedom of assembly, freedom of organization and association, freedom of religion and freedom of mobility. The democratic norms are essential as procedural norms.

The main argument for an institutional/procedural democracy norm and the more substantial democracy norms in rights and liberties is based on the idea that too much focus on the former may lead to missing out on other important rights and liberties. For example, states that have free and fair elections may still have other serious, undemocratic traits. Pseudodemocracies, illiberal democracies, semidemocracies or competitive authoritarian states combine democratic and authoritarian elements, where they may be superficially democratic in procedure, but fundamentally authoritarian in practice.[16]

Robert Dahl suggests that contestation and participation are essential characteristics of the democracy norm.[17] Contestation refers to the procedural processes of free and fair elections that result in organized competition between opposing political forces, while participation refers to the right of all people to participate either as voters or as contestants in the voting process. Yet merely having procedural mechanisms in place and declaring a right for people to vote are by themselves not enough in a substantive democratic society.

What is required is active support for basic civil liberties – such as free speech, freedom to organize and join associations, and freedom to publish one's views – in order to make the procedural and participatory processes meaningful for the democratic norm.[18] Liberal democracies support minority rights regardless of cultural, ethnic or religious affiliations, multiple channels for political expression beyond parties, and elections and free access to information. Democratic norms demand freedom of belief, opinion, discussion, speech, publication and assembly, demonstration, political equality and support for the rule of law. Sørensen summarizes the democracy norms embedded in a liberal democracy:

> Meaningful and extensive *competition* among individuals and organized groups (especially political parties) for all effective positions of government power, at regular intervals and excluding the use of force.
>
> A highly inclusive level of political *participation* in the selection of leaders and policies, at least through regular and fair elections, such that no major (adult) social group is excluded.
>
> A level of *civil and political liberties* – freedom of expression, freedom of the press, freedom to form and join organizations – sufficient to ensure the integrity of political competition and participation.[19]

Democracies share fundamental commonalities regarding the political role of citizens, though they may differ concerning institutional arrangements. So, if we claim to support the concept of a civil and moral society, then there is a complementary obligation to promote democracy. All democracies have at their core a requirement for representation by the people. Representation may take many forms and it means different things to different people, but in the end the public voice must be meaningfully engaged with the civil politic. Political representation concerns the role of the state functioning on behalf of its citizens and for the state to act based on the rule of law.

The popular engagement in politics is enhanced through a participatory culture and an institutional arrangement of checks and balances, transparency and legal guidelines and constraints. The inherited power of the people in democracies embeds, to a large extent, human security issues. As a consequence, democracies are better protectors and promoters of human security compared to most other regimes.

The UN has been active in the promotion of democratic reforms, and the 1945 UN Charter identified a range of rights and liberties to be promoted and protected by sovereign states. The Charter's preamble describes the UN's role as 'reaffirm[ing] faith in fundamental human rights, in the dignity and worth of the human person, in the equal rights of men and women and of nations large and small.'[20] Member states of the UN committed themselves to promote and protect civil and political rights within their state borders including; freedom of religion, speech, assembly and political participation, equality before the law and protection against arbitrary arrest and detention.[21] The former secretary-general, Boutros Boutros Ghali argued in the mid-1990s that democracy was good governance and that democracy promotion was essential to improve the engagement between citizens and the public politic.[22]

The UN, at its UN General Assembly in 2000, set out the millennium development goals declaring the support for democracy and human rights as fundamental values for good governance.[23] The UN and regional organizations such as the African Union (AU), the European Union (EU) and the Organization of American States (OAS) continue to push for the support of wide ranging democratic reforms. The EU community is an example of a democratic 'agent' in international politics where shared democratic norms and democratic cohesiveness has spilled over into regional and international politics.[24]

The founding ideas to the development of the EU as a norm-community may be found in UN *Universal Declaration of Human Rights* of 1948 and the development of the *International Covenant on Civil and Political Rights* of 1966.[25] The *Universal Declaration* and the *Covenant* set out eight principles for democratic progression including periodic and genuine democratic elections, the right to stand for election, universal suffrage, the right to vote and equal suffrage to express the free will of voters. The EU also adopted the universal principles stressed in Article 21 of the *Universal Declaration*:

> The will of the people shall be the basis of the authority of government; this will shall be expressed in periodic and genuine elections which shall be by universal and equal suffrage and shall be held by secret ballot or by equivalent free voting procedures.[26]

EU policy is founded on the preservation of democracy as proposed in Article 237 of the Treaty of Rome and further articulated in the 1962 *Birkelbach* report of the political committee of the European Parliament.[27] The Treaty of Rome implicitly set out the functionalities of a norm-community that adheres to the fundamentals of the democracy process. In the 1970s, changes in Southern European states led to a new debate on the conditions and requirements to enter such a norm-community.

In 1978, the European Council stressed that 'respect for and maintenance of representative democracy and human rights in each Member State are essential elements of membership in the European Communities'.[28] This statement was intended to guide Southern European states by setting certain standards that must be met should they wish to become member states of the EU. However, the council did not set out the specific conditions that had to be met in order to achieve these principles, so democracy and the pursuit of human rights continued to be fuzzy concepts. This resulted in most of the attention being directed towards substantive economic and administrative capacities, rather than democratic progression.

The Copenhagen Criteria of 1993 marked a change in European political affairs by formalizing certain prerequisites to become an EU member state. It stipulated the requirement to undergo market and other economic reforms in addition to democracy progression. This broadened the prerequisite base with the result that potential EU partners needed to introduce economic reforms in conjunction with democracy progression. These criteria were formally included in the Maastricht Treaty of 1993. A further democracy clause was added in 1995 that allowed for the suspension of aid and trade provisions to states that failed to undertake democratic reforms. Such reforms were considered essential for EU relations with all non-EU states.[29]

In 1999, Article 6 of the Amsterdam Treaty reaffirmed that the EU was based on liberty, democracy, respect for human rights and adherence to the rule of law.[30] In May 2001, the EU's report, *The European Union's Role in Promoting Human Rights and Democratisation in Third Countries*, again stated that the EU was founded on the principles of democracy and human rights as fundamental freedoms. It emphasized that such criteria was now consolidated and that sanctions could be used against those who did not respect these criteria.

The EU's articulation and formalization of democracy norms, both within the European Community and with potential community members, has been a catalyst in the progression of the democratic ideal. However, the EU has also demonstrated some serious double standards.[31] For example, core EU member states have been notably silent regarding the behaviour of a number of brutal, dictatorial regimes in the former European colonial areas in Africa. The Rwanda crisis discussed in previous chapters was perhaps the most tragic example of European failure to even censure the increasing levels of violence leading up to the genocide in 1994.

It is essential that democratic entities, in single states and/or in a union of states, continue to promote democracy. It opens for the possibility of developing a more just and civilized international order. It is also essential for the overall well-being of citizens of the world. There are at least three good reasons to push for democratic governance to promote human security.

These reasons in the following section provide a direct linkage between the expansion of democratic governments to the spread of human security within countries. We have chosen to address such linkages in terms of R2P through democratic norms in popular representation, peace and prosperity.

R2P through Democratic Norms: The Big Three

Challenges to human security are far more serious in nondemocratic regimes compared to democratic regimes. Nondemocratic regimes either neglect or totally ignore the fundamental requirements that democratic systems often take for granted. The capacity for citizens to engage in the public politic is ruthlessly suppressed, and efforts to engage in free speech, valid and meaningful electoral processes and freedom to associate are usually put down with draconian efficiency. The previous discussions regarding the progression from weak state to failing state, then perhaps to failed state status, relates to essential contributions for any democratic system: popular representation, peace and prosperity. The protection of these three Ps is critical, for without such support the progression toward democratic norms is mostly just idealistic theory.

Popular representation

One of the most fundamental ideas behind human security and democratic governance is political contestation and participation. This includes contestation by aspiring political candidates to political office and participation by the citizens in the public politic and in the selection of their political representatives. It is through the citizen's popular participation in free and fair elections where political candidates contest and achieve political support in order to legitimize their mandate for popular representation. The democratic procedures and values behind popular participation and contestation are based upon negotiation, compromise and the orderly transfer of power. Provided that popular representation is genuine and that citizens are prepared to engage with the political process, then such a political culture fosters debate, compromise and negotiation, rather than violence and physical confrontation.

The political culture of democratic regimes is inherently self-correcting because it is based on such negotiation and compromise. Political candidates who aspire to political office must articulate their values as well as their policies and procedures in order to achieve public support. This in turn promotes trust between citizens and elected officials. If this trust is violated, then citizens are able to openly voice their concerns and formally declare their intentions for change at the next election. When political leaders disagree, then disputes are settled and the people's preferences taken into account without recourse to violence. In sum, the democratic culture fosters political compromise to resolve conflicts.

Democratic decision making requires time, consideration of alternatives and ultimately the approval of citizens. Nondemocratic, authoritarian decision making has no such constraints. Decisions are made on the whims of the ruling elite and any consideration of alternatives is limited to supporting their power base. The approval of citizens is not sought, nor is it needed when the ultimate authority is the political master's gun. In democracies it is the voice of the people that matters and it is in the interests of their political servants to cater to the needs and welfare of citizens. Any kind of mistreatment of the people may result in the loss of political power.

Popular representativeness is beneficial for human rights in the sense that the people are defined as the political engine in democracies therefore they have the highest political value. Each citizen is sovereign with a wide range of political rights and civil liberties. Democracies incorporate the fundamental idea that there are such things as universal human rights and democratic mechanisms are designed to protect such rights.[32]

The political culture of democracies supports human prosperity and enhances civil society. An important part of a prosperous democracy is a vital, dynamic civil society where people may freely engage in the public discourse regarding their own security and the welfare of the state as a whole. Democracies are structured to mobilize support for political and social ideas and reforms, act as stimuli to the political parties and leaders and to be the watchdogs against the misuse of political power. It is in the nature of a vibrant civil society to identify then call for political action upon mistreatments by governments and officials that may play out as harmful to individuals or groups of people.

The fact finding and educating role of a civil society is a very important countermeasure against human rights abuses and political misuse of power. A dynamic civil society will promote democratization through popular organizations that educate citizens into political consciousness about politics and society, and involve them in the day-to-day political activities. Such a society serves as a training ground for democratic values, institutions and means and helps to foster the citizen's engagement with the political process.[33]

Peace

Democratic governance is beneficial to R2P due to its peace-prone character. Firstly, democracies consist of institutional checks and balances that aim to moderate the behaviour of political leaders and other representatives. A democratic constitution that formalizes the structure and processes of governments typically separates the powers of the judiciary, the legislature and the executive so that each branch provides a check and balance against the other. Peace is maintained and conflict avoided by political leaders being required to engage with all branches of representative government, with the judiciary, and ultimately with the citizens. Presidents and prime ministers in democracies are dependent on the political and judicial branches to declare, conduct and finance wars, which makes the engagement in military ventures far more complicated than in dictatorial regimes.

Civilian control over the military is another important feature of a democracy. The judiciary has a critical role to play in a democracy. The judicial branch maintains the rule of law. Politicians and others who aim to circumvent legal processes must first deal with the interpretations and rulings of the judiciary. Such judicial interpretations and rulings must be fully supported by both the citizens and their elected representatives to be an effective check and balance against the executive and the legislature.[34]

Secondly, democratic governance is also peace prone in the sense that democracies are, for the most part, mostly transparent regarding the workings of government.[35] Such transparency assists predictability in political decision making and in the policy-making process. Foreign governments and peoples also benefit from the transparency that is apparent in democratic systems because they can see how and why domestic and foreign policy develops. They may not agree with some or even many decisions made by a particular government, but they do have the benefit of not only observing a more open and accountable system of government, but also that such openness helps to educate all about the value of accountability and transparency.

It is perhaps this transparency factor in democratic systems that most reduces perceptions of threat and antagonism to enhance confidence building between societies that may have very different cultures and beliefs. By comparison, the closed-door policies of dictatorial regimes are far less transparent and much less predictable. This raises the perception of threat and the possibility of conflict when important security decisions are made in secret and according to the whims of only a few.[36] Democracies do not engage in military conflicts with other democracies. Only when they are directly threatened will democracies enter into military conflict with anyone, and even then with a great deal of reluctance. Wars are good business for a few, but they are very bad business for the many.

Democracies do engage in other forms of conflict where there are clearly winners and losers: favoured trading arrangements with one party but not with all, rapacious consumerism that demands access to limited resources, and discrimination (deliberate or not) against certain cultural or societal practices deemed inferior or in some other way to be unacceptable. Democracies are to an extent inherently self-correcting if military conflict becomes a possibility. Citizens do not lightly authorize their elected officials to undertake military adventurism and officials may be removed from office if the public will is strong enough.[37,38] No such constraints concern autocratic regimes unless citizens stage an outright rebellion. Should such a rebellion appear to be taking place, then a quick and ruthless military response usually quickly dampens any enthusiasm for an uprising.

Democracy promotion aims to link security to state survival in order to support both state security and human security. Political leaders may also then focus on domestic democratic reforms rather than being concerned about external threats to security because the overall level of regional and wider security is enhanced. A secured environment at the national, regional and global levels may also allow for the transfer of resources from the military sector into important development sectors in order to enhance human security. None of these factors are possible without political trust, confidence and tolerance among the population. In sum, political development is to a significant extent conditioned by internal and external security. Both rely on each other.[39]

Prosperity

The development of democratic norms is a preventive strategy for R2P in the sense that it fosters socioeconomic prosperity. The increasing number of democracies in the world has resulted in an overall increase in global wealth. Democracies in general are much more effective and prosperous socioeconomic entities than dictatorial regimes. Autocratic states are much less likely to economically and socially prosper because development is stifled either through dictatorial ineptitude or because the citizens see little scope for progression. Failed or failing states tend to have severe social and economic challenges that directly impact the citizen's capacity for a good life. Sheer daily survival is the priority.[40]

Democratic regimes have a convergence between the public politic, societal development and economic progression. Economic interdependence through financial exchanges, trade and investments makes violent conflict much less likely because there is a vested interest for all parties to work and prosper together. Economic integration, the opportunity to engage new markets, to invest and to find new economic partners all require a stable political and social environment. Economic prosperity leads to further co-operation and willingness for negotiation that further assist the democratic process, which then becomes self-perpetuating.

Democratic systems and their associated free market systems have a number of similarities regarding how they operate. Both are based on the notion of freedom and pluralism aiming at political and economic alternatives. The economic developments of welfare, socioeconomic pluralism and individual choices have a complementary relationship with democratization that result in a parallel trend of improvement or downfall.[41] By comparison, autocratic systems that rely on state ownership and centralized control of the means of production tend to have less economic prosperity because entrepreneurial initiatives are suppressed and citizens see little point in expending extra effort purely for the benefit of the state.[42] Progressive socioeconomic development requires functionality, flair and entrepreneurship that is lacking in most autocratic systems.[43]

Democracies are also more peace prone than most autocracies. While there may be divergence of views on whether democratic governance or free market forces are primarily responsible for this, the end result is the same. Prosperity may be measured in many different ways, but the key human security and social indicators are in the areas of education, health and living standards.[44]

Conclusion

Globalization has resulted in greater interdependence between states and an increased level of awareness about alternative political and economic regimes. From the late 1970s, the political legitimacy and progression of democratic norms has also resulted in a growing number of democracies in the world. Democracy norms have established rules, procedures and behaviours that are conducive to the positive development of human society. They have raised the expectations of people everywhere to strive for a more prosperous and better life. Democratic progression is multilayered and involves many different local, regional and global levels of engagement. Governmental institutions, NGOs, transnational organizations and institutions all contribute to the process. Some of these entities use negotiation and compromise as strategic development tools; others are more coercive and rely on both inclusion and exclusion strategies.

Although the push for democratic norms has intensified in the post–Cold War era, the historical and contemporary records show that the development of democratic norms is only one strategic interest among many others in international politics. This has at times led to selectivity of responses, the abuse of power and disagreements over when democratic norms should or should not be prioritized in relation to other strategic interests. If, however, democratic states see democratic norms as desirable universal norms and they encourage such norms peacefully throughout the world, then this is the best preventive strategy to human rights abuses and intra/interstate conflicts.

Chapter 6

CASE STUDY LIBYA: MOVING PRINCIPLE INTO ACTION?

The development of R2P from concept to principle then to formal ratification by the UN in 2005 has been a very difficult process. R2P critics continue to question whether the notion of R2P is anything more than a list of reasonable principles. That is, governments and policy makers may be willing to support the idea of R2P, but when the need for a practical application arises, then procrastination and inaction is the result. Despite these and many other challenges, the UN General Assembly formally endorsed R2P, and all of the five permanent UN Security Council members – China, France, Russia, the United Kingdom and the United States – supported R2P in Security Council Resolutions 1674 (2006) and 1894 (2009). In Chapter 3, we discussed the first direct application of R2P by the UN in 2007 to the humanitarian disaster in Darfur. We concluded that the international community's response in Darfur was much too slow, poorly implemented, and the outcome resulted in an ongoing humanitarian disaster.

By 2010, some African countries such as Côte d'Ivoire, Lesotho, Senegal, Guinea and Sierra Leone were making positive progress in the areas of popular civic engagement. Democracy promotion was improving in Burma, Bhutan, Mongolia and Tonga in the Asia Pacific region, but regressing in Central and Eastern Europe/Eurasia. People in North Africa and in many places throughout the Middle East struggled to have their governments recognize basic human rights and civil liberties. In late 2010, a groundswell of revolutionary protests and demonstrations erupted in many parts of the Arab world, leading to what has become known as the 'Arab Spring' uprisings. Egypt, Tunisia, Yemen, Algeria, Jordan, Syria and Libya were all confronted with significant civil unrest. There were a range of reasons why serious discontent swept through the Arab world. Rising food prices, extensive corruption by governments and civil authorities, high unemployment and levels of poverty, and increasing dissatisfaction (particularly by young people) regarding the concentration of power and wealth by self-serving autocrats, all served to ferment civil unrest. Social networking and the use of the Internet helped to coalesce unrest into a wider, regional expression of dissatisfaction against long-established regimes. Once again the international community struggled to deal with rapidly evolving events and the draconian response by many regimes to civil discontent.

This chapter is a case study of the 2011 civil war in Libya, which represented an intrastate conflict between Muammar Gaddafi loyalists and antiregime dissidents. Map 6.1 shows Libya. The Security Council's response to the rapidly escalating violence in Libya is presented and analysed with a view to assess the practical functionality of R2P. Official documents, particularly Security Council Resolutions 1970 (2011) and 1973 (2011), and speeches from the United Nations and world leaders, are scrutinized to provide an insight into whether the public rhetoric matched the behind-the-scenes diplomacy of the key stakeholders. The application of R2P in Libya was an important step in the development of a substantive norm that directly addresses the principles of protection and prevention. Despite the success of some important elements of R2P in Libya, there remains significant disagreement in the UN and among the major powers whether the formalization of R2P as a reactive response to conflict was effective and could be repeated elsewhere, or indeed whether the R2P rhetoric leading up to and during the conflict made any fundamental difference at all. The conflict in Libya also shows that the preventative aspect of R2P was almost totally reactive and 'prevention' was limited to trying to stop a rapidly deteriorating humanitarian situation from turning into something even worse. We conclude this chapter with eight lessons that could be learned from the application of R2P and the international response to the Libyan crisis.

Libya, 2010–11: Revolution and Aftermath

The first glimmers of significant, widespread public unrest began in Tunisia and Egypt with mass popular demonstrations taking place in almost all of the large cities. The scale and intensity of the demonstrations rapidly continued to build with people sharing a common desire for substantial political change. Consistent across almost all levels of society were demands for individual and collective rights, opposition to autocratic rule, and increasing frustration with the corruption of governments. The protests in Egypt and Tunisia resulted in political elections at the end of the year. In Libya, civil uprisings led to violent clashes with the existing regime. Autocratic regimes were increasingly being challenged throughout the Middle East for failing to identify and address serious areas of public concern.

The international community had a long-standing and complex engagement with Gaddafi prior to Libya's civil war in 2010–11.

Western countries in particular had a love–hate relationship with Gaddafi, vacillating between outright condemnation of his activities and behaviour to publically praising the volatile Arab leader for small improvements in his engagement with the rest of the global community. The late US president Ronald Reagan called him the 'mad dog of the Middle East', an unpredictable supporter of international terrorism and a rogue. Gaddafi was sanctioned and isolated as a result of his association with a range of terrorist activities against the West, such as the murder and injury of scores of American soldiers in the 1986 bombing of the La Belle nightclub in Germany, his support of the Irish Republican Army and the explosion of Pan Am Flight 103 over Lockerbie, Scotland in 1988. Yet at other times Gaddafi was considered to be a tolerable rogue, even a potential ally, who appeared to oppose the ideology of radical Islam. The West further tolerated Gaddafi because it wanted continued access to Libya's significant oil reserves. In 2003, Gaddafi announced that he would no longer pursue his nuclear program, and former British prime minister Tony Blair personally visited and embraced him, welcoming him back into the Western fold. This highly publicized visit was quickly followed by the US decision to restore diplomatic relations with Tripoli. The US declared that Gaddafi was once again someone that the West could openly accept and do business with. Prior to the civil war in Libya, France had close ties to the Libyan government and had signed many strategically important commercial agreements with Libya amounting to €10 billion in 2008. Gaddafi was also invited to speak to the United Nations in 2009.

By mid to late 2010, the relationship between most of the major powers and Gaddafi had significantly deteriorated as a result of his regime's brutal crackdown on mass popular protests. An important catalyst for the increasing number of protests and protestors was the imprisonment of the lawyer and human rights activist Fathi Terbil. Terbil was imprisoned because he agreed to represent the families of 1400 political prisoners killed during a prison riot in 1996.[1] On 5 March 2011, Libya's Transitional Council was established in Benghazi, where it proclaimed that Gaddafi's regime was illegitimate and had misused its power against the citizens of Libya. The establishment of the Transitional Council represented a serious challenge to Gaddafi's regime as well as a direct platform rallying international support for the idea of a liberated and potentially more democratized Libya. The council declared that Libya had come to a crossroads and a new political regime was needed to give the people of Libya a better future.[2] The French government immediately recognized the Transitional Council as the new representative body of Libya.[3]

The anti-Gaddafi rebel forces were poorly equipped and lacked organization, but they compensated for these deficiencies with widespread public support and the encouragement of large numbers of Libya's citizens. Gaddafi responded to the increasing number of demonstrations and demands for change with brutal efficiency, indiscriminately attacking rebel forces and civilians alike.[4] Libya quickly became polarized between Gaddafi loyalists in Tripoli and anti-Gaddafi rebels and supporters in Benghazi. As the conflict rapidly escalated, Gaddafi's forces, supported by heavy weapons and airpower, threatened to crush the rebellion as quickly as it had started. International attention that had been focused on earlier uprisings in Egypt, Tunisia and Yemen now shifted to the events unfolding in Libya. The five permanent Security Council members repeatedly referred to R2P and the need to protect the civilians in Libya against the onslaught from Gaddafi's military. The impetus for direct French, British and American involvement in Libya rapidly gained momentum, and they declared that it was legally necessary for the international community to protect civilians in accordance with the resolutions supporting R2P and the UN Charter.

The United Nations Security Council and the Application of R2P in Libya

In late 2010, the level of violence in Libya escalated. Graphic images of civilians suffering and dying were captured on individual cell phones and broadcast by the international media. The rapid pace and intensity of urban warfare between a motley collection of rebel forces trying to repel the heavily armed Libyan military resulted in urgent diplomatic discussions between the major powers. There were two immediate concerns. Firstly, large numbers of civilians were confined in highly populated areas between the two warring factions. Secondly, there were an increasing number of reports of Gaddafi's military forces indiscriminately using heavy weapons including tanks, artillery and aircraft against civilians trapped in the conflict zones. On 26 February 2011, the Security Council passed Resolution 1970, which condemned the violence perpetrated by the Libyan regime against the people of Libya.[5] Appendix II contains the full transcript of Resolution 1970.

The resolution identified Gaddafi and his regime as the main opponents to peace and freedom within the country and demanded that Gaddafi cease all military attacks against civilians. Resolution 1970 included an arms embargo, banned travel for top politicians in the regime and the freezing of international financial assets for most of Gaddafi's politicians and public servants. Paragraph 9 addressed the arms embargo: 'All member states shall immediately take the necessary measures to prevent the direct or indirect supply, sale or transfer to the Libyan Arab Jamahiriya.' This was followed by strict restrictions on travel for 16 members of the Gaddafi regime. In addition, Paragraph 15 ordered that 'all member states shall take the necessary measures to prevent the entry into or transit through their territories of individuals listed in Annex I of this resolution'.

Paragraph 17 froze the assets of core members of the Gaddafi regime: 'All member states shall freeze without delay all funds, other financial assets and economic resources which are in their territories, which are owned or controlled, directly or indirectly, by the individuals or entities listed in Annex II of this resolution.' There was no doubt that Resolution 1970 identified the Libyan regime as the primary threat to human security and was thereby violating the central tenants of R2P.[6] In the strongest possible diplomatic terms, Resolution 1970 labelled the abuses in Libya as crimes against humanity.

The problem was that pivotal parts of the resolution – the arms embargo, travel bans and frozen assets – were long-term sanctions rather than immediate measures that would halt the escalating brutality by the regime against Libyan civilians. Gaddafi continued to ignore the UN and the increasing demands by the international community to stop the attacks on civilians. In the spring of 2011, numerous reports of indiscriminate killings of civilians in the major population centres were passed to the international media from dissenters, NGOs and others in the conflict zones. The reports, many from independent observers, described how men, women and children were desperately trying to protect themselves against the regime's ground and air attacks. Gaddafi used heavy weapons against dissidents in Brega, Ajdabiya, Bin Jawad, Zawiyah and Ras Lanuf, but the rebel forces refused to surrender and the stalemate continued. The regime's persistent and indiscriminate use of heavy weapons against rebel forces meant that civilians trapped in the conflict zones had nowhere to escape the conflict and suffered significant loss of life.

By early March 2011, the major cities of Libya had become the main combat zones, with both sides repeatedly declaring victories. The reality was that territorial losses and gains changed almost daily. The international community looked on helplessly as the civilian death toll mounted and the spectre of a humanitarian disaster of mammoth proportions seemed imminent.[7] Rebel forces pleaded for heavy weapons support from the international community as the rebellion's momentum stalled in the face of the regime's military onslaught.[8] The call for armaments quickly changed to urgent requests for international military involvement on the grounds that Gaddafi had lost his legitimate right to rule and that the international community was obliged to help stop large-scale assaults against civilian communities. Britain and France, two of the permanent member states on the Security Council, argued in favour of international airstrikes against regime-loyal military forces. They also proposed implementing and defending a no-fly zone over Libya to stop Gaddafi from using his airpower against the major population centres, an idea supported by US Republican senator John McCain and former Democratic senator Joe Lieberman. Senator John Kerry, chairman of the US Senate Foreign Relations Committee, said, 'I believe that the global community cannot be on the sidelines while airplanes

Map 6.1 Libya and neighbouring states

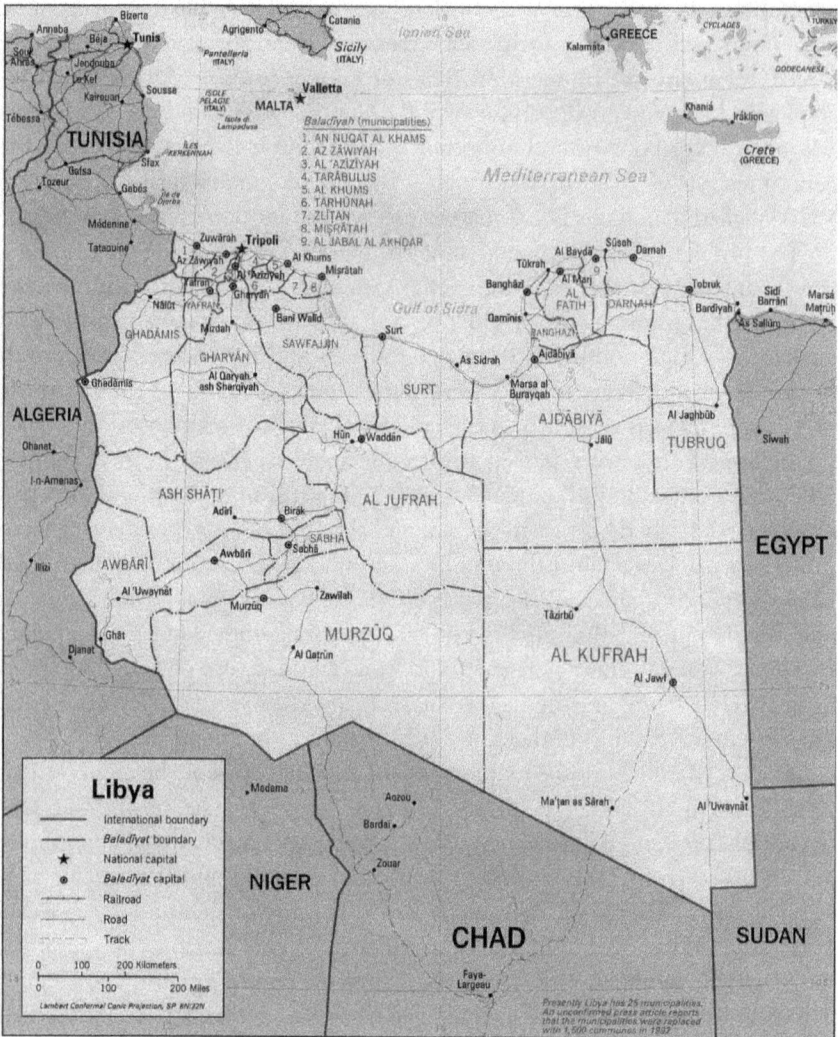

are allowed to bomb and strafe. A no-fly zone is not a long-term proposition, assuming the outcome is what all desire, and I believe we ought to be ready to implement it as necessary.' In addition, US president Barack Obama argued, 'There is a danger of a stalemate that, over time, could be bloody, and that is something that we are obviously considering. So what I want to make sure of is that the United States has full capacity to act, potentially rapidly.'[9]

By mid-March 2011, the possibility of direct military intervention in Libya by the international community dominated discussions in the UN and, on 12 March 2011, the Arab League agreed to ask the Security Council to vote for the implementation of a no-fly zone over Libya. The Arab League insisted that a no-fly zone must be enforced to limit the military capability of the Libyan regime and to stop the slaughter of civilians. If not, the league predicted an even worse civil and social catastrophe with further atrocities, and displaced Libyans fleeing into neighbouring countries. The UN High Commissioner for Refugees (UNHCR) noted that at least 300,000 people had already been forced to move to neighbouring states and an unknown number of others were displaced within the borders of Libya.[10] UN secretary-general Ban Ki-moon urged the international community for a rapid response to protect Libyan civilians from state violence and he asked the Security Council to agree to protective measures that would ensure the safety of the Libyan population.

On 17 March 2011, the Security Council responded with Resolution 1973. The full transcript of Resolution 1973 is in Appendix I. Resolution 1973 was a direct result of the failure of Resolution 1970 to force the Libyan government to comply with its demands.[11] Britain, France, the US, Bosnia–Herzegovina, Colombia, Gabon, Lebanon, Nigeria, Portugal and South Africa voted for the resolution, with abstentions from China, Russia, Brazil, Germany and India.

Resolution 1973 condemned the escalating human rights abuses and the increasing deprivations and suffering of the Libyan people. Although both resolutions declared that Gaddafi's attacks against civilians violated international humanitarian law and both emphasized the likelihood that these attacks could be defined as a crime against humanity, Resolution 1973 explicitly stated that the consequence of allowing Gaddafi to continue to rule would be widespread and significant loss of civilian life. Resolution 1973 redirected attention to the previous resolution by pointing out that taking action against the Gaddafi regime had broad international support, particularly from the Arab states. In addition, Resolution 1973 included a new requirement: the establishment of a no-fly zone over Libyan territory to stop Gaddafi's air force from bombing civilians. The secretary-general applauded both the new resolution and the no-fly zone.[12]

The Great Powers' Response to the Crisis in Libya

Resolution 1973 addressed the importance of implementing the agreed responses by using the phrase 'all necessary means'. However, the open-ended inference of this phrase led to significant disagreement within the Security Council. While Western countries seemed willing to use international ground forces in Libya, other Security Council members refused to consider the possibility of this type of intervention, pointing out that the resolution did not permit the direct deployment of military troops in Libya. Despite the overall agreement on the content of Resolution 1973, the major powers had different opinions on how much force and what type of force could legally be used to comply with the two resolutions. The Paris Summit to Support the Libyan People, organized by Herman Van Rompuy, the permanent president of the European Council, and Catherine Ashton, a representative of the European Union for Foreign Affairs, attempted to promote a common stance on what Resolution 1973 implied. The summit led to an agreement that a shared strategy needed to be developed. This agreement was signed by 10 countries: Belgium, Canada, Denmark, France, Italy, Norway, Qatar, Spain, the UK and the US.[13] The agreement was not signed by China or Russia. Although most nations present at the Paris summit agreed that urgent action was necessary to support the Libyan people, the degree of military involvement remained in dispute.

France and the UK took prominent positions during the ongoing talks and both urged that the international community must protect the Libyan civilian population against the atrocities perpetrated by the Gaddafi regime. They further proposed that direct military intervention was the only way to do this. The French government took the strongest position regarding the need for direct military action in Libya.[14] The French minister for foreign and European affairs, Alain Juppé, maintained close contact with the Libyan Transitional Council and the rebel leadership in order to constantly monitor the political and military situation on the ground. He worked hard to rally international support for the Transitional Council and made it clear that the French government was prepared to use all necessary means against Gaddafi as a consequence of the brutality of the Gaddafi regime against civilians.[15] He forcefully argued that Gaddafi's actions had undermined any legitimate right he might have to continue ruling Libya and that the international community was responsible to protect the Libyan people.[16]

Juppé spoke passionately at the press conference that preceded the final Security Council vote on Resolution 1973. His message was that France had had enough of Gaddafi's brutalities. Gaddafi's control of Libya had worsened the situation for civilians, and if he were allowed to continue his military assaults against the major population centres, then many more civilian casualties would be the result. Juppé stated his particular concern about the escalating military attacks against the city of Benghazi. To do nothing about the situation there would jeopardize the legitimacy of the UN Charter, and allowing Gaddafi to disregard the demands set out in Resolutions 1970 and 1973 would challenge the credibility of the international community itself. Juppé argued for international law to prevail. He pointed out that Gaddafi's air force had no enemies in the air and therefore could systematically attack cities to bomb civilians as well as potential rebel headquarters with total impunity. Juppé stressed the importance of the international community working together to safeguard basic international norms and that the UN proclaimed its values in order to combat tyranny and mass murder.[17]

The French government proposed that while protection of Libyan civilians must be the priority, the potential liberation of Libya from the Gaddafi regime would have important spillover effects on the region at large. Popular demonstrations were simultaneously taking place on the streets of most capitals within the Arab region, and these demonstrations could be indirectly supported by international action against Gaddafi. By supporting the popular demonstrations and uprising in Libya this would be an important symbolic act from the international community against any brutal regime that continued to harass and oppress its own people. France referred directly to the significant civil unrest in Egypt and Tunisia; doing nothing in Libya would lead to ongoing civilian atrocities. This would send a strong message to neighbouring regimes that Europe's democracies did not care about political rights and civil liberties in the Arab world. This would further undermine the hard won advances in democracy promotion and support for human rights worldwide. The UN would be discredited if it continued to claim to support basic rights and civil liberties, but did very little to ensure that such worthy ambitions were put into practice.[18]

France was keen to act upon what it saw as a historical period in the Middle East. The importance of allowing international law to prevail, to act upon the window of opportunity that had been provided, and to do so by promoting democracy and human rights were cornerstones of the French stand on Libya.[19] The arguments made by the French government were simultaneously echoed by the British. Strategic meetings and phone calls between Paris and London quickly resulted in an alliance against Gaddafi and a mutual consensus in favour of rapid military and diplomatic actions against the Libyan regime. Mirroring the French stand on Resolution 1973, UK prime minister David Cameron argued that the resolution was crucial in order to stop the slaughter. He stressed that Gaddafi had shown no signs of listening to his people or to the demands of international community. Gaddafi's dismissal of Resolution 1970 was a major sign of denial in terms of fundamental human rights, civil liberties and international law in general.[20]

The firm British support of the French position against the Libya regime was a significant development and this surprised many in the international community. The UK argued not only for military operations against the Libyan regime, but also that it was prepared to engage in direct military support to implement the resolution. This was contrary to Britain's previous support for Gaddafi. Prime minister Gordon Brown had written to Gaddafi in 2007 proclaiming that the relationship between the UK and Libya was excellent and that he was aware of Tony Blair's close personal relationship with the Gaddafis.[21] Brown further encouraged Gaddafi to make rapid progress in finalizing his contract to purchase the Jernas air defence system from Britain. The French government also changed its earlier position where it argued that the situation in Libya should be allowed to run its own course. The UK's past close friendship with Gaddafi and France's previous insistence that the events in Libya should be allowed to run their own course bore little resemblance to how both countries responded to the civil war erupting in Libya in 2010–11.

The British (and French) government's about turn on its close associations with the Libyan dictator was based on the rapid rise of regional popular and political support against Gaddafi and the violation of international law with regard to the serious abuse of civilian populations. Cameron stressed that there was a demonstrable need to stop the systematic use of regime-sponsored violence against civilians. The serious human rights abuses committed in Tripoli resulted in the British prime minister insisting that the international community must take a humanitarian position to stop further atrocities. Cameron repeatedly acknowledged the strong regional support for freedom and the Arab League's call for action against Gaddafi. The Arab League's unanimous position in favour of a no-fly zone was an important indication that the West and the Arab world shared common ground, at least on what to do about the Gaddafi regime.[22]

Although the need for military action was clear from the British and French point of view, Cameron struggled with the various alternatives concerning how to support a no-fly zone over Libya. He was well aware of the different and often confusing positions that the other major powers had taken regarding direct military intervention in Libya, and that Resolution 1973 did not directly allow for any interventionist ground troops. He also acknowledged that the sovereignty norm and the nonintervention norm in international law were cornerstones in international politics that could only be sidestepped for very good reasons, and only after substantial diplomatic efforts had failed. Cameron promoted interventionist action in Libya by the imposition of a no-fly zone, but he also agreed with the exclusion of further military action embedded in Resolution 1973. In accordance with the French position, Cameron argued that a moral and legal obligation to halt Gaddafi's indiscriminate violence against civilians existed. Doing nothing, Cameron argued, would betray people striving for democracy in Libya and around the world.[23]

The US had a more passive role at the beginning of the talks on what to do about the Libyan crisis and was preoccupied with its involvement in

Afghanistan and Iraq. The US was very reluctant to send American soldiers to yet another dangerous conflict zone.[24] The American people would not support what they saw as an unnecessary and most likely long, drawn-out foreign war in Libya. The US was in the midst of a painful economic recession with a rapidly expanding debt burden, therefore to engage in another costly war was domestically untenable. The most the US was prepared to consider was to act in a supporting role, provided that others, notably the British and the French, would do the heavy military lifting. By late February 2011, the US administration had agreed to be a participant regarding humanitarian intervention in Libya. President Barack Obama attempted to deflect accusations of being too slow to react to the Libyan crisis.[25] The US permanent representative to the UN cited humanitarian needs, human security and democracy as the key reasons for the American decision to vote in favour of direct intervention. Ambassador Susan Rice declared that the US administration saw no hope of change from Gaddafi; on the contrary, his harsh rhetoric against rebel forces and civilians signalled continued cruelty. The US argued that Resolution 1973 was a necessary platform for forcing a ceasefire and an immediate halt to the ongoing violence, as well as for safeguarding the rights and liberties of the Libyan people in the long run.[26]

The US and other NATO aircraft began launching military attacks against Gaddafi's forces immediately after there was collective agreement regarding how to implement the UN resolution. Obama argued that these military actions were being carried out in the name of the Libyan people and they were aimed at liberating them from tyranny. The US declared that its interests were squarely focused at the humanitarian cause of intervention and that American involvement was required from a moral and legal standpoint. Unless the international community acted decisively, the escalation of violence by regime forces would intensify against the major cities of Benghazi and Misrata, with further mass killings, thousands of wounded men, women and children, and perhaps hundreds of thousands of displaced civilians.[27]

While the US, France and Britain spoke as one about the necessity for direct humanitarian intervention, China and Russia remained opposed to such a strategy. Both acknowledged the need for the protection of civilians, but they disagreed that forcible intervention was the answer. They preferred to see a domestic solution that brought an end to Gaddafi's rule and that the state sovereignty of Libya should not be violated by foreign powers. China and Russia abstained from voting on Resolution 1973 and were quickly confronted by the international media. The Chinese UN ambassador, Li Baodong, acknowledged that Gaddafi's legitimacy as the ruler of Libya was under serious threat, but China was concerned over the implications of the open-ended phrase 'all necessary means'. Baodong said China suspected that a resolution allowing for military action could be misused by Western forces to intervene in Libya without acknowledging the fundamental international political principles of state sovereignty and nonintervention.[28]

Forcible foreign intervention in Libya was not acceptable to China. China agreed that the civil war had been caused by brutalities against the Libyan people by Gaddafi's regime and that Gaddafi had misused his power to such extent that he had no credibility as state leader, but this still did not open the door for external military intervention. China continued to point out the sanctity of a sovereign state and that the use of force would violate the sovereignty of Libya. The Libyan crisis was a domestic matter and must be solved domestically. International law and the UN Charter were, according to China, very clear on state jurisdiction and what was happening in Libya did not justify international interference in Libyan affairs. After China's strong rhetoric against forcible intervention, its decision not to use its veto power at the Security Council was unexpected. China explained its decision by referring to the rapidly deteriorating humanitarian crisis in Libya and Gaddafi's systematic attacks on major cities. More importantly, its decision was based on the view that the practice of brutally suppressing civil dissent was now a serious regional problem and it was therefore no longer solely a problem for the Libyans to resolve internally. There was now also widespread regional support from the Arab League and African Union member states to directly intervene in Libya. All these factors combined led the Chinese government to opt not to veto Resolution 1973.[29]

China, however, continued to express concern over how ultimately the UN resolution would be used against the Libyan regime and it accused Western powers on the Security Council of planning military actions beyond what the resolution allowed.[30] China argued that the Western military actions were resulting in further atrocities and civilian suffering, and that the NATO forces' actions were increasing the number of civilian causalities instead of promoting peace. China remained convinced that forcible intervention in Libya under what it saw to be the guise of humanitarian intervention and democracy promotion was a strategic plan by the West to expand its own geostrategic interests in the region and, in a time of global recession, assert control over strategic oil reserves in Libya.[31]

Russia also abstained rather than vetoed for many of the same reasons as China. Russia argued early in the negotiation process that the resolution would worsen the humanitarian situation rather than stopping the war. Russia consistently argued for alternatives to military action and stressed that the militarization of Libya would jeopardize the state-building process after Gaddafi was gone and the interventionist forces had left. Military intervention would inevitably lead to the arming of rebel forces and the destruction of important institutions and civil infrastructure, all of which would in the long term result in even more suffering for the Libyan people. A weakened and war-damaged Libya dominated by large numbers of armed militias would also have negative spillover effects into neighbouring states.

Russia continued to condemn Gaddafi and his regime by frequently speaking out in the international media, the domestic media and to the Security Council about the importance of protecting the Libyan people against the actions of the Gaddafi regime. Russia's support for the earlier resolution (1970) was a significant indication that Russia had no interest in seeing Gaddafi stay in power. Russia accused Gaddafi of using state terrorism against civilians and it saw Resolution 1970 as necessary and important. It clearly identified Gaddafi as the one to blame for the humanitarian catastrophe in Libya and established the UN's position that the crimes committed against the Libyans were unacceptable. Russia acknowledged that the good intentions behind the first resolution had not protected civilians nor had it ended the war and, although highly sceptical about the military aspects of Resolution 1973, Russia decided not to stop the resolution's passage in the Security Council.[32]

Both the Chinese and Russian governments argued that they had asked for but not received clarification on how UN Resolution 1973 would be implemented. The Russian government shared China's concern that installing a no-fly zone could lead to further military action by foreign forces.[33] The Russian president and foreign minister accused the other major powers of misinterpreting the resolution and misusing their position in the Security Council. They called on Western powers to refrain from further military action and from acting in any way that could jeopardize the future of Libya. Russia initially acknowledged that the main objective in implementing the no-fly zone and providing for an arms embargo was to protect civilians from further suffering, but then accused the Western powers of going too far in their military activities.[34]

Russian foreign minister Sergei Lavrov argued that coalition action in Libya had exceeded what had been sanctioned by the Security Council. The Russian envoy to the North Atlantic Council, led by Dmitry Rogozin, accused Western military planners of 'creativity' in how they were carrying out the limited mandate authorized by the Security Council.[35] Russia reacted to the bombing of Gaddafi family members in Tripoli by stating that such actions exceeded the intent of the UN mandate, which was to secure a no-fly zone and to protect civilians, not to attack Gaddafi's family. This accusation was echoed by Konstantin Kosachev, chairman of the International Affairs Committee in Russia's lower house of parliament, who argued that the NATO military actions against the Gaddafi family were of the same nature as Gaddafi's military strikes on civilians. That is, if the Libyan regime was conducting state terrorism by assaulting civilians, then NATO's military actions seemed to be remarkably similar. The Russian president, Dmitry Medvedev addressed a Russia/NATO meeting on Libya in the spring of 2011. He argued that the actions taken by Western nations far exceeded the framework of Resolution 1973 and he was extremely concerned that the arms embargo and the no-fly zone would lead to Western military ground troops in Libya.[36] His concern was shared by prime minister Vladimir Putin. Putin accused the West of relentlessly pushing for the politics of interventionism around the world, and that this was a US-led strategy against international law that destabilized international order and was intended to support Western national interests.[37]

The British prime minister, David Cameron, hosted an international conference on the Libyan crisis in London at the end of March 2011. The aim of the conference was to strengthen the political alliance and to justify Resolutions 1970 and 1973. More than 40 countries including all the major powers had expressed their support for the conference and for a discussion of what the resolutions contained and how they were to be carried out. The British government said that both resolutions had been necessary in order to protect Libyan civilians. They prevented Gaddafi from committing further atrocities against the people of Libya by enabling allied forces to stop him from attacking Benghazi. This had been an important argument for the final resolution. Many countries had foreseen a humanitarian catastrophe had Benghazi been attacked by the regime's ground forces and aircraft. Gaddafi had shown no mercy in previous attacks on Libyan cities and the city of Benghazi was next in line. An attack there would not only have led to thousands of deaths and injuries, but it would have destroyed the city's critical civil infrastructures. The immediate consequences would have been disastrous and the ramifications would continue well past the short term. The political debate on how to handle Gaddafi and his military forces continued long after resolutions 1970 and 1973 were implemented and the NATO coalition's action in Libya.

Gaddafi's actions were strongly condemned by all participating countries at the conference, which unanimously declared that he was no longer the legitimate ruler of Libya. They stressed the validity of the Transitional Council as Libya's new interim representative government and that Gaddafi's violent attacks against his own people had disqualified him as ruler. He no longer commanded any trust or support from the people and had shown no interest in serving them by providing security, welfare or representational leadership. As a consequence, the participating countries all declared that Gaddafi had lost his right to govern the country and that his behaviour needed to be scrutinized by the ICC.[38] His time as leader of Libya was up.

Some participating countries attending the conference proposed that to reduce Gaddafi's remaining time in power the Libyan opposition forces should be supplied with arms. Both China and Russia strongly opposed this controversial proposal. France, Britain and the US supported the proposal to arm the opposition forces and further suggested helping the rebels with training and strategic operations. These proposals were opposed by China and Russia, who pointed out that Resolution 1973 had explicitly called for an arms embargo and did not authorize the provision of arms and 'other support' to the rebels. The US, British and French leaders countered by stressing the importance of stopping Gaddafi before he was able to do further harm and that the immediate challenge was halting Gaddafi's military forces from their indiscriminate attacks on civilians in the cities of Misrata and Ras Lanuf.

The conference debates clearly showed that there was strong consensus for forcing Gaddafi out of power and having him sent to the ICC to answer for his actions, but the way that this was to be carried out was, as always, the contentious point. In the end the conference's intention to bolster support for action against Libya, or at least to unify consensus about what needed to be done, was unsuccessful. As the civil war and international involvement continued in Libya, the NATO forces by sheer necessity had to adapt to the unfolding situation on the ground. This adaptation meant that some of NATO's attacks, such as the attacks against Gaddafi's family and the regime's strongholds and ammunition supplies, were beginning to stretch the interpretation of what protecting civilians actually meant. Such attacks provoked loud condemnation, particularly from China and Russia. It was not until late October 2011, when rebel forces occupied Tripoli and Gaddafi had finally been captured and killed outside his hometown of Sirte, that the increasingly vocal debate between the Security Council member states diminished. The death of Gaddafi and the circumstances surrounding the event now triggered a new debate on why and how Gaddafi was killed. The UN responded by ordering an investigation into what had happened and why.

Lessons Learned: R2P and the Libyan Crisis

In this Libyan case study we have focused our attention on the international debates surrounding the different views on the validity of these two important resolutions, then more widely on the justifications presented or rejected regarding direct military engagement in Libya. *A first lesson learned* from the Libyan experience is that the lengthy diplomatic talks leading up to, and during, the implementation of UN Resolutions 1970 and 1973 resulted in needless loss of life. Gaddafi forces were fully engaged in the indiscriminate killing of rebels and civilians while the international community engaged in philosophical discussions about the value of state sovereignty and argued about real or imagined underlying agendas. This resulted in the Libyan civil war escalating to such an extent that only the relentless images in the international media of civilians trying to flee the Gaddafi onslaught seemed to prompt political leaders to stop talking and start acting. The behind the scenes diplomatic initiatives and squabbling about what to do, particularly during the early weeks of all out civil war in Libya, did not stop the heavy artillery or the blanket bombing of heavily populated, civilian areas by Gaddafi forces. While most of the major powers pressed for direct intervention both China and Russia argued for a domestic solution to the crisis. This continued despite everyone acknowledging that civilians were being slaughtered and that a significant humanitarian crisis was unfolding.

A *second lesson learned* is in the contemporary use of R2P as a strategic argument in crises such as Libya's. Despite disagreements on how to handle the Libyan crisis, many of the major powers argued for resolutions on Libya, including military action based on the notion of R2P. The three Western powers on the Security Council rarely used the term R2P in their official statements, but they shared common ground in calling for resolutions and military action to protect further civilian death and injury. This was intended to prevent regime forces from attacking more and more Libyan population centres. The protection and prevention dimensions of R2P were cornerstones of the French, British and American arguments regarding the Libya crisis. The fundamental message from everyone was that Gaddafi used brutal suppression against any dissent and that he had lost all domestic trust and international legitimacy. This situation required the international community to act.

A *third lesson learned* is how reference to the protection and prevention dimensions of R2P was not limited to an exclusively Western view of what both these terms are supposed to mean. The Arab League and the African Union clearly spoke out about the emergent need for international action against Gaddafi on the firm basis that protection of the Libyan people was the primary concern and that, as such protection was not being provided by the Gaddafi regime, Gaddafi was no longer the legitimate leader of Libya. Russia and China were much less forthright about the need for direct intervention, but they, too, strongly supported the protection dimension of the R2P ethos. All of the major powers were surprised by the speed and the scale of the uprisings during the Arab Spring, but they were even more worried about how far and how deep such a conflagration would spread. Resolution 1970 received significant support both within the Security Council and among members of NATO, the EU, the African Union and the Arab League.

The final decision to implement Resolution 1973 demonstrated how the Security Council was finally pushed into action by a region-wide call to protect the Libyan people and for the killing to stop. Resolution 1973 restated the restrictions outlined in Resolution 1970 and added the critical strategic step of establishing a no-fly zone against Gaddafi's air force. The wide regional support for both resolutions and the rapidly deteriorating humanitarian crisis in Libya led Russia and China to abstain from voting rather than to use their veto powers to negate the resolution before it could be mandated. Both Resolutions 1970 and 1973 symbolized a shared belief that international protection and prevention are integral parts of R2P and critical elements in contemporary politics. Political regimes are expected and bound to act in the service of their people.

A fourth lesson learned is the way most of the major powers tied protection and prevention to actions promoting democracy. Neither China nor Russia used this terminology or phrasing, but their rhetoric strongly supported protecting people against the excesses of their governments. By implication, if people rose up and refused to accept a long-held political status quo, this was still no reason for the excessive violence and brutality of a government intent on maintaining power. The other major powers all argued that a resolution to the Libyan crisis was an opportunity for more positive change in the Middle East. Democracy promotion was argued to be a moral responsibility to help free people from tyranny and oppression. Doing nothing, they argued, would be turning their backs on the norms and values on which civil and moral societies are founded.

A fifth lesson learned is that democratic states are much keener to practically execute the principles inherent in R2P than nondemocratic states. In the end, the practical implementation of the Security Council mandate defaulted to Western, prodemocratic countries. They were the ones who did the heavy lifting. Resolution 1973 was executed by NATO military forces led by the French and the British, with the support of the Americans. This NATO coalition enforced the no-fly zone over Libya and they protected the Libyan people by stopping the movement of Gaddafi's heavy weapons. World opinion held that the major democratic powers prevailed in their influence on the Security Council and in their diplomatic efforts to resolve the Libyan situation. Even if one was to argue that the democratic governments' effort to directly support the overthrow of Gaddafi was merely an opportunity for the spread of Western-style democratization, then the alternative needs to be carefully considered. That is, the brutal subjugation of a significant part of a society that disagrees with the regime, and the slaughter of anyone who does not fully support the regime. The choice between the two is stark. Airstrikes by Libyan forces on major population centres in Libya provoked the major powers to push for political change, but this was not done just because it was somehow a good democratic idea. China and Russia also very strongly supported the protection principles in R2P and urged political change in Libya. From a Western point of view, using military tools to force the overthrow of Gaddafi at this time and in this context was perhaps an inevitable final choice against a dictatorial regime that seemingly only understood the use of force.

A sixth lesson from the Libyan crisis is the normative power that democracies have when they are able to act multilaterally against dictatorial regimes. The diplomatic actions initiated by the French, British and Americans provided political strength for forcible intervention and for the application of soft power. The three democracies proclaimed the right for people to engage in the public politic, to express their opinions and to act against unjustifiable government policies. They argued for a human-centric approach to sovereignty and politics, and they disqualified the legitimacy of the Gaddafi regime based on his actions against his own people. They declared that state sovereignty was ultimately dependent on the support of citizens. When the democratic powers declared their common stand on Libya, they also established that the protection ethos was more than a developing norm. Protection is a substantive norm and it is based on a unity of shared standards and values regarding how international politics could and should be handled. Democratic institutions, norms and values descend from the people and democracy is all about people power. It is therefore a natural reaction among democracies to question the legitimacy of autocratic regimes. When such regimes forcibly conduct their political affairs against popular concerns, democracies are likely to challenge the fundamental legitimacy of the regime itself. Acting upon common democratic values and interests in the name of R2P is a powerful tool that reinforces the legitimacy of the state.

A seventh lesson learned is that, despite all nations accepting the value of R2P and formally endorsing the principles of protection and prevention, when it comes to practically implementing the critical elements of R2P it seems that there are always a long list of insurmountable problems standing in the way. China and Russia had, after years of diplomatic talks, accepted the R2P doctrine during the 2005 General Assembly and in the 2006 and 2009 Security Council meetings. Both supported Resolution 1970 and disavowed Gaddafi and his regime because of his brutality, yet when it came to direct action to stop his brutalities against his own people they baulked at the practicalities of how to do this. China and Russia did not fully embrace Resolution 1973, and while they may be applauded for abstaining rather than vetoing the mandate, the reality is that they did not vote in favour of the mandate either. Both China and Russia acknowledged that Gaddafi must stop the violence, but they claimed that this was a domestic political problem that needed to be solved through domestic politics. They approached the Libyan crisis from a traditional state-centric view of sovereignty and international nonintervention. China and Russia constantly questioned the other major powers' underlying motives for using force.

Our eighth lesson learned is how democracies often have underlying agendas in their foreign policies and rarely start with democracy promotion as a superior strategic interest. Military security, state security, geostrategic issues and economic and commercial incentives will usually trump concerns over rights and protections for ordinary people. The US initially stalled on becoming involved at all in the rapidly deteriorating situation in Libya. The US administration had concerns about engaging in yet another war after its many difficulties in Iraq and Afghanistan. America justified its reluctance based on an overstretched military, an exhausted economy and an American people who were fed up with being involved in unwinnable foreign wars. France, Britain and the US all courted Gaddafi when it suited them to have access to his oil reserves and as a possible ally in the war on terror. Concern over underlying agendas is always front and centre, regardless of the urgency or scale of humanitarian need.

Conclusion

Chapter 6 explored the Libyan crisis from a R2P perspective and how the major powers responded prior to and during international engagement in Libya. The Libyan crisis consisted of four groups of actors: the Gaddafi regime and pro-Gaddafi supporters, the rebel insurgents, the large numbers of Libyan people who supported regime change, and the international community attempting to deal with rapidly changing events in Libya. Domestically, the regime under the leadership of Gaddafi could no longer contain the popular uprising by the people and his response was immediate, indiscriminate and brutal. The lightly armed and outnumbered rebel forces were no match for the military capacity of the Libyan army and air force, yet they initially managed to hold out against overwhelming odds due to widespread public support. Internationally, the major powers struggled to come up with a coherent plan of how to respond to the Libyan disaster, which was increasing in severity almost on a daily basis. All agreed that the protection of the civilian population of Libya was a priority, but there were clear differences between the major powers about how to practically react.

The civil uprisings in Libya were in part inspired by other areas of civil unrest in the Arab world. The progression from civil protest to civil disobedience and then to all out civil war in Libya was to a significant extent as a result of the regime's crackdown on civil dissent. The brutality of Gaddafi's response resulted in widespread international condemnation and UN Security Council resolutions authorizing military action to protect the citizens of Libya. The Gaddafi regime and its supporters were quickly overwhelmed after British, French and US military action, and by September 2011 anti-Gaddafi insurgents had overrun Gaddafi's stronghold in Tripoli. Gaddafi fled to his hometown of Sirte, but was pursued by rebel forces and was killed on 20 October 2011.

The involvement of the Security Council was pivotal in the eventual removal of the Gaddafi regime. The phrasing of Resolutions 1970 and 1973 determined the success or otherwise of a mandate to intervene in the hostilities. Resolution 1970 was adopted unanimously by the Security Council. It condemned the use of lethal force by the Gaddafi regime against the Libyan people and authorized a range of sanctions against government officials. Resolution 1973 was more categorical, authorizing the international community's subsequent military engagement against the Libyan dictator. China and Russia's objection to the resolution was based on their insistence that forcible and direct intervention by the international community in Libya would result in even more death and injury to the Libyan people. Their position changed from outright condemnation of Resolution 1973 to recognition of the wide regional support from the Arab League, the African Union and others for regime change and for the active protection of the Libyan people.

The contribution of the protection pillar of R2P to the events in Libya was demonstrated by the unanimous agreement by all the major powers that the protection of civilians was fundamental regarding how the international community responded to the activities of the Gaddafi regime. The preventative aspects of the R2P ethos are ineffective if they amount to little more than preventing an already dire situation from becoming worse. This is reactive prevention, not proactive prevention. Proactive prevention means not supporting despotic dictators such as Gaddafi and not ignoring decades of abuse by his regime against his own people and his selective support for extremist groups internationally. R2P has a critical weakness when proclamations of good intentions are not matched by action. The ongoing civil war and humanitarian disaster in Syria is only one example of rhetoric not being matched by action. Another serious challenge for R2P is that it will always be selective in how it is applied in the practical world. The strength of R2P is that it is formally recognized by most and may be called upon to bolster the activities of the international community in how it responds to extreme humanitarian need. R2P is more than a formal policy that may or may not be applied with varying levels of success. It is an important principle that supports the idea that a civil and moral society has a clear obligation to defend the weak and the innocent.

Chapter 7

CONCLUSION

This study approached human security by focusing on the development of R2P, and we argued that R2P implies legal and moral obligations for the international community to act in the interest of people's safety and welfare. Despite such legal and moral requirements being recognized by an increasing number of political actors, there remains a lack of political will to act. The case study we presented on Libya indicates that there was a general consensus, at least in this instance, on the principles and values of R2P by most of the UN Security Council members. Yet, the practical application of protection is fraught with many challenges, as the ongoing humanitarian disaster in Syria indicates. By late 2012, over 60,000 people have been killed in Syria's vicious civil war, and the international community's response has been limited to expressions of outrage and concern.

There has been a gradual shift towards a more human-centric approach in international relations. The state-centric approach and the sovereignty norm have dominated international relations throughout history, but after World War II, and particularly after the Cold War(s), there has been an evolving debate regarding the moral acceptability and legal validity of intervention into the affairs of a sovereign state. Attention has increasingly been directed towards these issues as the number of failing and failed states has increased. Such states lack the institutional capacity to provide security, prosperity and/ or representation by the people, and they are often severely challenged by intrastate and regional tensions, as well as violent internal upheavals between armed fractions and paramilitary groups. The collapse of internal and external sovereignty not only jeopardizes domestic politics but also international politics by providing black holes in the international landscape. As a consequence, there has been a growing concern for human security in the world, from Rwanda and Sudan in Africa, to Burma in Southeast Asia and the Balkans in Europe.

Wars within states, often named civil wars and/or ethnic wars, have called for greater attention by the international community as increasing numbers of civilians are subject to levels of extreme violence by government and nongovernment military forces alike. These conflicts have to large extent been characterized by ethnic cleansing, systematic rapes and torture. The atrocities of the 1990s in Rwanda, Ethiopia, Sudan and the Balkans, and the ongoing violence in Burma, Libya, Syria and Yemen, just to mention a few examples, continue to call for greater protection of civilians by the international community. As previously stated in this study, the UN Charter, Article 2 (4), prohibits 'the threat or use of force against the territorial integrity or political independence of any state, or in any other manner inconsistent with the Purposes of the United Nations'. However, Chapter VII of the UN Charter sets out two exceptions. The first is highlighted in Article 39, which declares the right of the Security Council to authorize the use of force to uphold international peace and stability. The other exception is set out in Article 51, which emphasizes the right of self-defence. As a consequence, the UN has embedded a clash of norms within the charter. That is, the charter explicitly stresses the sovereignty norm and the principle of nonintervention, but it also directly sets out the right to intervene if there is a major threat to international peace and security. One challenge among many is how to determine what a major threat to international peace actually means.

States are expected to protect basic human rights according to the UN Charter, and the right to sovereignty comes with an obligation for a state to deal with its citizens in a humane way. If this does not occur, then this opens the door to the legal justification of the humanitarian interventionist norm. The legal aspects of humanitarian intervention to protect human security have been addressed in this study. We have argued that regardless of the content of substantive or customary international law and how the UN Charter is interpreted, we all have a moral obligation to help people in circumstances where belligerents repeatedly and deliberately violate even the most basic of human rights. If we claim to support the concept of a civil and moral society, then the obligation to act is itself substantive. In this sense, ignoring human security is not an option; it is legally and morally addressed in the affirmative within the UN Charter and by numerous conventions and protocols.

As democratic governance culturally and institutionally derives from the people, this study has identified the crucial, strategic role for democratic states to act upon the legal and moral responsibility to protect and promote human security. We have argued that despite the differences between democracies, there are significant commonalities that embed human security into the political culture and institutions. The sovereignty of democracies continues to substantially develop since the most essential part of sovereignty is that it derives its authority from the people.

Recently the discourse has evolved on the need to prevent violence as a long-term initiative, rather than to view 'protection' only as a final desperate response after the atrocities have begun. Embracing the concept of a responsibility to prevent (R2Prevent) is proactive, and protection, whether based on some notion of responsibility or not, is mostly reactive. The prevention thesis has primarily been the result of democracies pushing for a greater overall focus on human security, and there is an urgent need for a reorientation in thinking away from the traditional focus on state-centric security norms to one where human security and prevention initiatives have a much more prominent role in international relations. If powerful states only pay lip service or ignore entirely important international humanitarian conventions and obligations, then there is little point in hectoring weaker states to change their behaviour. The international community may occasionally directly intervene in an effort to protect those already subject to widespread and extreme levels of violence, but when a situation has deteriorated to such a level, then prevention efforts, if they have occurred at all, have been far too little and much too late.

We have argued that what is needed is a change from traditional state security paradigms to grassroots human security embracing R2Prevent strategies. The notion of 'prevention' is complex and multifaceted, and there is no preventive silver bullet. How to prevent violence is perhaps the biggest challenge facing the international community. A great deal of research still needs to be done in this area. No one can argue that the best protection is not prevention. Yet most still see prevention as an adjunct to protection to try to stop events spiralling even further out of control, but this approach is merely reactive when prevention needs to occur much earlier. Those who dismiss long-term prevention as an overly vague, even incomprehensible, approach to international affairs substantially miss the point. The point and the reality is that much can be done to prevent mass atrocities and violence, but each circumstance is different and any preventative strategy is context specific. Such an approach is difficult and complex, but surely not incomprehensible. The prevention approach is a hard sell to those who look for short-term solutions to long-term problems, but it is not a hard sell to those who need food on the table, shelter, clean drinking water and the construction of basic public utilities.

This study has presented a number of 'lessons learned' in the application of R2P in Libya. Foremost among these is the requirement not only to acknowledge the principles and norms of R2P, but to turn expressions of outrage by the international community into action. Democracies are far keener to promote the notion of human security and R2P compared to authoritarian regimes, but too often the commitment and political will to act is lacking when competing interests are at stake. The ongoing civil unrest in North Africa and in parts of the Middle East symbolize the tension that exists in the application of R2P as a developing norm when the international community attempts to address the excesses of state behaviour in failing or failed states. In such states, catalysts for civil unrest that may lead to widespread uprisings vary widely and are often unpredictable. On the streets of Sidi Bouzid in Tunisia, the self-immolation of Mohammed Bouazizi, as a result of the confiscation of his fruit and vegetables business by the state, triggered violent demonstrations and riots by intellectuals, human rights activists and many others who were politically and socially marginalized. This one act by one individual was an important catalyst that triggered the Tunisian revolution and it was the beginning of several other Arab uprisings across the region. One individual's inability to sell his wares to provide money for food and housing for his family mobilized people within and across state borders in their demand for greater freedom and human security.

Many important, unresolved questions remain about the causes of civil unrest that lead to revolution and the application of R2P and R2Prevent in the contemporary world. A great deal of research remains to be done. Has R2P and the notion of human security played a substantive role not only as a response to civil unrest, but also in triggering the uprisings in the Middle East and elsewhere over the last two years? Has globalization and a greater awareness among citizens everywhere of their entitlements to the most basic of human rights become a triggering factor to the mass demonstrations seen across two regions of the world? Is the notion of human security a concept or a vision that encourages people on the streets to stand up against unjust regimes?

Another important area to explore is not only the role of the West, but the active engagement by all democracies in promoting and preventing human security in the zeitgeist of the Arab uprisings. What role, if any, have Western democracies come to play in supporting the mass demonstrations for freedom and security against dictatorial leadership? Are there any clear-cut foreign policy strategies among these democracies that directly link their support to prodemocratic forces on the ground, and if so, how may this be effectively implemented to support the basic human rights and liberties of states that are unwilling or unable to do so themselves? Even if such foreign policy initiatives exist or eventuate, how do we deal with the highly selective nature of any form of intervention?

The sheer waste of precious lives and the scarce resources of would-be interventionists and citizens at risk alike are the usual outcomes when protection becomes a priority in desperation. A focus on prevention is future-oriented and it does not rely on pyrrhic military or political victories that ultimately fail to protect those most at risk. An essential tool for such efforts is to put greater focus on the legal support for human security within the UN Charter and to build democracies. We argue that there is an increasing international understanding of the merits of democratic governance. The inherited power of the people in democracies embeds to a large extent human security issues.

Appendix I

UN RESOLUTION 1970

	Security Council	Distr.: General
		26 February 2011

Resolution 1970 (2011)

Adopted by the Security Council at its 6491st meeting, on 26 February 2011

The Security Council,

Expressing grave concern at the situation in the Libyan Arab Jamahiriya and condemning the violence and use of force against civilians,

Deploring the gross and systematic violation of human rights, including the repression of peaceful demonstrators, expressing deep concern at the deaths of civilians, and rejecting unequivocally the incitement to hostility and violence against the civilian population made from the highest level of the Libyan government,

Welcoming the condemnation by the Arab League, the African Union, and the Secretary General of the Organization of the Islamic Conference of the serious violations of human rights and international humanitarian law that are being committed in the Libyan Arab Jamahiriya,

Taking note of the letter to the President of the Security Council from the Permanent Representative of the Libyan Arab Jamahiriya dated 26 February 2011,

Welcoming the Human Rights Council resolution A/HRC/RES/S-15/1 of 25 February 2011, including the decision to urgently dispatch an independent international commission of inquiry to investigate all alleged violations of international human rights law in the Libyan Arab Jamahiriya, to establish the facts and circumstances of such violations and of the crimes perpetrated, and where possible identify those responsible,

Considering that the widespread and systematic attacks currently taking place in the Libyan Arab Jamahiriya against the civilian population may amount to crimes against humanity,

Expressing concern at the plight of refugees forced to flee the violence in the Libyan Arab Jamahiriya,

Expressing concern also at the reports of shortages of medical supplies to treat the wounded,

Recalling the Libyan authorities' responsibility to protect its population,

Underlining the need to respect the freedoms of peaceful assembly and of expression, including freedom of the media,

Stressing the need to hold to account those responsible for attacks, including by forces under their control, on civilians,

Recalling article 16 of the Rome Statute under which no investigation or prosecution may be commenced or proceeded with by the International Criminal Court for a period of 12 months after a Security Council request to that effect,

Expressing concern for the safety of foreign nationals and their rights in the Libyan Arab Jamahiriya,

Reaffirming its strong commitment to the sovereignty, independence, territorial integrity and national unity of the Libyan Arab Jamahiriya.

Mindful of its primary responsibility for the maintenance of international peace and security under the Charter of the United Nations,

Acting under Chapter VII of the Charter of the United Nations, and taking measures under its Article 41,

1. *Demands* an immediate end to the violence and calls for steps to fulfil the legitimate demands of the population;
2. *Urges* the Libyan authorities to:
   (a) Act with the utmost restraint, respect human rights and international humanitarian law, and allow immediate access for international human rights monitors;
   (b) Ensure the safety of all foreign nationals and their assets and facilitate the departure of those wishing to leave the country;
   (c) Ensure the safe passage of humanitarian and medical supplies, and humanitarian agencies and workers, into the country; and
   (d) Immediately lift restrictions on all forms of media;
3. *Requests* all Member States, to the extent possible, to cooperate in the evacuation of those foreign nationals wishing to leave the country;

ICC referral

4. *Decides* to refer the situation in the Libyan Arab Jamahiriya since 15 February 2011 to the Prosecutor of the International Criminal Court;

5. *Decides* that the Libyan authorities shall cooperate fully with and provide any necessary assistance to the Court and the Prosecutor pursuant to this resolution and, while recognizing that States not party to the Rome Statute have no obligation under the Statute, urges all States and concerned regional and other international organizations to cooperate fully with the Court and the Prosecutor;

6. *Decides* that nationals, current or former officials or personnel from a State outside the Libyan Arab Jamahiriya which is not a party to the Rome Statute of the International Criminal Court shall be subject to the exclusive jurisdiction of that State for all alleged acts or omissions arising out of or related to operations in the Libyan Arab Jamahiriya established or authorized by the Council, unless such exclusive jurisdiction has been expressly waived by the State;

7. *Invites* the Prosecutor to address the Security Council within two months of the adoption of this resolution and every six months thereafter on actions taken pursuant to this resolution;

8. *Recognizes* that none of the expenses incurred in connection with the referral, including expenses related to investigations or prosecutions in connection with that referral, shall be borne by the United Nations and that such costs shall be borne by the parties to the Rome Statute and those States that wish to contribute voluntarily;

Arms Embargo

9. *Decides* that all Member States shall immediately take the necessary measures to prevent the direct or indirect supply, sale or transfer to the Libyan Arab Jamahiriya, from or through their territories or by their nationals, or using their flag vessels or aircraft, of arms and related materiel of all types, including weapons and ammunition, military vehicles and equipment, paramilitary equipment, and spare parts for the aforementioned, and technical assistance, training, financial or other assistance, related to military activities or the provision, maintenance or use of any arms and related materiel, including the provision of armed mercenary personnel whether or not originating in their territories, and decides further that this measure shall not apply to:

(a) Supplies of non-lethal military equipment intended solely for humanitarian or protective use, and related technical assistance or training, as approved in advance by the Committee established pursuant to paragraph 24 below;

(b) Protective clothing, including flak jackets and military helmets, temporarily exported to the Libyan Arab Jamahiriya by United

Nations personnel, representatives of the media and humanitarian and development workers and associated personnel, for their personal use only; or

(c) Other sales or supply of arms and related materiel, or provision of assistance or personnel, as approved in advance by the Committee;

10. *Decides* that the Libyan Arab Jamahiriya shall cease the export of all arms and related materiel and that all Member States shall prohibit the procurement of such items from the Libyan Arab Jamahiriya by their nationals, or using their flagged vessels or aircraft, and whether or not originating in the territory of the Libyan Arab Jamahiriya;

11. *Calls upon* all States, in particular States neighbouring the Libyan Arab Jamahiriya, to inspect, in accordance with their national authorities and legislation and consistent with international law, in particular the law of the sea and relevant international civil aviation agreements, all cargo to and from the Libyan Arab Jamahiriya, in their territory, including seaports and airports, if the State concerned has information that provides reasonable grounds to believe the cargo contains items the supply, sale, transfer, or export of which is prohibited by paragraphs 9 or 10 of this resolution for the purpose of ensuring strict implementation of those provisions;

12. *Decides* to authorize all Member States to, and that all Member States shall, upon discovery of items prohibited by paragraph 9 or 10 of this resolution, seize and dispose (such as through destruction, rendering inoperable, storage or transferring to a State other than the originating or destination States for disposal) items the supply, sale, transfer or export of which is prohibited by paragraphs 9 or 10 of this resolution and decides further that all Member States shall cooperate in such efforts;

13. *Requires* any Member State when it undertakes an inspection pursuant to paragraph 11 above, to submit promptly an initial written report to the Committee containing, in particular, explanation of the grounds for the inspections, the results of such inspections, and whether or not cooperation was provided, and, if prohibited items for transfer are found, further requires such Member States to submit to the Committee, at a later stage, a subsequent written report containing relevant details on the inspection, seizure, and disposal, and relevant details of the transfer, including a description of the items, their origin and intended destination, if this information is not in the initial report;

14. *Encourages* Member States to take steps to strongly discourage their nationals from travelling to the Libyan Arab Jamahiriya to participate in activities on behalf of the Libyan authorities that could reasonably contribute to the violation of human rights;

Travel ban

15. *Decides* that all Member States shall take the necessary measures to prevent the entry into or transit through their territories of individuals listed in Annex I of this resolution or designated by the Committee established pursuant to paragraph 24 below, provided that nothing in this paragraph shall oblige a State to refuse its own nationals entry into its territory;

16. *Decides* that the measures imposed by paragraph 15 above shall not apply:

    (a) Where the Committee determines on a case-by-case basis that such travel is justified on the grounds of humanitarian need, including religious obligation;

    (b) Where entry or transit is necessary for the fulfilment of a judicial process;

    (c) Where the Committee determines on a case-by-case basis that an exemption would further the objectives of peace and national reconciliation in the Libyan Arab Jamahiriya and stability in the region; or

    (d) Where a State determines on a case-by-case basis that such entry or transit is required to advance peace and stability in the Libyan Arab Jamahiriya and the States subsequently notifies the Committee within forty-eight hours after making such a determination;

Asset freeze

17. *Decides* that all Member States shall freeze without delay all funds, other financial assets and economic resources which are on their territories, which are owned or controlled, directly or indirectly, by the individuals or entities listed in annex II of this resolution or designated by the Committee established pursuant to paragraph 24 below, or by individuals or entities acting on their behalf or at their direction, or by entities owned or controlled by them, and decides further that all Member States shall ensure that any funds, financial assets or economic resources are prevented from being made available by their nationals or by any individuals or entities within their territories, to or for the benefit of the individuals or entities listed in Annex II of this resolution or individuals designated by the Committee;

18. *Expresses* its intention to ensure that assets frozen pursuant to paragraph 17 shall at a later stage be made available to and for the benefit of the people of the Libyan Arab Jamahiriya;

19. *Decides* that the measures imposed by paragraph 17 above do not apply to funds, other financial assets or economic resources that have been determined by relevant Member States:

 (a) To be necessary for basic expenses, including payment for foodstuffs, rent or mortgage, medicines and medical treatment, taxes, insurance premiums, and public utility charges or exclusively for payment of reasonable professional fees and reimbursement of incurred expenses associated with the provision of legal services in accordance with national laws, or fees or service charges, in accordance with national laws, for routine holding or maintenance of frozen funds, other financial assets and economic resources, after notification by the relevant State to the Committee of the intention to authorize, where appropriate, access to such funds, other financial assets or economic resources and in the absence of a negative decision by the Committee within five working days of such notification;

 (b) To be necessary for extraordinary expenses, provided that such determination has been notified by the relevant State or Member States to the Committee and has been approved by the Committee; or

 (c) To be the subject of a judicial, administrative or arbitral lien or judgment, in which case the funds, other financial assets and economic resources may be used to satisfy that lien or judgment provided that the lien or judgment was entered into prior to the date of the present resolution, is not for the benefit of a person or entity designated pursuant to paragraph 17 above, and has been notified by the relevant State or Member States to the Committee;

20. *Decides* that Member States may permit the addition to the accounts frozen pursuant to the provisions of paragraph 17 above of interests or other earnings due on those accounts or payments due under contracts, agreements or obligations that arose prior to the date on which those accounts became subject to the provisions of this resolution, provided that any such interest, other earnings and payments continue to be subject to these provisions and are frozen;

21. *Decides* that the measures in paragraph 17 above shall not prevent a designated person or entity from making payment due under a contract entered into prior to the listing of such a person or entity, provided that the relevant States have determined that the payment is not directly or indirectly received by a person or entity designated pursuant to paragraph 17 above, and after notification by the relevant States to the Committee of the intention to make or receive such payments or to authorize, where appropriate, the unfreezing of funds, other financial assets or economic resources for this purpose, 10 working days prior to such authorization;

Designation criteria

22. *Decides* that the measures contained in paragraphs 15 and 17 shall apply to the individuals and entities designated by the Committee, pursuant to paragraph 24 (b) and (c), respectively;

    (a) Involved in or complicit in ordering, controlling, or otherwise directing, the commission of serious human rights abuses against persons in the Libyan Arab Jamahiriya, including by being involved in or complicit in planning, commanding, ordering or conducting attacks, in violation of international law, including aerial bombardments, on civilian populations and facilities; or

    (b) Acting for or on behalf of or at the direction of individuals or entities identified in subparagraph (a).

23. *Strongly encourages* Member States to submit to the Committee names of individuals who meet the criteria set out in paragraph 22 above;

New Sanctions Committee

24. *Decides* to establish, in accordance with rule 28 of its provisional rules of procedure, a Committee of the Security Council consisting of all the members of the Council (herein "the Committee"), to undertake to following tasks:

    (a) To monitor implementation of the measures imposed in paragraphs 9, 10, 15, and 17;

    (b) To designate those individuals subject to the measures imposed by paragraphs 15 and to consider requests for exemptions in accordance with paragraph 16 above;

    (c) To designate those individuals subject to the measures imposed by paragraph 17 above and to consider requests for exemptions in accordance with paragraphs 19 and 20 above;

    (d) To establish such guidelines as may be necessary to facilitate the implementation of the measures imposed above;

    (e) To report within thirty days to the Security Council on its work for the first report and thereafter to report as deemed necessary by the Committee;

    (f) To encourage a dialogue between the Committee and interested Member States, in particular those in the region, including by inviting representatives of such States to meet with the Committee to discuss implementation of the measures;

    (g) To seek from all States whatever information it may consider useful regarding the actions taken by them to implement effectively the measures imposed above;

(h) To examine and take appropriate action on information regarding alleged violations or non-compliance with the measures contained in this resolution;

25. *Calls upon* all Member States to report to the Committee within 120 days of the adoption of this resolution on the steps they have taken with a view to implementing effectively paragraphs 9, 10, 15 and 17 above;

Humanitarian assistance

26. Calls upon all Member States, working together and acting in cooperation with the Secretary General, to facilitate and support the return of humanitarian agencies and make available humanitarian and related assistance in the Libyan Arab Jamahiriya, and requests the States concerned to keep the Security Council regularly informed on the progress of actions undertaken pursuant to this paragraph, and expresses its readiness to consider taking additional appropriate measures, as necessary, to achieve this;

Commitment to review

27. Affirms that it shall keep the Libyan authorities' actions under continuous review and that it shall be prepared to review the appropriateness of the measures contained in this resolution, including the strengthening, modification, suspension or lifting of the measures, as may be needed at any time in light of the Libyan authorities' compliance with relevant provisions of this resolution;

28. Decides to remain actively seized of the matter.

Annex I

Travel Ban

1. Al-Baghdadi, Dr Abdulqader Mohammed
   Passport number: B010574. Date of birth: 01/07/1950.
   Head of the Liaison Office of the Revolutionary Committees. Revolutionary Committees involved in violence against demonstrators.
2. Dibri, Abdulqader Yusef
   Date of birth: 1946. Place of birth: Houn, Libya.
   Head of Muammar Qadhafi's personal security. Responsibility for regime security. History of directing violence against dissidents.
3. Dorda, Abu Zayd Umar
   Director, External Security Organisation. Regime loyalist. Head of external intelligence agency.

4. Jabir, Major General Abu Bakr Yunis
   Date of birth: 1952. Place of birth: Jalo, Libya.
   Defence Minister. Overall responsibility for actions of armed forces.
5. Matuq, Matuq Mohammed
   Date of birth: 1956. Place of birth: Khoms.
   Secretary for Utilities. Senior member of regime. Involvement with
   Revolutionary Committees. Past history of involvement in suppression of
   dissent and violence.
6. Qadhaf Al-dam, Sayyid Mohammed
   Date of birth: 1948. Place of birth: Sirte, Libya.
   Cousin of Muammar Qadhafi. In the 1980s, Sayyid was involved in the
   dissident assassination campaign and allegedly responsible for several deaths
   in Europe. He is also thought to have been involved in arms procurement.
7. Qadhafi, Aisha Muammar Date of birth: 1978.
   Place of birth: Tripoli, Libya.
   Daughter of Muammar Qadhafi. Closeness of association with regime.
8. Qadhafi, Hannibal Muammar
   Passport number: B/002210. Date of birth: 20/09/1975. Place of birth:
   Tripoli, Libya.
   Son of Muammar Qadhafi. Closeness of association with regime.
9. Qadhafi, Khamis Muammar
   Date of birth: 1978. Place of birth: Tripoli, Libya.
   Son of Muammar Qadhafi. Closeness of association with regime.
   Command of military units involved in repression of demonstrations.
10. Qadhafi, Mohammed Muammar
    Date of birth: 1970. Place of birth: Tripoli, Libya.
    Son of Muammar Qadhafi. Closeness of association with regime.
11. Qadhafi, Muammar Mohammed Abu Minyar
    Date of birth: 1942. Place of birth: Sirte, Libya.
    Leader of the Revolution, Supreme Commander of Armed Forces.
    Responsibility for ordering repression of demonstrations, human rights abuses.
12. Qadhafi, Mutassim
    Date of birth: 1976. Place of birth: Tripoli, Libya.
    National Security Adviser. Son of Muammar Qadhafi. Closeness of
    association with regime.
13. Qadhafi, Saadi
    Passport number: 014797. Date of birth: 25/05/1973. Place of birth:
    Tripoli, Libya.
    Commander Special Forces. Son of Muammar Qadhafi. Closeness of
    association with regime. Command of military units involved in repression
    of demonstrations.

14. Qadhafi, Saif al-Arab
    Date of birth: 1982. Place of birth: Tripoli, Libya.
    Son of Muammar Qadhafi. Closeness of association with regime.
15. Qadhafi, Saif al-Islam
    Passport number: B014995. Date of birth: 25/06/1972. Place of birth:
    Tripoli, Libya.
    Director, Qadhafi Foundation. Son of Muammar Qadhafi. Closeness of
    association with regime. Inflammatory public statements encouraging
    violence against demonstrators.
16. Al-Senussi, Colonel Abdullah
    Date of birth: 1949. Place of birth: Sudan.
    Director Military Intelligence. Military Intelligence involvement in
    suppression of demonstrations. Past history includes suspicion of
    involvement in Abu Selim prison massacre. Convicted in absentia for
    bombing of UTA flight. Brother-in-law of Muammar Qadhafi.

Annex II

Asset Freeze

1. Qadhafi, Aisha Muammar
   Date of birth: 1978. Place of birth: Tripoli, Libya.
   Daughter of Muammar Qadhafi. Closeness of association with regime.
2. Qadhafi, Hannibal Muammar
   Passport number: B/002210. Date of birth: 20/09/1975. Place of birth:
   Tripoli, Libya.
   Son of Muammar Qadhafi. Closeness of association with regime.
3. Qadhafi, Khamis Muammar
   Date of birth: 1978. Place of birth: Tripoli, Libya.
   Son of Muammar Qadhafi. Closeness of association with regime.
   Command of military units involved in repression of demonstrations.
4. Qadhafi, Muammar Mohammed
   Abu Minyar Date of birth: 1942. Place of birth: Sirte, Libya.
   Leader of the Revolution, Supreme Commander of Armed Forces.
   Responsibility for ordering repression of demonstrations, human rights
   abuses.
5. Qadhafi, Mutassim
   Date of birth: 1976. Place of birth: Tripoli, Libya.
   National Security Adviser. Son of Muammar Qadhafi. Closeness of
   association with regime.

6. Qadhafi, Saif al-Islam
   Passport number: B014995. Date of birth: 25/06/1972. Place of birth: Tripoli, Libya.
   Director, Qadhafi Foundation. Son of Muammar Qadhafi. Closeness of association with regime. Inflammatory public statements encouraging violence against demonstrators.

Appendix II

UN RESOLUTION 1973

	Security Council	Distr.: General
		17 March 2011

Resolution 1973 (2011)

**Adopted by the Security Council at its 6498th meeting,
on 17 March 2011**

The Security Council,

Recalling its resolution 1970 (2011) of 26 February 2011,

Deploring the failure of the Libyan authorities to comply with resolution 1970 (2011),

Expressing grave concern at the deteriorating situation, the escalation of violence, and the heavy civilian casualties,

Reiterating the responsibility of the Libyan authorities to protect the Libyan population and *reaffirming* that parties to armed conflicts bear the primary responsibility to take all feasible steps to ensure the protection of civilians,

Condemning the gross and systematic violation of human rights, including arbitrary detentions, enforced disappearances, torture and summary executions,

Further condemning acts of violence and intimidation committed by the Libyan authorities against journalists, media professionals and associated personnel and *urging* these authorities to comply with their obligations under international humanitarian law as outlined in resolution 1738 (2006),

Considering that the widespread and systematic attacks currently taking place in the Libyan Arab Jamahiriya against the civilian population may amount to crimes against humanity,

Recalling paragraph 26 of resolution 1970 (2011) in which the Council expressed its readiness to consider taking additional appropriate measures, as necessary, to facilitate and support the return of humanitarian agencies and make available humanitarian and related assistance in the Libyan Arab Jamahiriya,

Expressing its determination to ensure the protection of civilians and civilian populated areas and the rapid and unimpeded passage of humanitarian assistance and the safety of humanitarian personnel,

Recalling the condemnation by the League of Arab States, the African Union, and the Secretary General of the Organization of the Islamic Conference of the serious violations of human rights and international humanitarian law that have been and are being committed in the Libyan Arab Jamahiriya,

Taking note of the final communiqué of the Organization of the Islamic Conference of 8 March 2011, and the communiqué of the Peace and Security Council of the African Union of 10 March 2011 which established an ad hoc High Level Committee on Libya,

Taking note also of the decision of the Council of the League of Arab States of 12 March 2011 to call for the imposition of a no-fly zone on Libyan military aviation, and to establish safe areas in places exposed to shelling as a precautionary measure that allows the protection of the Libyan people and foreign nationals residing in the Libyan Arab Jamahiriya,

Taking note further of the Secretary-General's call on 16 March 2011 for an immediate cease-fire,

Recalling its decision to refer the situation in the Libyan Arab Jamahiriya since 15 February 2011 to the Prosecutor of the International Criminal Court, and *stressing* that those responsible for or complicit in attacks targeting the civilian population, including aerial and naval attacks, must be held to account,

Reiterating its concern at the plight of refugees and foreign workers forced to flee the violence in the Libyan Arab Jamahiriya, *welcoming* the response of neighbouring States, in particular Tunisia and Egypt, to address the needs of those refugees and foreign workers, and *calling on* the international community to support those efforts,

Deploring the continuing use of mercenaries by the Libyan authorities,

Considering that the establishment of a ban on all flights in the airspace of the Libyan Arab Jamahiriya constitutes an important element for the protection of civilians as well as the safety of the delivery of humanitarian assistance and a decisive step for the cessation of hostilities in Libya,

Expressing concern also for the safety of foreign nationals and their rights in the Libyan Arab Jamahiriya,

Welcoming the appointment by the Secretary General of his Special Envoy to Libya, Mr Abdel-Elah Mohamed Al-Khatib and supporting his efforts to find a sustainable and peaceful solution to the crisis in the Libyan Arab Jamahiriya,

Reaffirming its strong commitment to the sovereignty, independence, territorial integrity and national unity of the Libyan Arab Jamahiriya,

Determining that the situation in the Libyan Arab Jamahiriya continues to constitute a threat to international peace and security,

Acting under Chapter VII of the Charter of the United Nations,

1. *Demands* the immediate establishment of a cease-fire and a complete end to violence and all attacks against, and abuses of, civilians;

2. *Stresses* the need to intensify efforts to find a solution to the crisis which responds to the legitimate demands of the Libyan people and *notes* the decisions of the Secretary-General to send his Special Envoy to Libya and of the Peace and Security Council of the African Union to send its ad hoc High Level Committee to Libya with the aim of facilitating dialogue to lead to the political reforms necessary to find a peaceful and sustainable solution;

3. *Demands* that the Libyan authorities comply with their obligations under international law, including international humanitarian law, human rights and refugee law and take all measures to protect civilians and meet their basic needs, and to ensure the rapid and unimpeded passage of humanitarian assistance;

Protection of civilians

4. *Authorizes* Member States that have notified the Secretary-General, acting nationally or through regional organizations or arrangements, and acting in cooperation with the Secretary-General, to take all necessary measures, notwithstanding paragraph 9 of resolution 1970 (2011), to protect civilians and civilian populated areas under threat of attack in the Libyan Arab Jamahiriya, including Benghazi, while excluding a foreign occupation force of any form on any part of Libyan territory, and *requests* the Member States concerned to inform the Secretary-General immediately of the measures they take pursuant to the authorization conferred by this paragraph which shall be immediately reported to the Security Council;

5. *Recognizes* the important role of the League of Arab States in matters relating to the maintenance of international peace and security in the region, and bearing in mind Chapter VIII of the Charter of the United Nations, requests the Member States of the League of Arab States to cooperate with other Member States in the implementation of paragraph 4;

No Fly Zone

6. *Decides* to establish a ban on all flights in the airspace of the Libyan Arab Jamahiriya in order to help protect civilians;

7. *Decides further* that the ban imposed by paragraph 6 shall not apply to flights whose sole purpose is humanitarian, such as delivering or facilitating the delivery of assistance, including medical supplies, food, humanitarian workers and related assistance, or evacuating foreign nationals from the Libyan Arab Jamahiriya, nor shall it apply to flights authorised by paragraphs 4 or 8, nor other flights which are deemed necessary by States acting under the authorisation conferred in paragraph 8 to be for the benefit of the Libyan people, and that these flights shall be coordinated with any mechanism established under paragraph 8;

8. *Authorizes* Member States that have notified the Secretary-General and the Secretary-General of the League of Arab States, acting nationally or through regional organizations or arrangements, to take all necessary measures to enforce compliance with the ban on flights imposed by paragraph 6 above, as necessary, and *requests* the States concerned in cooperation with the League of Arab States to coordinate closely with the Secretary General on the measures they are taking to implement this ban, including by establishing an appropriate mechanism for implementing the provisions of paragraphs 6 and 7 above,

9. *Calls upon* all Member States, acting nationally or through regional organizations or arrangements, to provide assistance, including any necessary overflight approvals, for the purposes of implementing paragraphs 4, 6, 7 and 8 above;

10. *Requests* the Member States concerned to coordinate closely with each other and the Secretary-General on the measures they are taking to implement paragraphs 4, 6, 7 and 8 above, including practical measures for the monitoring and approval of authorised humanitarian or evacuation flights;

11. *Decides* that the Member States concerned shall inform the Secretary-General and the Secretary-General of the League of Arab States immediately of measures taken in exercise of the authority conferred by paragraph 8 above, including to supply a concept of operations;

12. *Requests* the Secretary-General to inform the Council immediately of any actions taken by the Member States concerned in exercise of the authority conferred by paragraph 8 above and to report to the Council within 7 days and every month thereafter on the implementation of this resolution, including information on any violations of the flight ban imposed by paragraph 6 above;

Enforcement of the arms embargo

13. *Decides that* paragraph 11 of resolution 1970 (2011) shall be replaced by the following paragraph: "Calls upon all Member States, in particular

States of the region, acting nationally or through regional organisations or arrangements, in order to ensure strict implementation of the arms embargo established by paragraphs 9 and 10 of resolution 1970 (2011), to inspect in their territory, including seaports and airports, and on the high seas, vessels and aircraft bound to or from the Libyan Arab Jamahiriya, if the State concerned has information that provides reasonable grounds to believe that the cargo contains items the supply, sale, transfer or export of which is prohibited by paragraphs 9 or 10 of resolution 1970 (2011) as modified by this resolution, including the provision of armed mercenary personnel, *calls upon* all flag States of such vessels and aircraft to cooperate with such inspections and authorises Member States to use all measures commensurate to the specific circumstances to carry out such inspections";

14. *Requests* Member States which are taking action under paragraph 13 above on the high seas to coordinate closely with each other and the Secretary-General and *further requests* the States concerned to inform the Secretary-General and the Committee established pursuant to paragraph 24 of resolution 1970 (2011) ("the Committee") immediately of measures taken in the exercise of the authority conferred by paragraph 13 above;

15. *Requires* any Member State whether acting nationally or through regional organisations or arrangements, when it undertakes an inspection pursuant to paragraph 13 above, to submit promptly an initial written report to the Committee containing, in particular, explanation of the grounds for the inspection, the results of such inspection, and whether or not cooperation was provided, and, if prohibited items for transfer are found, further requires such Member States to submit to the Committee, at a later stage, a subsequent written report containing relevant details on the inspection, seizure, and disposal, and relevant details of the transfer, including a description of the items, their origin and intended destination, if this information is not in the initial report;

16. *Deplores* the continuing flows of mercenaries into the Libyan Arab Jamahiriya and *calls upon* all Member States to comply strictly with their obligations under paragraph 9 of resolution 1970 (2011) to prevent the provision of armed mercenary personnel to the Libyan Arab Jamahiriya;

Ban on flights

17. *Decides* that all States shall deny permission to any aircraft registered in the Libyan Arab Jamahiriya or owned or operated by Libyan nationals or companies to take off from, land in or overfly their territory unless the particular flight has been approved in advance by the Committee, or in the case of an emergency landing;

18. *Decides that* all States shall deny permission to any aircraft to take off from, land in or overfly their territory, if they have information that provides reasonable grounds to believe that the aircraft contains items the supply, sale, transfer, or export of which is prohibited by paragraphs 9 and 10 of resolution 1970 (2011) as modified by this resolution, including the provision of armed mercenary personnel, except in the case of an emergency landing;

Asset freeze

19. *Decides* that the asset freeze imposed by paragraph 17, 19, 20 and 21 of resolution 1970 (2011) shall apply to all funds, other financial assets and economic resources which are on their territories, which are owned or controlled, directly or indirectly, by the Libyan authorities, as designated by the Committee, or by individuals or entities acting on their behalf or at their direction, or by entities owned or controlled by them, as designated by the Committee, and *decides further* that all States shall ensure that any funds, financial assets or economic resources are prevented from being made available by their nationals or by any individuals or entities within their territories, to or for the benefit of the Libyan authorities, as designated by the Committee, or individuals or entities acting on their behalf or at their direction, or entities owned or controlled by them, as designated by the Committee, and directs the Committee to designate such Libyan authorities, individuals or entities within 30 days of the date of the adoption of this resolution and as appropriate thereafter;

20. *Affirms* its determination to ensure that assets frozen pursuant to paragraph 17 of resolution 1970 (2011) shall, at a later stage, as soon as possible be made available to and for the benefit of the people of the Libyan Arab Jamahiriya;

21. *Decides* that all States shall require their nationals, persons subject to their jurisdiction and firms incorporated in their territory or subject to their jurisdiction to exercise vigilance when doing business with entities incorporated in the Libyan Arab Jamahiriya or subject to its jurisdiction, and any individuals or entities acting on their behalf or at their direction, and entities owned or controlled by them, if the States have information that provides reasonable grounds to believe that such business could contribute to violence and use of force against civilians;

Designations

22. *Decides* that the individuals listed in Annex I shall be subject to the travel restrictions imposed in paragraphs 15 and 16 of resolution 1970 (2011),

and *decides* further that the individuals and entities listed in Annex II shall be subject to the asset freeze imposed in paragraphs 17, 19, 20 and 21 of resolution 1970 (2011);

23. *Decides* that the measures specified in paragraphs 15, 16, 17, 19, 20 and 21 of resolution 1970 (2011) shall apply also to individuals and entities determined by the Council or the Committee to have violated the provisions of resolution 1970 (2011), particularly paragraphs 9 and 10 thereof, or to have assisted others in doing so;

Panel of Experts

24. *Requests* the Secretary-General to create for an initial period of one year, in consultation with the Committee, a group of up to eight experts ("Panel of Experts"), under the direction of the Committee to carry out the following tasks:

(a) Assist the Committee in carrying out its mandate as specified in paragraph 24 of resolution 1970 (2011) and this resolution;

(b) Gather, examine and analyse information from States, relevant United Nations bodies, regional organisations and other interested parties regarding the implementation of the measures decided in resolution 1970 (2011) and this resolution, in particular incidents of non-compliance;

(c) Make recommendations on actions the Council, or the Committee or State, may consider to improve implementation of the relevant measures;

(d) Provide to the Council an interim report on its work no later than 90 days after the Panel's appointment, and a final report to the Council no later than 30 days prior to the termination of its mandate with its findings and recommendations;

25. *Urges* all States, relevant United Nations bodies and other interested parties, to cooperate fully with the Committee and the Panel of Experts, in particular by supplying any information at their disposal on the implementation of the measures decided in resolution 1970 (2011) and this resolution, in particular incidents of non-compliance;

26. *Decides* that the mandate of the Committee as set out in paragraph 24 of resolution 1970 (2011) shall also apply to the measures decided in this resolution;

27. *Decides* that all States, including the Libyan Arab Jamahiriya, shall take the necessary measures to ensure that no claim shall lie at the instance of the Libyan authorities, or of any person or body in the Libyan Arab Jamahiriya, or of any person claiming through or for the benefit of any

such person or body, in connection with any contract or other transaction where its performance was affected by reason of the measures taken by the Security Council in resolution 1970 (2011), this resolution and related resolutions;

28. *Reaffirms* its intention to keep the actions of the Libyan authorities under continuous review and underlines its readiness to review at any time the measures imposed by this resolution and resolution 1970 (2011), including by strengthening, suspending or lifting those measures, as appropriate, based on compliance by the Libyan authorities with this resolution and resolution 1970 (2011).

29. *Decides* to remain actively seized of the matter.

Libya: UNSCR proposed designations

Number Name	Justification	Identifiers
Annex I: Travel Ban		
1. QUREN SALIH QUREN AL QADHAFI	Libyan Ambassador to Chad. Has left Chad for Sabha. Involved directly in recruiting and coordinating mercenaries for the regime.	
2. Colonel AMID HUSAIN AL KUNI	Governor of Ghat (South Libya). Directly involved in recruiting mercenaries.	
Annex II: Asset Freeze		
1. Dorda, Abu Zayd Umar	Position: Director, External Security Organisation	
2. Jabir, Major General Abu Bakr Yunis	Position: Defence Minister	**Title:** Major General **DOB:** --/--/1952. **POB:** Jalo, Libya
3. Matuq, Matuq Mohammed	Position: Secretary for Utilities	**DOB**: --/--/1956. **POB**: Khoms
4. Qadhafi, Mohammed Muammar	Son of Muammar Qadhafi. Closeness of association with regime	**DOB**: --/--/1970. **POB**: Tripoli, Libya
5. Qadhafi, Saadi	Commander Special Forces. Son of Muammar Qadhafi. Closeness of association with regime. Command of military units involved in repression of demonstrations	**DOB**: 25/05/1973. **POB**: Tripoli, Libya

(Continued)

Number Name	Justification	Identifiers
6. Qadhafi, Saif al-Arab	Son of Muammar Qadhafi. Closeness of association with regime	**DOB**: --/--/1982. **POB**: Tripoli, Libya
7. Al-Senussi, Colonel Abdullah	Position: Director Military Intelligence	**Title**: Colonel **DOB**: --/--/1949. **POB**: Sudan

Entities

1. Central Bank of Libya	Under control of Muammar Qadhafi and his family, and potential source of funding for his regime.	
2. Libyan Investment Authority	Under control of Muammar Qadhafi and his family, and potential source of funding for his regime.	**a.k.a**: Libyan Arab Foreign Investment Company (LAFICO) **Address**: 1 Fateh Tower Office, No 99 22nd Floor, Borgaida Street, Tripoli, Libya, 1103
3. Libyan Foreign Bank	Under control of Muammar Qadhafi and his family and a potential source of funding for his regime.	
4. Libyan Africa Investment Portfolio	Under control of Muammar Qadhafi and his family, and potential source of funding for his regime.	**Address**: Jamahiriya Street, LAP Building, PO Box 91330, Tripoli, Libya
5. Libyan National Oil Corporation	Under control of Muammar Qadhafi and his family, and potential source of funding for his regime.	**Address**: Bashir Saadwi Street, Tripoli, Tarabulus, Libya

NOTES

Chapter 1   Introduction

1 United Nations General Assembly, *2005 World Summit Outcome*, A/60/L.1, United Nations World Summit, 24 October 2005, 3, 30.

2 Hampson and Malone, 'Improving the UN's Capacity for Conflict Prevention', *International Peacekeeping* 9, 1 (2002): 78.

3 Carnegie Commission on Preventing Deadly Conflict, *Preventing Deadly Conflict: Final Report with Executive Summary* (Washington, DC: 1997), xviii–xxviii.

4 Bellamy, Williams and Griffin, *Understanding Peacekeeping*, 2nd edition (Cambridge: Polity Press/Blackwell, 2010), 155.

5 Hampson and Malone, 'Conflict Prevention', 77.

6 Rummel, *Death by Government* (New Brunswick, NJ: Transactions, 1994), 2–15.

7 International Law Commission, *Report of the International Law Commission on the Work of its Fifty-third Session*, UN Doc. A/56/10, (New York: 2001), 32.

8 United Nations Security Council, S/RES/1973 (2011), 2.

Chapter 2   State versus Human Security: The Great Debate

1 For a comprehensive review of the discourse, see: Hehir, *Humanitarian Intervention After Kosovo: Iraq, Darfur and the Record of Global Civil Society* (Houndmills, Basingstoke: Palgrave Macmillan, 2008).

2 Collins, *Contemporary Security Studies* (Oxford and New York: Oxford University Press, 2007), 132.

3 Brunnée and Toope, 'Norms, Institutions, and UN Reform: The Responsibility to Protect', *Journal of International Law and International Relations* 2 (2006): 128.

4 Ibid.

5 Gallie, 'Essentially Contested Concepts', *Proceedings of the Aristotelian Society* 56 (1956): 167–98.

6 Williams, 'Security Studies: An Introduction', in *Security Studies: An Introduction* (London: Routledge, 2008), 5.

7 For a useful overview, see: Booth, *Theory of World Security* (New York: Cambridge University Press, 2007). See also: Cottey, *Security in the New Europe* (Basingstoke and New York: Palgrave Macmillan, 2007).

8 Krasner, 'Rethinking the Sovereign State Model', *Review of International Studies* 27, 5 (2001): 17–42.

9 United Nations, *United Nations Charter* (New York: United Nations, 1945), 1–80.

10 For a useful discussion on the development of foreign policy analysis, see Merritt, *Foreign Policy Analysis* (D. C. Heath: Lexington Books, 1976).

11 Carlsnaes, 'The Agency-Structure Problem in Foreign Policy Making', *International Studies Quarterly* 36, 3 (1992): 245–70. See also: Hudson and Vore, 'Foreign Policy Analysis Yesterday, Today, and Tomorrow', *Mershon International Studies Review* 39, 2 (1995): 209–38; Neack, Hey and Patrick, *Foreign Policy Analysis: Continuity and Change in its Second Generation* (Englewood Cliffs: Prentice Hall, 1995); Breuning, *Foreign Policy Analysis: A Comparative Introduction* (New York: Palgrave Macmillan, 2007).

12 Two classical studies on state security are: Waltz, *Theory of International Politics* (New York: McGraw-Hill, 1979); Waltz, *Man, the State, and War: A Theoretical Analysis* (New York: Columbia University Press, 2001).

13 For a thorough presentation of causes to and consequences of the Cold War, see: Gaddis, *The Cold War: A New History* (London: Penguin, 2007); Gaddis, *We Now Know: Rethinking Cold War History* (New York: Oxford University Press, 1998).

14 Mayall, 'Non-intervention, Self-determination and the "New World Order"', *International Affairs* 67, 3 (1991): 421–9. See also: Onuf, 'The Principle of Nonintervention, the United Nations, and the International System', *International Organization* 25, 2 (1971): 209–27.

15 Walker, *The Cold War: A History* (New York: Henry Holt, 1995), 29–59, 252–78. See also: Gaddis, *The Cold War: A New History*; Cowley, *The Cold War: A Military History* (New York: Random House, 2009).

16 Krasner, 'Sharing Sovereignty: New Institutions for Collapsed and Failing States', *International Security* 29, 2 (2004): 85. See also: Krasner, *Sovereignty: Organized Hypocrisy* (Princeton: Princeton University Press, 1999), 3–43, 43–73.

17 Huntington, 'Will More Countries Become Democratic?', *Political Science Quarterly* 99, 2 (1984): 193–218.

18 Helman and Ratner, 'Saving Failed States', *Foreign Policy Analysis* 89 (Winter 1992–93): 3–20; Wade, 'Failing States and Cumulative Causation in the World System', *International Political Science Review* 26, 1 (2005): 17–36.

19 Weber, 'Power, Authority and Imperative Control', in *The Theory of Social and Economic Organizations*, ed. Parsons (New York: Free Press, 1964), 152–66. For a comparative and contextual debate on sovereignty, see Krasner, 'Sharing Sovereignty: New Institutions for Collapsed and Failing States', *International Security* 29, 2 (2004): 85–120.

20 Fukuyama, 'The Imperative of State-Building', *Journal of Democracy* 15, 2 (2004), 17–31.

21 Englehart, 'State Capacity, State Failure, and Human Rights', *Journal of Peace Research* 46, 2 (2009): 163–80.

22 For a discussion on the concept of failed states, see: Rotberg, *When States Fail: Causes and Consequences* (Princeton: Princeton University Press, 2004).

23 Kaldor, *New and Old Wars: Organized Violence in a Global Era* (Stanford: Stanford University Press, 2007), 1–231.

24 For an analysis of the national–international linkage, see: Jackson, *Quasi-states: Sovereignty, International Relations, and the Third World* (Cambridge: Cambridge University Press, 1990). See also: Zartman, *Collapsed State: The Disintegration and Restoration of Legitimate Authority* (Boulder: Lynne Rienner, 1995).

25 Chauvet and Paul, 'What Are the Preconditions for Turnarounds in Failing States?', *Conflict Management and Peace Science* 25, 4 (2008): 332–48. See also: Newman,

'Peacebuilding as Security in "Failing" and Conflict-Prone States', *Journal of Intervention and Statebuilding* 4, 3 (2010): 305–22.

26 Eizenstat, Porter and Weinstein, 'Rebuilding Weak States', *Foreign Affairs* 84 (2005): 134–47.

27 Jackson, 'The State and Internal Conflict', *Australian Journal of International Affairs* 55 (2001): 65–81.

28 For an insightful study on national unity, see: Rustow, 'Transitions to Democracy: Toward a Dynamic Model', in *Transitions to Democracy*, ed. Anderson (New York: Columbia University Press, 1999), 1–316.

29 Eizenstat, Porter and Weinstein, 'Rebuilding Weak States', 134–47. See also: Jackson, 'The State and Internal Conflict', 65–81.

30 Eizenstat, Porter and Weinstein, 'Rebuilding Weak States', 134–47.

31 Jackson, 'The State and Internal Conflict', 65–81.

32 Milliken and Krause, 'State Failure, Collapse and Reconstruction: Concepts, Lessons and Strategies', *Development and Change* 5 (2002): 753–74. See also: Cowen and Coyne, 'Postwar Reconstruction: Some Insights from Public Choice and Institutional Economics', *Constitutional Political Economy* 16 (2005): 31–48; *Weak and Failing States: Evolving Security Threats and US Policy*, CRS Report for Congress (Washington, DC, 2008), 1–37.

33 For a discussion on state functionality, see: Rotberg, *When States Fail: Causes and Consequences*.

34 Moore, 'UN Peacekeeping: A Glass Half Empty, Half Full', *Bulletin of the Atomic Scientists* 51, 2 (1995): 22–3.

35 For a useful over view of these conflicts, see: Pellatt, *Nagorno-Karabakh, Abkhazia and Chechnya: Violence and Autonomy in Eurasia's Secessionist Conflicts* (Ottawa: Library and Archives Canada, 2009). See also: Seely, *Russo-Chechen Conflict, 1800–2000: A Deadly Embrace* (New York: Frank Cass, 2005).

36 For an extended analysis of the dissolution of Yugoslavia, see Rogel, *The Breakup in Yugoslavia and the War in Bosnia* (Westport: Greenwood Press, 1998); Rogel, *The Breakup of Yugoslavia and its Aftermath* (Westport: Greenwood Press, 2004).

37 Bangura, 'Politicized Ethnicities Versus Tribal Etnicities: Examples from Liberia, Rwanda and Sierra Leone', in *The Politics Ethnicity and National Identity*, ed. Saha (New York: Peter Lang 2007), 121–38. See also: Mamdani, *When Victims Become Killers: Colonialism, Nativism, and the Genocide in Rwanda* (Princeton: Princeton University Press, 2001).

38 Vaccaro, 'The Politics of Genocide: Peacekeeping and Disaster Relief in Rwanda', in *UN Peacekeeping, American Policy and the Uncivil Wars of the 1990s*, ed. Durch (New York: St Martin's Press, 1996), 367–409.

39 Grunfeld and Huijboom, *The Failure to Prevent Genocide in Rwanda: The Role of Bystanders* (Leiden: Martinus Nijhoff, 2007), 107, 214–16.

40 Totten, Bartrop and Jacobs, *Dictionary of Genocide* (Westport: Greenwood Press, 2008), 381.

41 Piiparinen, *The Transformation of UN Conflict Management: Producing Images of Genocide from Rwanda to Darfur and Beyond* (London and New York: Routledge, 2010), 129.

42 Molony, 'Response to Rwanda "Too Little, Too Late"', *Independent* (Ireland), 8 April 2004. Online: http://www.independent.ie/world-news/africa/response-to-rwanda-too-little-too-late-175164.html (accessed 12 December 2011).

43 The History Place, 'Genocide in the 20th Century: Rwanda 1994 800,000 Deaths'. Online: http://www.historyplace.com/worldhistory/genocide/rwanda.htm (accessed 20 November 2011).

44 Cordial and Rosandhaug, *Post-Conflict Property Restitution: The Approach in Kosovo and Lessons Learned for Future International Practice* (Leiden: Koninklijke Brill NV, 2008), 10–11. See also: Crnobrnja, *The Yugoslav Drama* (London: I.B. Tauris, 1996), 174–89, 266–85.

45 Bell, *Peace Agreements and Human Rights* (Oxford: Oxford University Press, 2000), 98–112.

46 For a presentation of the escalation of violence in Kosovo, see: Silander, *United Nations Interim Mission in Kosovo: Standards Before Status: A Policy of Catch 22* (Saarbrucken: VDM Verlag, 2009). See also: IICK, *The Kosovo Report: Conflict, International Response, Lessons Learned* (Oxford: Oxford University Press, 2000).

47 North Atlantic Council, *Statement on Kosovo* (Washington, DC, 23–24 April 1999).

48 Henriksen, *NATO's Gambling: Combining Diplomacy and Airpower in the Kosovo Crisis 1998–1999* (Annapolis: Naval Institute Press, 2007), 7. See also: Krieger, *The Kosovo Conflict and International Law: An Analytical Documentation 1974–1999* (Cambridge: Cambridge University Press, 2001), 304.

49 Silander, *United Nations Interim Mission in Kosovo*, 161.

50 'NATO's Role in Relation to the Conflict in Kosovo', NATO, 15 July 1999. Online: http://www.nato.int/docu/handbook/2001/hb050305.htm (accessed 25 December 2011).

51 Janzekovic, *The Use of Force in Humanitarian Intervention: Morality and Practicalities* (London: Ashgate, 2006), 159–85.

52 Daalder, 'Emerging Answers: Kosovo, NATO, and the Use of Force', *Brookings Review* 17, 3 (1999): 22–5.

53 For a review of arguments, see: Independent International Commission, *Why Conditional Independence? The Follow-up of the Kosovo Report* (Stockholm: Palme International Centre and Global Reporting, 2001), 1–48; IICK, *The Kosovo Report*.

54 Glennon, 'The New Interventionism: The Search for a Just International Law', *Foreign Affairs* (May/June 1999): 1.

55 Wheeler and Bellamy, 'Humanitarian Intervention in World Politics', in *The Globalization of World Politics: An Introduction to International Relations*, ed. Baylis (Oxford: Oxford University Press, 2001), 522–39. See also: Wheeler, *Saving Strangers: Humanitarian Intervention in International Society* (Oxford: Oxford University Press, 2000); Cottey, *Security in the New Europe*.

56 Fukuyama, 'Building Democracy After Conflict: Stateness First', *Journal of Democracy* 1 (2005): 84–8.

57 Kondoch, 'The United Nations Administration of East Timor', *Journal of Conflict and Security Law* 6, 2 (2001): 245–65.

58 Coleman, *International Organisations and Peace Enforcement: The Politics of International Legitimacy* (Cambridge: Cambridge University Press, 2007), 5–9.

59 Matheson, 'United Nations Governance of Postconflict Societies', *American Journal of International Law* 95, 1 (2001): 76–7.

60 Strohmeyer, 'Collapse and Reconstruction of a Judicial System: The United Nations Missions in Kosovo and East Timor', *American Journal of International Law* 95, 1 (2001): 46–63.

61 Failed States Index, *Foreign Policy*, 16 May 2012.

62 Janzekovic, 'Global Democratic Governance: One Step Forward, Two Steps Back', *Social Alternatives* 29, 2 (2010): 64–9.

63 Failed States Index, *Foreign Policy*, 16 May 2012.

64 Ibid. See also: Coyne, 'Reconstructing Weak and Failed States: Foreign Intervention and the Nirvana Fallacy', *Foreign Policy Analysis* 2, 4 (2006): 343–60; Mazrui, 'The Blood of Experience: The Failed State and Political Collapse in Africa', *World Policy Journal* 12, 1 (1995): 28–34; Rotberg, 'Failed States in a World of Terror', *Foreign Affairs* 81, 4 (2002): 127–40.

65 Ibid. See also: Englebert and Denis, 'Postconflict Reconstruction in Africa: Flawed Ideas About Failed States', *International Security* 32, 4 (2008): 106–39; Charlton and May, 'Warlords and Militarism in Chad', *Review of African Political Economy* 16 (1989): 45–6, 12–25.

66 Ibid. See also: Bechtold, *Politics in the Sudan: Parliamentary and Military Rule in an Emerging African Nation* (New York: Praeger, 1976); Abel, *Southern Sudan: Too Many Agreements Dishonoured* (Exeter: Ithaca Press, 1990).

67 Hayden, *Cosmopolitan Global Politics* (Aldershot: Ashgate, 2005), 71.

68 Mandal, 'Some New Directions in Regional Geography', in *Patterns of Regional Geography: An International Perspective*, ed. Mandal (New Delhi: Concept, 1990), 67–8.

69 Meadows et al., *The Limits to Growth: A Report for the Club of Rome's Project on the Predicament of Mankind* (New York: Potomac Associates, 1972), 22–5.

70 Brandt, *North-South: A Programme for Survival: Report of the Independent Commission on International Development Issues* (London: Pan Books, 1980), 1.

71 Independent Commission on Disarmament and Security Issues, *Common Security: A Blueprint for Survival* (New York: Simon and Schuster, 1982), 172.

72 For an extended discussion on security, see Buzan, *People, States and Fear: The National Security Problem in International Relations* (Brighton: Wheatsheaf, 1983), 1–262. See also: Shaw, 'There is No Such Thing as Society: Beyond Individualism and Statism in International Security Studies', *Review of International Studies* 19, 2 (1994): 159–76.

73 Waldron, 'The Rule of International Law', *Harvard Journal of Law and Public Policy* 30, 1 (2006): 24.

74 Buzan, *People, States and Fear*, 15–18; Buzan, Waever and Wilde, *Security: A New Framework for Analysis* (Boulder: Lynne Rienner, 1998).

75 Peoples and Vaughan, *Critical Security Studies: An Introduction* (New York: Routledge, 2010), 89–166. See also: Kerr, 'Human Security', in *Contemporary Security Studies*, ed. Collins (New York: Oxford University Press, 2010), 121–36.

76 For further details on these areas, see UNDP, *Human Development Report 1994* (New York: Oxford University Press for the UNDP, 1994), 1–226.

77 Boutros-Ghali, *An Agenda for Development 1995: With Related UN Documents* (New York: United Nations, 1995), 1–132. See also: Boutros-Ghali, *An Agenda for Peace* (New York: United Nations, 1992).

78 Annan, *Secretary-General's Annual Report to the General Assembly* (New York: United Nations, 20 September 1999).

79 Murphy, *Humanitarian Intervention: The United Nations in an Evolving World Order* (Philadelphia: University of Pennsylvania Press, 1996), 282–95. See also: McFaul, 'Democracy Promotion as a World Value', *Washington Quarterly* 28, 1 (2004): 147–63.

80 Prime Minister's Office Sweden, *Common Responsibility in the 1990s: The Stockholm Initiative on Global Security and Governance* (Stockholm, 22 April 1991), 2–3.

81 UNDP, *United Nations Human Development Report 1994* (New York: Oxford University Press, 1994), 22–3.

82 Mahbub ul Haq, 'New Imperatives of Human Security', RGICS paper no. 17, Rajiv Gandhi Institute for Contemporary Studies (New Delhi, 1994), 2–19.

83 Human Security Centre and University of British Columbia, *Human Security Report* (New York: Oxford University Press, 2005), 1–170; UNDP, *Human Development Report* (New York: United Nations, 1999), 1–172.

84 Ogata and Sen, *Human Security Now* (New York: United Nations, 2003), 2.

85 Alkire, *A Conceptual Framework for Human Security* (Oxford: Centre for Research on Inequality, Human Security and Ethnicity, 2003), 20–25.

86 Bookmiller and Bookmiller, 'Canada and the Human Security Network (1998–2010): RIP?', *British Journal of Canadian Studies* 23, 2 (2010): 248.

87 Small, *Human Security and the New Diplomacy: Protecting People, Promoting Peace*, ed. McRae and Hubert (Montreal and London: McGill-Queen's University Press, 2001), 233–4.

88 Bookmiller and Bookmiller, 'Canada and the Human Security Network', 248.

89 Ibid.

90 Kerim, 'International Institutions Must Empower the Individual', *Hindu*, 15 April 2008. Online: http://www.hindu.com/2008/04/15/stories/2008041554930900.htm (accessed 3 February 2011).

Chapter 3   Responsibility: Protection and Prevention

1 ICISS, *The Responsibility to Protect: Report of the International Commission on Intervention and State Sovereignty* (Ottawa, ON, Canada, 2001).

2 Crocker, Hampson and Aall, *Leashing the Dogs of War: Conflict Management in a Divided World* (Washington, DC: United States Institute of Peace Press, 2007), 511.

3 ICISS, *The Responsibility to Protect*, 1–108.

4 Ibid., 71.

5 Bellamy and Wheeler, 'Humanitarian Intervention in World Politics', in *The Globalization of World Politics: An Introduction to International Relations*, ed. Baylis and Smith, 3rd edition (Oxford and New York: Oxford University Press, 2005), 537–8.

6 Dagne, *Sudan: The Crisis in Darfur and Status of the North–South Peace Agreement: CRS Report for Congress* (RL33574) (Washington, DC, 15 June 2011).

7 United Nations Security Council, S/RES/1769 (2007), 1–6.

8 Galbreath, 'International Regimes and Organisations', in *Issues in International Relations*, ed. Salmon and Imber, 2nd edition (London and New York: Routledge, 2008), 134.

9 Crocker, Hampson and Aall, *Leashing the Dogs of War*, 511.

10 Bellamy, *Responsibility to Protect: The Global Effort to End Mass Atrocities* (Cambridge: Polity Press, 2009), 6.

11 Buzan, 'A Reductionist, Idealistic Notion that Adds Little Analytical Value', *Security Dialogue* 35, 3 (2004): 360–70.

12 Ban Ki-moon, address in Berlin, 'Responsible Sovereignty: International Cooperation for a Changed World' (New York, 2008), 5.

13 Groenewold, Porter and Médecins sans frontières, *World in Crisis: The Politics of Survival at the End of the Twentieth Century* (London and New York: Routledge, 1997), xxiv. See also: Hannikainen, *Peremptory Norms (Jus Cogens) in International Law: Historical Development,*

Criteria, Present Status (Helsinki: Finnish Lawyers' Pub. Co., University of Lapland, 1988), 353.

14 Johnstone, 'Law-Making Through the Operational Activities of International Organizations', *George Washington International Law Review* 40, 1 (2008): 94.

15 Evans, 'Rethinking Collective Action: The Responsibility to Protect and a Duty to Prevent', American Society of International Law, proceedings of the Annual Meeting, 2004, 78.

16 Holzgrefe and Keohane, *Humanitarian Intervention: Ethical, Legal, and Political Dilemmas* (Cambridge and New York: Cambridge University Press, 2003), 205–16.

17 Abbott, 'Rights and Responsibilities: Resolving the Dilemma of Humanitarian Intervention', *Journal of Humanitarian Assistance* (2005): 1.

18 Annan, 'Two Concepts of Sovereignty', press release GA/9595, *Economist*, 18 September 1999, 49–50. See also: Annan, *We the Peoples: The Role of the United Nations in the 21st Century* (New York: United Nations, 2000), 43–53; Annan, 'Sustaining the Earth in the New Millennium: The UN Secretary-General Speaks Out', *Environment* 42, 8 (2000): 20; United Nations General Assembly, *Implications of International Response to Events in Rwanda, Kosovo Examined by Secretary-General, in Address to General Assembly*, GA/9595 (New York, 1999).

19 Nasu, *International Law on Peacekeeping: A Study of Article 40 of the UN Charter* (Leiden and Boston: Martinus Nijhoff, 2009), 225. See also: Henderson, *The Persistent Advocate and the Use of Force: The Impact of the United States upon the* Jus ad Bellum *in the post–Cold War Era* (Farnham, Surrey and Burlington, VT: Ashgate, 2012), 126.

20 ICISS, *The Responsibility to Protect*, xi.

21 IICK, *The Kosovo Report: Conflict, International Response, Lessons Learned* (Oxford: Oxford University Press, 2000), 193.

22 Wheeler, 'Legitimating Humanitarian Intervention: Principles and Procedures', *Melbourne Journal of International Law* 2, 2 (2001): 566.

23 Garrigues, *The Responsibility to Protect: From an Ethical Principle to an Effective Policy* (Madrid: Fundación para las Relaciones Internacionales y el Diálogo Exterior, 2007), 3–4.

24 Chataway, 'Towards Normative Consensus on Responsibility to Protect', *Griffith Law Review* 16, 1 (2007): 196–97. See also: Abbott, 'Rights and Responsibilities', 8.

25 United Nations General Assembly, *Agenda Item 55: Follow-up to the Outcome of the Millennium Summit*, A/59/565 (New York, 2 December 2004), 21–2, 56.

26 United Nations, *A More Secure World: Our Shared Responsibility: Report of the High-Level Panel on Threats, Challenges and Change* (New York, 2004), 56–7.

27 United Nations, *A More Secure World: Our Shared Responsibility: Report of the High-Level Panel on Threats, Challenges and Change* (New York, 2004), viii.

28 Bieber and Daskalovski, *Understanding the War in Kosovo* (London and Portland: Frank Cass, 2003), 134–135. See also: Claude and Weston, *Human Rights in the World Community: Issues and Action*, 3rd edition (Philadelphia: University of Pennsylvania Press, 2006), 407.

29 Welsh, 'The 2005 International Policy Statement', *International Journal* 61, 4 (2006): 926.

30 Danish Ministry of Foreign Affairs, *Evaluation: Humanitarian and Rehabilitation Assistance to Kosovo, 1999–2003*, (Copenhagen, 2004), 24.

31 United Nations General Assembly, *The Peacebuilding Commission*, A/RES/60/180 (New York, 30 December 2005).

32 Toope, Theis, Anaya and Charlesworth, 'Contemporary Conceptions of Customary International Law' (American Society of International Law, proceedings of the Annual Meeting, 1998), 9.

33 Ibid.
34 Slaughter, 'Security, Solidarity, and Sovereignty: The Grand Themes of UN Reform', *American Journal of International Law* 99, 3 (2005): 627.
35 Arbour, 'The Responsibility to Protect as a Duty of Care in International Law and Practice', *Review of International Studies* 34, 3 (2008): 457–8.
36 Stahn, 'Responsibility to Protect: Political Rhetoric or Emerging Legal Norm?', *American Journal of International Law* 101, 1 (2007): 100–101.
37 Ekiyor, 'The Responsibility to Protect (R2P): A Way Forward – or Rather Part of the Problem?', *Foreign Voices* 1 (2008): 3–4.
38 Kyung-wha Kang, *16th Special Session of the Human Rights Council on 'The Situation of Human Rights in the Syrian Arab Republic'* (New York, 29 April 2011), 1–2.
39 United Nations General Assembly, *The Current Human Rights Situation in the Syrian Arab Republic in the Context of Recent Events*, A/HRC/RES/S-16/1 (New York, 29 April 2011), 1–3.
40 United Nations General Assembly, *Report of the United Nations High Commissioner for Human Rights on the Situation of Human Rights in the Syrian Arab Republic*, A/HRC/18/53 (New York, 15 September 2011), 1–24.
41 Ibid.
42 United Nations General Assembly, *Human Rights Situations that Require the Council's Attention*, A/HRC/RES/21/26 (New York, 28 September 2011), 1–4.
43 United Nations, press conference on Independent International Commission of Inquiry on Syria (New York, 16 October 2012), 1–2.
44 'Security Council Draft Resolution Against Syria Vetoed', United Nations News and Media, 4 October 2012.
45 Foreign Affairs Committee, *Fourth Report of the 1999–2000 Session* (London, 23 May 2000).
46 United Nations Security Council, S/RES/1199 (1998), 1–2. On the imposition of an arms embargo against Yugoslavia, see also: United Nations Security Council, S/RES/1160 (1998), 1–2.
47 Hendrickson, 'Crossing the Rubicon', *NATO Review* (Autumn 2005).
48 Danish Ministry of Foreign Affairs, 'Evaluation: Humanitarian and Rehabilitation Assistance to Kosovo, 1999–2003', 7–9.
49 Six Nation Contact Group, Interim Agreement for Peace and Self-Government in Kosovo, Rambouillet, France, 23 February 1999, 39–52.
50 Ibid.
51 Ibid.
52 Foreign Affairs Committee, *Fourth Report of the 1999–2000 Session*.
53 Hudson, *Justice, Intervention, and Force in International Relations: Reassessing Just War Theory in the 21st Century* (London and New York: Routledge, 2009), 140–42.
54 Hosmer, *The Conflict Over Kosovo: Why Milošević Decided to Settle When He Did* (Santa Monica, CA: Rand, 2001), 12–13.
55 Little and Wickham-Jones, *New Labour's Foreign Policy: A New Moral Crusade?* (Manchester: Manchester University Press, 2000), 135–136.
56 United Nations Security Council, S/RES/1199 (1998), 1–2.
57 Javier Solana, quoted in Tierney, *Accommodating National Identity: New Approaches in International and Domestic Law* (The Hague and Boston: Kluwer Law International, 2000), 124.

58 Youngs, 'Kosovo: The Diplomatic and Military Options' (research paper 98/93, London: House of Commons, 27 October 1998), 14–16.

59 Primakov, press statement, Russian Public TV, BBC Summary of World Broadcasts, Moscow, March 2009.

60 Youngs, 'Kosovo', 14.

61 Jentleson, 'A Responsibility to Protect', *Harvard International Review* 28, 4 (2007): 20.

62 Abbott, 'Rights and Responsibilities', 4.

63 Blair, speech delivered at the Chicago Economic Club, Chicago, quoted in 'The Blair Doctrine', PBS Newshour, 22 April 1999.

64 Ibid.

65 Blair, 'Kosovo', *Commons Hansard Debates*, col. 161–2 (23 March 1999).

66 Waller and Drezov, *Kosovo: The Politics of Delusion* (London: Frank Cass, 2001), 81. See also: Krieger, *The Kosovo Conflict and International Law: An Analytical Documentation 1974–1999* (Cambridge: Cambridge University Press, 2001), 305.

67 Johnstone, 'Law-Making', 94.

68 United Nations Security Council, Resolution S/PV.3989 (New York, 24 October 1999), 1–16.

69 United Nations Security Council, S/1999/328, Draft Resolution by Belarus, India and Russian Federation (New York, 26 March 1999), 1.

70 United Nations Security Council, Resolution S/PV.3989 (New York, 24 October 1999), 6.

71 Lambeth, *NATO's Air War for Kosovo: A Strategic and Operational Assessment* (Santa Monica, CA: Rand, 2001), 222. See also: Blitz, *War and Change in the Balkans: Nationalism, Conflict and Cooperation* (Cambridge and New York: Cambridge University Press, 2006), 156.

72 Thakur, *The United Nations, Peace and Security: From Collective Security to the Responsibility to Protect* (Cambridge and New York: Cambridge University Press, 2006), 214. See also: Schnabel and Thakur, 'Unbridled Humanitarianism: Between Justice, Power, and Authority', in *Kosovo and the Challenge of Humanitarian Intervention: Selective Indignation, Collective Action, and International Citizenship*, ed. Schnabel and Thakur (Tokyo and New York: United Nations University Press, 2000), 499.

73 For an extended analysis, read IICK, *The Kosovo Report*.

74 ICISS, *The Responsibility to Protect*, xi. See also: Chataway, 'Towards Normative Consensus', 194.

75 Mayersen, *The Responsibility to Prevent: Opportunities, Challenges and Strategies for Operationalisation* (Brisbane, Queensland: Asia-Pacific Centre for the Responsibility to Protect, 2010), 9–11.

76 Ban Ki-moon, address to Stanley Foundation Conference on the responsibility to protect, United Nations News Centre, New York, 18 January 2012.

77 Welsh and Sharma, 'Policy Brief: Operationalizing the Responsibility to Prevent', Oxford Institute for Ethics, Law and Armed Conflict (ELAC), 2012, 4.

78 Ibid.

79 Tutu, 'Taking the Responsibility to Protect', *New York Times*, 9 November 2008. See also: Feinstein and Slaughter, 'A Duty to Prevent', *Foreign Affairs* 83, 1 (2004): 136.

80 Rothschild, 'What is Security?', *Daedalus* 124, 3 (1995): 72–3.

81 Bellamy, 'Conflict Prevention and the Responsibility to Protect', *Global Governance* 14, 2 (2008): 142.

82 UNHCR, *The Causes of Conflict and the Promotion of Durable Peace and Sustainable Development in Africa*, UN doc. no. A/52/87-S/1998/318.

83 Evans, 'Rethinking Collective Action', 83.

84 Benjamin, 'Last Resort: Bridging Protection and Prevention', *International Journal on World Peace* 26, 4 (2009): 51–2.
85 Thakur, *United Nations*, 257.
86 UNHCR, 'Global Appeal 2011 (update) – Iraq', New York, 2010b. See also: UNHCR, '2011 UNHCR Country Operations Profile – Iraq', New York, 2010a.
87 Burnham et al., 'Mortality After the 2003 Invasion of Iraq: A Cross-Sectional Cluster Sample Survey', *The Lancet* 368, 9545 (2006): 7. See also: Iraq Family Health Survey Study Group, 'Violence-Related Mortality in Iraq from 2002 to 2006', *New England Journal of Medicine* 358, 5 (2008): 484. Fischer, CRS Report to Congress RS22537: Iraqi Civilian Deaths estimates, Washington, DC, 2008; Reynolds, 'Huge Gaps Between Iraq Death Estimates', BBC News, 20 October 2006.
88 Rogers, 'Wikileaks Iraq: Data Journalism Maps Every Death', *Guardian*, 23 October 2010.
89 'Iraqi Deaths from Violence in 2010: Analysis of the Year's Civilian Death Toll from Iraq Body Count', IBC, 30 December 2010, 1–2.
90 'Three Times as Many Injuries as Deaths Have Been Reported', IBC, 2010.
91 Rogers, 'Wikileaks Iraq: What's Wrong With the Data?', *Guardian*, 25 October 2010.
92 For an explanation of how civilian war related injuries may be calculated, see IBC, 'Three Times as Many Injuries as Deaths Have Been Reported'.
93 Rafiq and Merrell, 'Telemedicine in Extreme Conditions: Disasters, War, and Remote Sites', in *Telemedicine for Trauma, Emergencies, and Disaster Management*, ed. Latifi (Norwood, MA: Artech House, 2010), 163–4.
94 McInnes, 'A Different Kind of War? September 11 and the United States' Afghan War', *Review of International Studies* 29, 2 (2003), 174. See also: Bush, State of the Union Address, Washington, DC, 29 January 2002.
95 Kapur, *The Fall of a Superpower: Betrayal and Shattered Dreams of a Nation and Its People* (Indianapolis: Wordclay, 2008), 123. See also: Bell, *The Truth that Sticks: New Labour's Breach of Truth* (Thriplow: Icon, 2007), 116.

Chapter 4 State Responsibility, Human Security and International Law

1 Sassoli, 'State Responsibility for Violations of International Humanitarian Law', *International Review of the Red Cross* 84, 846 (2002): 401.
2 Hartley, *European Union Law in a Global Context: Text, Cases, and Materials* (Cambridge and New York: Cambridge University Press, 2004), 132. See also: Wessel and Wouters, *Multilevel Regulation and the EU: The Interplay Between Global, European, and National Normative Processes* (Leiden and Boston: Martinus Nijhoff, 2008), 373.
3 Hartley, *European Union Law*, 133.
4 Fritz, *Career Preparation and Opportunities in International Law*, ed. Williams, 2nd edition (Washington, DC: American Bar Association, 1984), 125.
5 van Ert, 'Using Treaties in Canadian Courts', *Canadian Yearbook of International Law* 38 (2000), 7. See also: Ellis, *The Origin, Structure and Working of the League of Nations* (Clark, NJ: The Lawbook Exchange, 2003), 281; Scott, 'International Law in Legal Education', *Columbia Law Review* 4, 6 (1904): 409.

6 Mokhtari, 'The New American Encounter with International Human Rights Norms: The Road After Abu Ghraib', *Proceedings of the Annual Meeting (American Society of International Law)* 100 (2006): 151–4.

7 Schachter, Sørensen and Steiner, 'Theory and Reality in International Law', *Proceedings of the Annual Meeting (American Society of International Law)* 75 (1981): 144.

8 Sinclair, 'Vienna Conference on the Law of Treaties', *International and Comparative Law Quarterly* 19, 1 (1970): 65.

9 Setear, 'Treaties, Custom, Iteration, and Public Choice', *Chicago Journal of International Law* 5, 2 (2005): 715.

10 Toope et al., 'Contemporary Conceptions of Customary International Law', *Proceedings of the Annual Meeting (American Society of International Law)* 92 (1998): 38.

11 Schachter, Sørensen and Steiner, 'Theory and Reality in International Law', 143. See also: Nevins, 'Contesting the Boundaries of International Justice: State Countermapping and Offshore Resource Struggles between East Timor and Australia', *Economic Geography* 80, 1 (2004): 16; and Jack Goldsmith disagrees with the views of Toope, et al. and Schachter et al.: Goldsmith and Posner, 'A Theory of Customary International Law', *University of Chicago Law Review* 66, 4 (1999): 1115.

12 Schwebel, 'The Compliance Process and the Future of International Law', *Proceedings of the Annual Meeting (American Society of International Law)* 75 (1981): 183.

13 Drinan, *The Mobilization of Shame: A World View of Human Rights* (New Haven: Yale University Press, 2001), 32.

14 Ibid.

15 Chayes and Chayes, *The New Sovereignty: Compliance with International Regulatory Agreements* (Cambridge, MA: Harvard University Press, 1995), 25–6.

16 ICJ, Article 38 of the Statute of the International Court of Justice, The Hague (Netherlands), 1974.

17 Roberts, 'Traditional and Modern Approaches to Customary International Law: A Reconciliation', *American Journal of International Law* 95, 4 (2001): 757.

18 Malanczuk and Akehurst, *Akehurst's Modern Introduction to International Law*, 7th edition (London and New York: Routledge, 1997), 44.

19 Sands, *Principles of International Environmental Law*, 2nd edition (Cambridge and New York: Cambridge University Press, 2003), 149. See also: ICJ, 'ICJ Decision in North Sea Continental Shelf Cases (Continental Shelf Boundaries; Relationship of Multilateral Treaties, Custom, and International Law)', *American Society of International Law* 8, 2 (1969): 362; and ICJ, Fisheries Jurisdiction Case (*United Kingdom v. Iceland*), Judgment of 25 July 1974, The Hague (Netherlands).

20 Andrew, 'A Compliance-Based Theory of International Law', *California Law Review* 90, 6 (2002): 1874.

21 Meron, 'Revival of Customary Humanitarian Law', *American Journal of International Law* 99, 4 (2005): 817.

22 Bothe, 'Customary International Humanitarian Law: Some Reflections on the ICRC Study', *Yearbook of International Humanitarian Law* 8 (2005): 154.

23 Baxter, 'Some Existing Problems of Humanitarian Law in the Concept of International Armed Conflict: Further Outlook 1 and Further Outlook 2' (Proceedings of the International Symposium on Humanitarian Law, Brussels, 1974).

24 American Law Institute, *Restatement of the Law, the Foreign Relations Law of the United States*, rev. and enl. edition (St Paul, MN: American Law Institute Publishers, 1987).

25 Slomanson, *Fundamental Perspectives on International Law*, 5th edition (Belmont, CA: Thomson/Wadsworth, 2007), 10–12.

26 Meron, 'On the Inadequate Reach of Humanitarian and Human Rights Law and the Need for a New Instrument', *American Journal of International Law* 77 (1983): 592–3.

27 Meron, 'The Humanization of Humanitarian Law', *American Journal of International Law* 94, 2 (2000): 243.

28 Quoted in Rogers, 'War Crimes Trials Under the Royal Warrant: British Practice 1945–1949', *International and Comparative Law Quarterly* 39, 4 (1990): 782–3.

29 See Schindler and Toman, *The Laws of Armed Conflicts: A Collection of Conventions, Resolutions, and Other Documents*, 4th rev. and completed edition (Leiden and Boston: Martinus Nijhoff, 2004), xli, 1493.

30 Pictet, 'The New Geneva Conventions for the Protection of War Victims', *American Journal of International Law* 45, 3 (1951): 462.

31 Henckaerts, 'Study on Customary International Humanitarian Law', *American Society of International Law* 87 (2005): 423.

32 See Red Cross, 'Meeting of the Intergovernmental Group of Experts for the Protection of War Victims, Geneva, 23–27 January 1995, Recommendation II', *International Review of the Red Cross* 310 (1996): 84.

33 Kuper, *International Law Concerning Child Civilians in Armed Conflict* (Oxford New York: Clarendon Press and Oxford University Press, 1997), 31. See also, Meron, 'The Humanization of Humanitarian Law', 240.

34 Meron, 'The Humanization of Humanitarian Law', 241.

35 Gardam, 'The Contribution of the International Court of Justice to International Humanitarian Law', *Leiden Journal of International Law* 14 (2001): 351.

36 Dinah, 'Righting Wrongs: Reparations in the Articles on State Responsibility', *American Journal of International Law* 96, 4 (2002): 838.

37 Pradt, *The Congress of Vienna* (London: S. Leigh, 1816), 16–27.

38 United Nations, *The Work of the International Law Commission*, 7th edition (New York: United Nations, 2007). See also: Phillimore, *Commentaries upon International Law* (Littleton, CO: F. B. Rothman, 1985), 157.

39 For an extensive list of conferences and conventions, and the progressive development of legal instruments of international law, see: United Nations, 'United Nations Documents on the Development and Codification of International Law: Supplement to American Journal of International Law', *American Journal of International Law* 41, 4 (1947).

40 Ratner and Abrams, *Accountability for Human Rights Atrocities in International Law: Beyond the Nuremberg Legacy*, 2nd edition (Oxford and New York: Oxford University Press, 2001), 4.

41 García-Amador and Sohn, *Recent Codification of the Law of State Responsibility for Injuries to Aliens* (Dobbs Ferry, NY: Oceana Publications, 1974), 128. See also: García-Amador, 'Responsibility of the State for Injuries Caused in its Territory to the Person or Property of Aliens,' UN Doc. A/CN.4/SER.A/1961/Add.1, *Yearbook of the International Law Commission* 2 (1961): 46.

42 United Nations General Assembly, *Responsibility of States for Internationally Wrongful Acts*, A/56/83 (New York, 28 January 2002), 2.

43 Bodansky and Crook, 'Symposium: The ILC's State Responsibility Articles – Introduction and Overview', *American Journal of International Law* 96, 4 (2002): 773.

44 James, 'The ILC's Articles on Responsibility of States for Internationally Wrongful Acts: A Retrospect', *American Journal of International Law* 96, 4 (2002): 875.

45 Pellet, 'Between Codification and Progressive Development of the Law: Some Reflections from the ILC', *International Law FORUM du droit international* 6, 1 (2004), 23.

46 Bodansky and Crook, 'Symposium', 775.

47 Sinclair, 'Vienna Conference on the Law of Treaties', 47–50.

48 Ramcharan, *The International Law Commission: Its Approach to the Codification and Progressive Development of International Law* (The Hague: Nijhoff, 1977), ix. See also: Graefrath, 'The International Law Commission Tomorrow: Improving its Organization and Methods of Work', *American Journal of International Law* 85, 4 (1991): 595.

Chapter 5   Promoting Democratic Norms for Protection and Prevention

1 Schimmelfennig, 'Introduction – The Impact of International Organizations on the Central and Eastern Eruopean States: Conceptual and Theoretical Issues', in *Norms and Nannies: The Impact of International Organizations on the Central and East European States*, ed. Linden (Lanham: Rowman & Littlefield, 2002), 6–8. See also: Finnemore and Sikkink, 'International Norm Dynamics and Political Change', *International Organization* 52, 4 (1998): 887–917; Huntington, *The Third Wave – Democratization in the Late Twentieth Century* (Norman: University of Oklahoma Press, 1991), 1–343; Fukuyama, *Historiens slut och den sista människan* (Stockholm: Norstedt, 1992), 1–414.

2 For analysis on the spread of democracies, see: Huntington, *The Third Wave*, 1–343. See also: Diamond, 'Is the Third Wave Over?', *Journal of Democracy* 7, 3 (1996): 20–37; Huntington, 'Democracy for the Long Haul?', *Journal of Democracy* 7, 2 (1996): 3–13. For complementary reading, see: Diamond, 'Is Pakistan the (Reverse) Wave of the Future?', *Journal of Democracy* 11, 3 (2000): 91–106; Fukuyama, *Historiens slut och den sista människan*, 1–414.

3 Hinnebusch, 'Authoritarian Persistence, Democratization Theory and the Middle East: An Overview and Critique', *Democratization* 13, 3 (2006).

4 Caporaso, 'Changes in the Westphalian Order: Territory, Public Authority, and Sovereighnty', in *Continuity and Change in the Westphalian Order*, ed. Caporaso (Malden: Blackwell, 2000), 1–28. See also, Spruyt, 'The End of Empire and the Extension of the Westphalian System: The Normative Basis of the Modern State Order', in *Continuity and Change in the Westphalian Order*, ed. Caporaso (Malden: Blackwell, 2000), 62–92.

5 For an analysis of the remaking of international order, see: Ikenberry, *After Victory: Institutions, Strategic Restraint, and the Rebuilding of Order After Major Wars* (Princeton and Oxford: Princeton University Press, 2001), 1–293.

6 Eayrs, 'The Atlantic Conference and Its Charter: A Canadian's Reflections', in *The Atlantic Charter*, ed. Brinkley and Facey-Crowther (New York: St Martin's Press, 1994), 151–72. See also: Whitehead, 'International Aspects of Democratization', in *Transitions from Authoritarian Rule: Comparative Perspectives*, ed. O'Donnell et al. (Baltimore and London: The Johns Hopkins University Press, 1986), 1–190.

7 For a review of the Truman Doctrine and its consequences on US foreign policy, read: Weiner, *The Truman Doctrine: Background and Presentation* (Ann Harbor: Claremont Graduate School, 1967).

8 For views on democracy promotion, see: Carothers, *Aiding Democracy Abroad: The Learning Curve* (Washington, DC: Carnegie Endowment for International Peace, 1999), 1–411; Lowe, *Idea to Reality: NED at 25* (Washington, DC: National Endowment for Democracy, 2011).

9 McFaul, 'Democracy Promotion as a World Values', *Washington Quarterly* 28, 1 (2004): 155–6.

10 Ibid, 148–52.

11 Risse and Sikkink, 'The Socialization of International Human Rights Norms into Domestic Practices: Introduction', in *The Power of Human Rights and Domestic Change*, ed. Risse (Cambridge: Cambrdige University Press, 1999), 7. See also, Finnemore and Sikkink, 'International Norm Dynamics', 887–917.

12 Schimmelfennig, 'Introduction', 6–8.

13 Ibid. See also: McFaul, 'Democracy Promotion as a World Value', 147–63.

14 Schumpeter, *Capitalism, Socialism and Democracy* (New York: Harper, 1942), 1–432.

15 Linz and Stepan, *Problems of Democratic Transition and Consolidation: Southern Europe, South America, and Post-Communist Europe* (Baltimore: Johns Hopkins University Press, 1996), 3. For further studies on electoral democracy, see also: Huntington, *The Third Wave*, 1–343; Schumpeter, *Capitalism, Socialism and Democracy*, 1–432; Diamond, 'Defining and Developing Democracy', in *The Democracy Sourcebook*, ed. Dahl (Cambridge and London: MIT Press, 2003), 1–556.

16 Diamond, 'Thinking about Hybrid Regimes', *Journal of Democracy* 13, 2 (2002): 21–35; Levitsky and Way, 'The Rize of Authoritarianism', *Journal of Democracy* 13, 2 (2002): 51–65.

17 For a well-known definition of democracy, see: Dahl, *Participation and Opposition* (New York and London: Yale University, 1971): 1–267.

18 Freedom House, *Freedom in the World Survey* (Washington, DC: Freedom House, 2011); See also, Diamond, 'Defining and Developing Democracy', 1–556.

19 Sørensen, *Democracy and Democratization: Processes and Prospects in a Changing World* (Boulder: Westview Press, 1993), 12–13.

20 UN Charter, 1–80.

21 Ibid.

22 For an extended discussion on the arguments provided by the former secretary-general, see: Boutros-Ghali, *An Agenda for Development 1995: With Related UN Documents* (New York: United Nations, 1995), 1–132.

23 United Nations, *United Nations Millenium Goals* (New York, 2000). See also: Pogge, 'The First United Nations Millennium Development Goal: A Cause for Celebration?', *Journal of Human Development* 5, 3 (2004): 377–97.

24 European Commission, *The European Union's Role in promoting Human Rights and Democratisation in Third Countries* (Brussels, 2001), 1–28.

25 United Nations, *Universal Declaration on Human Rights* (10 December 1948). See also, Office of the United Nations High Commissioner for Human Rights, *International Covenant on Civil and Political Rights* (New York, 1966), 1–14.

26 United Nations, *Universal Declaration on Human Rights*.

27 European Community, Treaty of Rome (1949/1957), 1–80. See also, Birkelbach, *Report by Willi Birkelbach on the Political and Institutional Aspects of Accession to or Association with the Community* (European Parliamentary Assembly, 19 December 1961).

28 The European Council, *Copenhagen Summit 1978* (Copenhagen, 1978), 1–26.

29 Horng, 'The Human Rights Clause in the European Union's External Trade and Development Agreements', *European Law Journal* 9, 5 (2003): 1. See also: Gillespie and Youngs, 'Themes in European Democracy Promotion', in *European Union and Democracy Promotion: The Case of North Africa*, ed. Gillespie and Youngs (London and Portland: Frank Cass, 2002), 1–219.

30 European Union, Treaty of Amsterdam (Brussels, 1997), 1–148.

31 See: Smith, *European Union Foreign Policy in a Changing World* (Malden: Polity Press, 2008), 137–41.

32 For data and analysis on popular participation and peace, see: Russett, *Grasping the Democratic Peace: Principles for a Post–Cold War World* (Princeton: Princeton University Press, 1993), 1–184; Weart, *Never at War: Why Democracies Will Not Fight Each Other* (New Haven: Yale University Press, 1998); Ravlo and Gleditsch, *Colonial War and the Globalization of Democratic Values* (Copenhagen: ECPR, 2000), 1–47; Maoz and Russett, 'Normative and Structural Causes of Democratic Peace 1946–1986', *American Political Science Review* 87, 3 (1993): 624–38.

33 For views on the role of civil society, see: Carothers, *Aiding Democracy Abroad*, 1–411; Köchler, *Democracy and the International Rule of Law: Propositions for an Alternative World Order* (Vienna and New York: Springer-Verlag, 1995), 1–170.

34 Carothers, *Aiding Democracy Abroad*, 1–411. See also: Eklit, *Electoral Systems for Emerging Democracies: Experiences and Suggestions* (Copenhagen: Danish Ministry of Foreign Affairs, 1997).

35 Gelpi and Griesdorf, 'Winners or Losers? Democracies in International Crisis, 1918–1994', *American Political Science Review* 95, 3 (2001): 633–47.

36 Levy and Razin, 'It Takes Two: An Explanation for the Democratic Peace', *Journal of European Economic Association* 2, 1 (2004): 1–29.

37 Ravlo and Gleditsch, *Colonial War*, 1–47. See also, Doyle, 'Three Pillars of the Liberal Peace', *American Political Science Review* 99, 3 (2005): 463–66.

38 Russett, *Grasping the Democratic Peace*, 1–184.

39 Levy, 'The Causes of War: A Review of Theories and Evidence' in *Behavior, Society, and Nuclear War*, ed. Tetlock et al. (Oxford: Oxford University Press, 1989), 270. See also, Doyle, 'Liberalism and World Politics', *American Political Science Review* 80, 4 (1986): 1151–69. Diamond, 'Promoting Democracy', *Foreign Policy* 92, 87 (1992): 25–46; Pravda, Introduction to *Democratic Consolidation in Eastern Europe – International and Transnational Factors, vol. 2*, ed. Zielonka and Pravda (Oxford and New York: Oxford University Press, 2001), 1–568.

40 Hegre, 'Disentangling Democracy and Development as Determinants of Armed Conflict' (paper presented at the Annual Meeting of the International Studies Association, Portland, Oregon, 27 February 2003), 1–48; Weede, 'The Diffusion of Prosperity and Peace by Globalization', *Independent Review* 9, 2 (2004): 165–86.

41 For a discussion on the linkage between political and economic development, see Pravda, Introduction, 1–568.

42 Diamond, 'Promoting Democracy', 25–46.

43 Hegre, 'Development and the Liberal Peace: What Does It Take to Be a Trading State?', *Journal of Peace Research* 47, 2 (2000): 155–65.

44 Hegre, 'Disentangling Democracy', 1–48. See also: Oneal and Russett, *Causes of Peace: Democracy, Interdependence, and International Organizations, 1885–1992* (Annual Meeting of the American Political Science Association, San Francisco, 2001); Goenner, 'Uncertainty of the Liberal Peace', *Journal of Peace Research* 41, 5 (2004): 589–605.

Chapter 6 Case Study Libya: Moving Principle into Action?

1 Nyheter, 'Detta har hänt: striderna i Libyen', DN.se, 21 March 2011, 1.

2 Libyan Interim National Council, 'Introducing the Council', Libyan Interim National Council – Official Website, 2011.

3 Nyheter, 'Detta har hänt', 1.

4 'Libya Civil War – No Fly Zone', GlobalSecurity.org, 4 April 2011.

5 Rice, *Remarks by Ambassador Susan E. Rice, U. S. Permanent Representative to the United Nations, at the Security Council Stakeout on UN Security Council Resolution 1973* (17 March 2011).

6 UN Security Council, *Peace and Security in Africa* (New York, 2011), 1–10.

7 'Libya Civil War – No Fly Zone', GlobalSecurity.org.

8 Lévy, 'Behind the Scenes of France's Lead on Libya', *New Perspectives Quarterly* 28, 2 (2011): 48–51.

9 'Libya Civil War – No Fly Zone', GlobalSecurity.org.

10 UNHCR, 'UNHCR Global Appeal 2011 (update): Iraq', UNHCR.org, 1 December 2010.

11 UN Security Council, Resolution 1973 (2011), S/RES/1973 (2011), (7 July 2011), 1–8.

12 Ban, quoted in 'Libya: Ban Welcomes Security Council Authorization of Measures to Protect Civilians', UN News Centre, 18 March 2011.

13 IISS, *Libya: Direct Military Hits, Unclear Political Targets* (IISS, 2011), 1–3.

14 'Gaddafi Visit Seals French Deals', BBC News, 10 December 2007.

15 Juppé, quoted in 'Libya: Adoption of Resolution 1973', France in Canada: French Embassy in Canada, 17 March 2011.

16 Ibid. See also Juppé, *Statement by Mr. Alain Juppé, Ministre d'Etat, Minister of Foreign and European Affairs before the U. N. Security Council* (New York, 15 May 2011).

17 Juppé, 'Libya: Adoption of Resolution 1973'.

18 Ibid.

19 Ibid.

20 Cameron, quoted in 'Libya: David Cameron Statement on U. N. Resolution', BBC News, 18 March 2011.

21 Birrell, 'Devastating Secret Files Reveal Labour Lies Over Gaddafi: Dictator Warned of Holy War if Lockerbie Bomber Megrahi Died in Scotland', *Daily Mail*, 4 September 2011.

22 Cameron, quoted in 'Libya: David Cameron Statement on U. N. Resolution', BBC News, 18 March 2011.

23 Ibid.

24 'Libya Civil War – No Fly Zone', GlobalSecurity.org.

25 O'Hanlon 2011:1–2.

26 Rice, *Remarks by Ambassador Susan E. Rice*; Obama, *Remarks by the President on Libya: Convention Brasil 21 Center Brasilia*, Brazil, 19 March 2011; Obama, quoted in 'Obama on Libya: This is Not What We Wanted', CBS News World, 4 April 2011.

27 Obama, quoted in 'Not Acting in Libya "would have been a betrayal of who we are"', CNN, 28 March 2011.

28 Baodong, '"China has serious difficulty with part of the resolution," envoy says', English.news.cn, 18 March 2011.

29 Ibid.

30 Buckley, 'China Intensifies Condemnation of Libya Airstrikes', Reuters, 6 April 2011.

31 Goodenough, 'Russia, China Accuse West of Exceeding U. N. Resolution; Makes Libyan Crisis Worse', CNSnews.com, 8 July 2011.

32 Mendeleyev, 'Why Russia Voted to Abstain on Libya "No-Fly" Resolution', The Mendeleyev Journal (blog), 16 June 2011.

33 'Russia Accuses NATO of Going Beyond U. N. Resolution on Libya', RT.com, 17 April 2011; 'Russia Slams Libya Attack', *Bangkok Post*, 20 March 2011.

34 Mendeleyeev, 'Why Russia Voted to Abstain'.
35 Chernichenko, 'No to Creative Interpretations of Resolution 1973', The Voice of Russia, 30 March 2011.
36 Abbott, 'Rights and Responsibilities: Resolving the Dilemma of Humanitarian Intervention', *Journal of Humanitarian Assistance* 7 (2005): 5.
37 Radhuyin, 'Sitting on the Fence', *Frontline* 28, 8 (2011): 1–2.
38 Nyheter, 'Detta har hänt', 1.

BIBLIOGRAPHY

Abbott, C. 'Rights and Responsibilities: Resolving the Dilemma of Humanitarian Intervention'. *Journal of Humanitarian Assistance* (2005).

Abel, A. *Southern Sudan: Too Many Agreements Dishonoured*. Exeter: Ithaca Press, 1990.

Africa Legal Brief. 'NATO Violating UN Resolution 1973 – Russia'. 2 May 2011.

Alkire, S. *A Conceptual Framework for Human Security*. Centre for Research on Inequality, Human Security and Ethnicity, Oxford. Online: http://www.crise.ox.ac.uk/pubs/workingpaper2.pdf (accessed 12 March 2012).

American Law Institute. *Restatement of the Law, the Foreign Relations Law of the United States*, rev. and enl. edition. St Paul, MN: American Law Institute Publishers, 1987.

Andrew, T. G. 'A Compliance-Based Theory of International Law'. *California Law Review* 90, 6 (2002).

Annan, K. 'Sustaining the Earth in the New Millennium: The UN Secretary-General Speaks Out'. *Environment* 42, 8 (2000).

———. 'Two Concepts of Sovereignty'. Press release GA/9595. *Economist*, 18 September 1999. Online: http://www.economist.com/node/324795 (accessed 12 March 2012).

———. *In Larger Freedom: Towards Development, Security and Human Rights For All*, UN Doc. A/59/2005. New York: United Nations, 2005. Online: http://www.un.org/News/Press/docs/1999/19990920.ga9595.html (accessed 12 March 2012).

———. *Secretary-General's Annual Report to the General Assembly*. New York: United Nations, 20 September 1999. Online: http://www.un.org/News/Press/docs/1999/19990920.sgsm7136.html (accessed 15 February 2012).

———. *We the Peoples: The Role of the United Nations in the 21st Century*. New York: United Nations, 2000. Online: http://www.un.org/millennium/sg/report/full.htm (accessed 12 March 2012).

Arbour, L. 'The Responsibility to Protect as a Duty of Care in International Law and Practice'. *Review of International Studies* 34, 3 (2008).

Ban Ki-moon. Quoted in 'Libya: Ban Welcomes Security Council Authorization of Measures to Protect Civilians'. UN News Centre, 18 March 2011. Online: http://www.un.org/apps/news/story.asp?NewsID=37809&Cr=libya&Cr1 (accessed 11 April 2011).

———. 'Responsible Sovereignty: International Cooperation for a Changed World'. Address in Berlin, 15 July 2008. Online: http://www.brookings.edu/events/2008/07/15-mgi (accessed 12 January 2012).

———. *Address to Stanley Foundation Conference on the Responsibility to Protect*. United Nations News Centre, 18 January 2012. Online: http://www.un.org/apps/news/infocus/sgspeeches/search_full.asp?statID=1433 (accessed 19 December 2012).

Bangkok Post. 'Russia Slams Libya Attack'. 20 March 2011. Online: http://www.bangkok post.com/breakingnews/227700/russia-slams-indiscriminate-use-of-force (accessed 20 December 2012).

Bangura, A. K. 'Politicized EthnicitiesVersus Tribal Etnicities: Examples from Liberia, Rwanda and Sierra Leone'. In *The Politics Ethnicity and National Identity*. Ed. Santosh C. Saha. New York: Peter Lang, 2007.

Baodong, L. '"China has serious difficulty with part of the resolution," Envoy Says'. English.news.cn, 18 March 2011. Online: http://news.xinhuanet.com/english2010/ world/2011-03/18/c_13784748.htm (accessed 12 December 2011).

Baxter, R. 'Some Existing Problems of Humanitarian Law in the Concept of International Armed Conflict: Further Outlook 1 and Further Outlook 2'. Proceedings of the International Symposium on Humanitarian Law, Brussels, 1974. Online: http://www. it4sec.org/node/4385 (accessed 11 July 2011).

BBC News. 'Gaddafi Visit Seals French Deals'. 10 December 2007. Online: http://news. bbc.co.uk/2/hi/africa/7135788.stm (accessed 12 December 2012).

Bechtold, P. *Politics in the Sudan: Parliamentary and Military Rule in an Emerging African Nation.* New York: Praeger, 1976.

Bell, C. *Peace Agreements and Human Rights.* Oxford: Oxford University Press, 2000.

Bell, M. *The Truth that Sticks: New Labour's Breach of Truth.* Thriplow: Icon, 2007.

Bellamy, A. 'Conflict Prevention and the Responsibility to Protect'. *Global Governance* 14, 2 (2008).

———. *Responsibility to Protect: The Global Effort to End Mass Atrocities.* Cambridge: Polity Press, 2009.

Bellamy, A. and J. Wheeler. 'Humanitarian Intervention in World Politics'. In *The Globalization of World Politics: An Introduction to International Relations.* Ed. John Baylis and Steve Smith, 3rd edition. Oxford and New York: Oxford University Press, 2005.

Bellamy, A., P. Williams and S. Griffin. *Understanding Peacekeeping*, 2nd edition. Cambridge: Polity Press, 2010.

Benjamin, D. 'Last Resort: Bridging Protection and Prevention'. *International Journal on World Peace* 26, 4 (2009).

Bieber, F. and C. Daskalovski. *Understanding the War in Kosovo.* London and Portland: Frank Cass, 2003.

Birkelbach, W. *Report by Willi Birkelbach on the Political and Institutional Aspects of Accession to or Association with the Community.* European Parliamentary Assembly, 19 December 1961. Online: http://www.ena.lu/report_willi_birkelbach_political_institutional_aspects_ accession_association_with_community_december_1961-020006013.html (accessed 20 February 2012).

Birrell, I. 'Devastating Secret Files Reveal Labour Lies Over Gaddafi: Dictator Warned of Holy War if Lockerbie Bomber Megrahi Died in Scotland'. *Daily Mail*, 4 September 2011. Online: http://www.dailymail.co.uk/news/article-2033460/Secret-files-Labour- lied-Gaddafi--warned-holy-war-Megrahi-died-Scotland.html (accessed 12 December 2012).

Blair, T. 'Kosovo'. *Commons Hansard Debates*, col. 161–2 (23 March 1999). Online: http://www. publications.parliament.uk/pa/cm199899/cmhansrd/vo990323/debindx/90323-x. htm (accessed 28 December 2011).

———. Speech delivered at the Chicago Economic Club, Chicago. Quoted in 'The Blair Doctrine'. PBS Newshour, 22 April 1999. Online: http://www.pbs.org/newshour/bb/ international/jan-june99/blair_doctrine4-23.html (accessed 15 January 2012).

Blitz, B. *War and Change in the Balkans: Nationalism, Conflict and Cooperation*. Cambridge and New York: Cambridge University Press, 2006.

Bodansky, D. and J. Crook. 'Symposium: The ILC's State Responsibility Articles – Introduction and Overview'. *American Journal of International Law* 96, 4 (2002).

Bookmiller, R. and K. Bookmiller. 'Canada and the Human Security Network (1998–2010): RIP?'. *British Journal of Canadian Studies* 23, 2 (2010).

Booth, K. *Theory of World Security*. New York: Cambridge University Press, 2007.

Bothe, M. 'Customary International Humanitarian Law: Some Reflections on the ICRC Study'. *Yearbook of International Humanitarian Law* 8 (2005).

Boutros-Ghali, Boutros. *An Agenda for Peace*. New York: United Nations, 1992. Online: http://www.un.org/Docs/SG/agpeace.html (accessed 9 November 2011).

———. *An Agenda for Development 1995: With Related UN Documents*. New York: United Nations, 1995.

Brandt, W. *North-South: A Programme for Survival: Report of the Independent Commission on International Development Issues, 1980*. London: Pan Books, 1992.

Breuning, M. *Foreign Policy Analysis: A Comparative Introduction*. New York: Palgrave Macmillan, 2007.

Brunnée, J. and S. Toope. 'Norms, Institutions, and UN Reform: The Responsibility to Protect'. *Journal of International Law and International Relations* 2 (2006).

Buckley, C. *China Intensifies Condemnation of Libya Airstrikes*, Reuters, 6 April 2011. Online: http://www.reuters.com/article/2011/03/21/us-china-libya-idUSTRE72K0LX20110321 (accessed 18 March 2012).

Burnham, G., R. Lafta, S. Doocy and L. Roberts. 'Mortality After the 2003 Invasion of Iraq: A Cross-Sectional Cluster Sample Survey'. *The Lancet* 368, 9545 (2006).

Bush, G. State of the Union Address, Washington, DC, 29 January 2002. Online: http://georgewbush-whitehouse.archives.gov/news/releases/2002/01/20020129-11.html (accessed 20 January 2012).

Buzan, B. *People, States and Fear: The National Security Problem in International Relations*. Brighton: Wheatsheaf, 1983.

———. *People, States and Fear: An Agenda for International Security Studies in the Post–Cold War Era*. London: Harvester Wheatsheaf, 1991.

———. 'A Reductionist, Idealistic Notion that Adds Little Analytical Value'. *Security Dialogue* 35, 3 (2004).

Buzan, B., O. Waever and J. D. Wilde. *Security: A New Framework for Analysis*. Boulder: Lynne Rienner, 1998.

Cameron, D. Quoted in 'Libya: David Cameron Statement on UN Resolution'. BBC News, 18 March 2011. Online: http://www.bbc.co.uk/news/uk-politics-12786225 (accessed 12 February 2012).

Caporaso, J. A. 'Changes in the Westphalian Order: Territory, Public Authority, and Sovereignty'. In *Continuity and Change in the Westphalian Order*. Ed. James A. Caporaso. Malden: Blackwell, 2000.

Carlsnaes, W. 'The Agency-Structure Problem: in Foreign Policy Making'. *International Studies Quarterly* 36, 3 (1992).

Carnegie Commission on Preventing Deadly Conflict. *Preventing Deadly Conflict: Final Report with Executive Summary*. Washington, DC, 1997.

Carothers, T. *Aiding Democracy Abroad: The Learning Curve*. Washington, DC: Carnegie Endowment for International Peace, 1999.

Carsten, S. 'Responsibility to Protect: Political Rhetoric or Emerging Legal Norm?'. *American Journal of International Law* 101, 1 (2007).

Charltona, R. and R. Mayb. 'Warlords and Militarism in Chad'. *Review of African Political Economy* 16 (1989).

Chataway, T. 'Towards Normative Consensus on Responsibility to Protect'. *Griffith Law Review* 16, 1 (2007).

Chauvet, L. and C. Paul. 'What are the Preconditions for Turnarounds in Failing States?'. *Conflict Management and Peace Science* 25, 4 (2008).

Chayes, A. and A. H. Chayes. *The New Sovereignty: Compliance with International Regulatory Agreements*. Cambridge, MA: Harvard University Press, 1995.

Chernichenko, A. 'No to Creative Interpretations of Resolution 1973'. The Voice of Russia, 30 March 2011. Online: http://english.ruvr.ru/2011/03/30/48213883.html (accessed 20 September 2011).

Claude, R. and B. Weston. *Human Rights in the World Community: Issues and Action*, 3rd edition. Philadelphia, PA: University of Pennsylvania Press, 2006.

Coleman, K. *International Organisations and Peace Enforcement: The Politics of International Legitimacy*. Cambridge: Cambridge University Press, 2007.

Collins, A. *Contemporary Security Studies*. Oxford and New York: Oxford University Press, 2007.

Cordial, M. and K. Rosandhaug. *Post-Conflict Property Restitution: The Approach in Kosovo and Lessons Learned for Future International Practice*. Leiden: Koninklijke Brill NV, 2008.

Cottey, A. *Security in the New Europe*. Basingstoke and New York: Palgrave Macmillan, 2007.

Cowen, T. and C. J. Coyne. 'Postwar Reconstruction: Some Insights from Public Choice and Institutional Economics'. *Constitutional Political Economy* 16 (2005).

Cowley, R. *The Cold War: A Military History*. New York: Random House, 2009.

Coyne, C. 'Reconstructing Weak and Failed States: Foreign Intervention and the Nirvana Fallacy'. *Foreign Policy Analysis* 2, 4 (2006).

Crnobrnja, M. *The Yugoslav Drama*. London: I.B. Tauris, 1996.

Crocker, C., F. Hampson and P. Aall. *Leashing the Dogs of War: Conflict Management in a Divided World*. Washington, DC: United States Institute of Peace Press, 2007.

CRS (Congressional Research Service). *Weak and Failing States, Evolving Security Threats and U.S. Policy*. Report for Congress, Washington, DC, 2008.

Daalder, I. 'Emerging Answers: Kosovo, NATO, and the Use of Force'. *Brookings Review* 17, 3 (1999).

Dagne, T. 2010, *Sudan: The Crisis in Darfur and Status of the North–South Peace Agreement: CRS Report for Congress*. Washington, DC, 15 June 2011. Online: http://www.fas.org/sgp/crs/row/RL33574.pdf (accessed 12 October 2011).

Dahl, R. *Participation and Opposition*. New York and London: Yale University, 1971.

Danish Ministry of Foreign Affairs. *Evaluation: Humanitarian and Rehabilitation Assistance to Kosovo, 1999–2003*. Copenhagen, 2004. Online: http://www.um.dk/Publikationer/Danida/English/Evaluations/Kosovo2005/Kosovo.pdf (accessed 1 July 2011).

Diamond, L. 'Promoting Democracy'. *Foreign Policy* 92, 87 (1992).

⸺· 'Is the Third Wave Over?'. *Journal of Democracy* 7, 3 (1996).

⸺· 'Is Pakistan the (Reverse) Wave of the Future?'. *Journal of Democracy* 11, 3 (2000).

⸺· 'Thinking about Hybrid Regimes'. *Journal of Democracy* 13, 2 (2002).

⸺· 'Defining and Developing Democracy'. In *The Democracy Sourcebook*. Ed. R. Dahl, I. Shapiro, A. J. Cheibub. Cambridge, MA and London: MIT Press, 2003.

Dinah, S. 'Righting Wrongs: Reparations in the Articles on State Responsibility'. *American Journal of International Law* 96, 4 (2002).

Doyle, M. 'Liberalism and World Politics'. *American Political Science Review* 80, 4 (1986).

Doyle, M. 'Three Pillars of the Liberal Peace'. *American Political Science Review* 99, 3 (2005).

Drinan, R. *The Mobilization of Shame: A World View of Human Rights.* New Haven: Yale University Press, 2001.

Eayrs, J. 'The Atlantic Conference and Its Charter: A Canadian's Reflections'. In *The Atlantic Charter.* Ed. D. Brinkley and D. R. Facey-Crowther. New York: St Martin's Press, 1994.

Eizenstat, S., J. Porter and J. Weinstein. 'Rebuilding Weak States'. *Foreign Affairs* 84 (2005).

Ekiyor, T. and M. O'Connell. International SEF Symposium 2007, The Development and Peace Foundation, Bonn, Germany, 29–30 November 2007.

Eklit, J. *Electoral Systems for Emerging Democracies: Experiences and Suggestions.* Copenhagen: Danish Ministry of Foreign Affairs, 1997.

Ellis, C. H. *The Origin, Structure and Working of the League of Nations.* Clark, NJ: The Lawbook Exchange, 2003.

Englebert, P. and M. Denis. 'Postconflict Reconstruction in Africa: Flawed Ideas about Failed States'. *International Security* 32, 4 (2008).

Englehart, N. 'State Capacity, State Failure, and Human Rights'. *Journal of Peace Research* 46, 2 (2009).

Ert, G. van. 'Using Treaties in Canadian Courts'. *Canadian Yearbook of International Law* 38 (2000).

European Commission. *The European Union's Role in Promoting Human Rights and Democratisation in Third Countries.* Brussels: European Commission, 2001. Online: http://www. initiativeforpeacebuilding.eu/resources/Communication_on_Promoting_democracy_ and_HR.pdf (accessed 12 September 2011).

European Council. *Copenhagen Summit 1978.* Copenhagen, 1978. Online: http://aei.pitt. edu/1440/ (accessed 12 November 2011).

European Community. Treaty of Rome. 1949/1957. Online: http://ec.europa.eu/economy_ finance/emu_history/documents/treaties/rometreaty2.pdf (accessed 15 December 2011).

European Union. Treaty of Amsterdam. 1997. Online: http://www.europarl.europa.eu/ topics/treaty/pdf/amst-en.pdf (accessed 11 January 2012).

Evans, G. 'Rethinking Collective Action: The Responsibility to Protect and a Duty to Prevent'. *Proceedings of the Annual Meeting (American Society of International Law)* (2004).

Feinstein, L. and A.-M. Slaughter. 'A Duty to Prevent' *Foreign Affairs* 83, 1 (2004).

Finnemore, M. and K. Sikkink. 'International Norm Dynamics and Political Change'. *International Organization* 52, 4 (1998).

Fischer, H. *CRS Report to Congress RS22537: Iraqi Civilian Deaths Estimates.* Washington, DC, 2008. Online: http://www.cdi.org/pdfs/crs%20on%20civilian%20casualties%202007. pdf (accessed 19 February 2012).

Foreign Affairs Committee. *Fourth Report of the 1999–2000 Session.* London, 23 May 2000. Online: http://www.publications.parliament.uk/pa/cm199900/cmselect/ cmfaff/28/2802.htm (accessed 23 November 2011).

Foreign Policy. Failed States Index. 16 May 2012. Online: http://www.foreignpolicy.com/ failed_states_index_2012_interactive (accessed 16 December 2012).

Freedom House. *Freedom in the World Survey.* Washington, DC: Freedom House, 2011. Online: http://www.freedomhouse.org/template.cfm?page=277 (accessed 12 January 2012).

Fritz, K. *Career Preparation and Opportunities in International Law*. Ed. Williams, 2nd edition. Washington, DC: American Bar Association, 1984.

Fukuyama, F. *Historiens slut och den sista människan*. Stockholm: Norstedt, 1992.

———. 'The Imperative of State-Building'. *Journal of Democracy* 15, 2 (2004).

———. 'Building Democracy After Conflict: Stateness First'. *Journal of Democracy* 1 (2005).

Gaddis, J. *We Now Know: Rethinking Cold War History*. New York: Oxford University Press, 1998.

———. *The Cold War: A New History*. London: Penguin, 2007.

Galbreath, D. 'International Regimes and Organisations'. In *Issues in International Relations*, 2nd edition. Ed. T. Salmon and M. Imber. London and New York: Routledge, 2008.

Gallie, W. 'Essentially Contested Concepts'. *Proceedings of the Aristotelian Society* 56 (1956).

García-Amador, F. V. 'Responsibility of the State for Injuries Caused in its Territory to the Person or Property of Aliens', UN Doc. A/CN.4/SER.A/1961/Add.1. *Yearbook of the International Law Commission* 2 (1961).

García-Amador, F. V. and L. Sohn. *Recent Codification of the Law of State Responsibility for Injuries to Aliens*. Dobbs Ferry, NY: Oceana Publications, 1974.

Gardam, J. 'The Contribution of the International Court of Justice to International Humanitarian Law'. *Leiden Journal of International Law* 14 (2001).

Garrigues, J. *The Responsibility to Protect: From an Ethical Principle to an Effective Policy*. Madrid: The Fundación para las Relaciones Internacionales y el Diálogo Exterior, 2007. Online: http://www.responsibilitytoprotect.org/files/responsibilidad.proteger.pdf (accessed 12 January 2012).

Gelpi, C. and M. Griesdorf. 'Winners or Losers? Democracies in International Crisis, 1918–1994'. *American Political Science Review* 95, 3 (2001).

Gillespie, R. and R. Youngs. 'Themes in European Democracy Promotion'. In *European Union and Democracy Promotion: The Case of North Africa*. Ed. Richard Gillespie and Richard Youngs. London and Portland: Frank Cass, 2002.

Glennon, M. 'The New Interventionism: The Search for a Just International Law'. *Foreign Affairs* (May/June 1999).

GlobalSecurity.org. 'Libya Civil War – No Fly Zone'. 4 April 2011. Online: http://www.globalsecurity.org/military/world/war/libya-civil-war-nfz.htm (accessed 15 March 2012).

Goenner, C. 'Uncertainity of the Liberal Peace'. *Journal of Peace Research* 41, 5 (2004).

Goldsmith, J. and E. Posner. 'A Theory of Customary International Law'. *University of Chicago Law Review* 66, 4 (1999).

Goodenough, P. 'Russia, China Accuse West of Exceeding UN Resolution; Makes Libyan Crisis Worse'. CNSnews.com, 8 July 2011. Online: http://grendelreport.posterous.com/russia-china-note-west-exceeds-un-libyan-reso (accessed 20 September 2011).

Graefrath, B. 'The International Law Commission Tomorrow: Improving its Organization and Methods of Work'. *American Journal of International Law* 85, 4 (1991).

Groenewold, J., E. Porter and Médecins sans frontières. *World in Crisis: The Politics of Survival at the End of the Twentieth Century*. London and New York: Routledge, 1997.

Grunfeld, F. and A. Huijboom. *The Failure to Prevent Genocide in Rwanda: The Role of Bystanders*. Leiden: Martinus Nijhoff and Biggleswade, 2007.

The Hague, Netherlands, 1974. Online: http://www.icj-cij.org/documents/index.php?p1=4&p2=2&p3=0 (accessed 1 January 2011).

Hampson, F. and D. Malone. 'Improving the UN's Capacity for Conflict Prevention'. *International Peacekeeping* 9, 1 (2002).

Hannikainen, L. *Peremptory Norms (jus cogens) in International Law: Historical Development, Criteria, Present Status.* Helsinki: Finnish Lawyers' Pub. Co., University of Lapland, 1988.

Hartley, T. *European Union Law in a Global Context: Text, Cases, and Materials.* Cambridge and New York: Cambridge University Press, 2004.

Hayden, P. *Cosmopolitan Global Politics.* Aldershot: Ashgate, 2005.

Hegre, H. 'Development and the Liberal Peace: What Does It Take to Be a Trading State?'. *Journal of Peace Research* 47, 2 (2000).

———. 'Disentangling Democracy and Development as Determinants of Armed Conflict'. Paper presented at the Annual Meeting of the International Studies Association. Portland, Oregon, 27 February 2003.

Hehir, A. *Humanitarian Intervention after Kosovo: Iraq, Darfur and the Record Of Global Civil Society.* Basingstoke: Palgrave Macmillan, 2008.

Helman, G. and S. Ratner. 'Saving Failed States'. *Foreign Policy Analysis* 89 (Winter 1992–93).

Henckaerts, J.-M. 'Study on Customary International Humanitarian Law'. *American Society of International Law* 87 (2005).

Henderson, C. *The Persistent Advocate and the Use of Force: The Impact of the United States upon the jus ad bellum in the Post–Cold War Era.* Farnham, Surrey and Burlington, VT: Ashgate, 2012.

Hendrickson, R. C. 'Crossing the Rubicon'. *NATO Review* (Autumn 2005). Online: http://www.nato.int/docu/review/2005/issue3/english/history_pr.html (accessed 19 February 2012).

Henriksen, D. *NATO's Gambling: Combining Diplomacy and Airpower in the Kosovo Crisis 1998–1999.* Annapolis: Naval Institute Press, 2007.

Hinnebusch, R. 'Authoritarian Persistence, Democratization Theory and the Middle East: An Overview and Critique'. *Democratization* 13, 3 (2006).

History Place, The. 'Genocide in the 20th Century: Rwanda 1994 800,000 Deaths'. Online: http://www.historyplace.com/worldhistory/genocide/rwanda.htm (accessed 20 November 2011).

Holzgrefe, J. and R. Keohane. *Humanitarian Intervention: Ethical, Legal, and Political Dilemmas.* Cambridge and New York: Cambridge University Press, 2003.

Horng, D.-C. 'The Human Rights Clause in the European Union's External Trade and Development Agreements'. *European Law Journal* 9, 5 (2003).

Hosmer, S. *The Conflict Over Kosovo: Why Milosevic Decided to Settle When He Did.* Santa Monica, CA: Rand, 2001.

Hudson, K. *Justice, Intervention, and Force in International Relations: Reassessing Just War Theory in the 21st Century.* London and New York: Routledge, 2009.

Hudson, V. and C. Vore. 'Foreign Policy Analysis Yesterday, Today, and Tomorrow'. *Mershon International Studies Review* 39, 2 (1995).

Human Security Centre and University of British Columbia. *Human Security Report.* New York Oxford University Press, 2005.

Huntington, S. 'Will More Countries Become Democratic?'. *Political Science Quarterly* 99, 2 (1984).

———. *The Third Wave – Democratization in the Late Twentieth Century.* Norman: University of Oklahoma Press, 1991.

———. 'Democracy for the Long Haul?'. *Journal of Democracy* 7, 2 (1996).

International Institute for Strategic Studies. *Libya: Direct Military Hits, Unclear Political Targets.* IISS, 2011.

Ikenberry, J. *After Victory: Institutions, Strategic Restraint, and the Rebuilding of Order After Major Wars.* Princeton and Oxford: Princeton University Press, 2001.

Independent Commission on Disarmament and Security Issues. *Common Security: A Blueprint for Survival.* New York: Simon and Schuster, 1982.

Independent International Commission on Kosovo. *The Kosovo Report: Conflict, International Response, Lessons Learned.* Oxford: Oxford University Press, 2000.

———. *The Follow-up of the Kosovo Report: Why Conditional Independence?* Palme International Centre and Global reporting, Stockholm, 2001. Online: http://www.kulturserver-hamburg.de/home/illyria/kosovocommission.org_report_english_2001.pdf (accessed 12 February 2012).

International Commission on Intervention and State Sovereignty. *The Responsibility to Protect: Report of the International Commission on Intervention and State Sovereignty.* Ottawa, ON, 2001. Online: http://www.iciss.ca/pdf/Commission-Report.pdf (accessed 1 December 2011).

International Court of Justice. 'I.C.J. Decision in North Sea Continental Shelf Cases (Continental Shelf Boundaries; Relationship of Multilateral Treaties, Custom, and International Law)', *American Society of International Law* 8, 2 (1969).

———. Article 38 of the Statute of the International Court of Justice. The Hague, Netherlands, 1974.

———. *Fisheries Jurisdiction Case (United Kingdom V. Iceland).* The Hague, Netherlands, 25 July 1974. Online: http://www.icj-cij.org/docket/index.php?sum=304&code=ai&p1=3&p2=3&case=55&k=9d&p3=5 (accessed 20 December 2011).

International Law Commission. *Report of the International Law Commission on the Work of its Fifty-third Session,* UN Doc. A/56/10. New York, 2001.

Iraq Body Count. 'Three Times as Many Injuries as Deaths Have Been Reported'. 7 August 2003. Online: http://www.iraqbodycount.org/analysis/beyond/indifference-to-injury/3 (accessed 20 February 2012).

———. 'Iraqi Deaths from Violence in 2010: Analysis of the Year's Civilian Death Toll from Iraq Body Count'. 30 December 2010. Online: http://www.iraqbodycount.org/analysis/numbers/2010/ (accessed 20 February 2012).

Iraq Family Health Survey Study Group. 'Violence-Related Mortality in Iraq from 2002 to 2006'. *New England Journal of Medicine* 358, 5 (2008).

Jackson, R. *Quasi-states: Sovereignty, International Relations, and the Third World.* Cambridge: Cambridge University Press, 1990.

———. 'The State and Internal Conflict'. *Australian Journal of International Affairs* 55 (2001).

James, C. 'The ILC's Articles on Responsibility of States for Internationally Wrongful Acts: A Retrospect'. *American Journal of International Law* 96, 4 (2002).

Janzekovic, J. *The Use of Force in Humanitarian Intervention: Morality and Practicalities.* London: Ashgate, 2006.

———. 'Global Democratic Governance: One Step Forward, Two Steps Back'. *Social Alternatives* 29, 2 (2010).

Jentleson, B. 'A Responsibility to Protect'. *Harvard International Review* 28, 4 (2007).

Johnstone, I. 'Law-Making through the Operational Activities of International Organizations'. *George Washington International Law Review* 40, 1 (2008).

Juppé, A. Quoted in 'Libya: Adoption of Resolution 1973'. France in Canada: French Embassy in Canada, 17 March 2011. Online: http://www.ambafrance-ca.org/spip.php?article3888 (accessed 1 December 2011).

———. *Statement by Mr Alain Juppé, Ministre d'Etat, Minister of Foreign and European Affairs before the UN Security Council.* New York, 15 May 2011. Online: http://www.diplomatie.gouv.fr/en/spip.php?page=article_imprim&id_article=15238 (accessed 1 December 2011).

Kaldor, M. *New and Old Wars: Organized Violence in a Global Era*. Stanford: Stanford University Press, 2007.

Kapur, A. *The Fall of a Superpower: Betrayal and Shattered Dreams of a Nation and Its People*. Indianapolis: Wordclay, 2008.

Kellerhals, M. 'U.N. Security Council Approves No-Fly Zone over Libya'. IIP Digital, 25 March 2011. Online: http://iipdigital.usembassy.gov/st/english/article/2011/03/201 10317210213elrem2.422076e-02.html#axzz1QfOofY9v (accessed 9 November 2011).

Kerim, S. 'International Institutions Must Empower the Individual'. *The Hindu*, 15 April 2008. Online: http://www.hindu.com/2008/04/15/stories/2008041554930900.htm (accessed 3 February 2011).

Kerr, P. 'Human Security'. In *Contemporary Security Studies*. Ed. Alan Collins. New York: Oxford University Press, 2010.

Köchler, H. *Democracy and the International Rule of Law: Propositions for an Alternative World Order*. Vienna and New York: Springer-Verlag, 1995.

Kondoch, B. 'The United Nations Administration of East Timor'. *Journal of Conflict and Security Law* 6, 2 (2001).

Krasner, S. *Sovereignty: Organized Hypocrisy*. Princeton: Princeton University Press, 1999.

———. 'Rethinking the Sovereign State Model'. *Review of International Studies* 27, 5 (2001).

———. 'Sharing Sovereignty: New Institutions for Collapsed and Failing States'. *International Security* 29 (2004).

Krieger, H. *The Kosovo Conflict and International Law: An Analytical Documentation 1974–1999*. Cambridge: Cambridge University Press, 2001.

Kuper, J. *International Law Concerning Child Civilians in Armed Conflict*. Oxford and New York: Clarendon Press and Oxford University Press, 1997.

Kyung-wha Kang. *16th Special Session of the Human Rights Council on 'The Situation of Human Rights in the Syrian Arab Republic': Statement by the Deputy High Commissioner for the Human Rights Council Special Session on Syria*. New York, 29 April 2011. Online: http://www. ohchr.org/en/NewsEvents/Pages/DisplayNews.aspx?NewsID=10968&LangID=E (accessed 20 December 2012).

Lambeth, B. *NATO's Air War for Kosovo: A Strategic and Operational Assessment*. Santa Monica, CA: Rand, 2001.

Levitsky, S. and L. Way. 'The Rise of Authoritarianism'. *Journal of Democracy* 13, 2 (2002).

Lévy, B.-H. 'Behind the Scenes of France's Lead on Libya'. *New Perspectives Quarterly* 28, 2 (2011).

Levy, G. and R. Razin. 'It Takes Two: An Explanation for the Democratic Peace'. *Journal of European Economic Association* 2, 1 (2004).

Levy, J. 'The Causes of War: A Review of Theories and Evidence'. In *Behavior, Society, and Nuclear War*. Ed. P. E. Tetlock, J. L. Husbands, R. Jervis, P. C. Stern and C. Tilly. 1989.

Libyan Interim National Council. 'Introducing the Council'. Libyan Interim National Council Official Website, 2011. Online: http://ntclibya.org/english/about/ (accessed 12 June 2011).

Linz, J. and A. Stepan. *Problems of Democratic Transition and Consolidation: Southern Europe, South America, and Post-Communist Europe*. Baltimore: Johns Hopkins University Press, 1996.

Little, R. and M. Wickham-Jones. *New Labour's Foreign Policy: A New Moral Crusade?* Manchester: Manchester University Press, 2000.

Lowe, R. *Idea to Reality: NED at 25*. Washington, DC: National Endowment for Democracy, 2011. Online: http://www.ned.org/about/history (accessed 15 December 2011).

Mahbub ul Haq. 'New Imperatives of Human Security'. RGICS paper no. 17. Rajiv Gandhi Institute for Contemporary Studies (RGICS), New Delhi, 1994. Online: http://rgics.org/working_papers_old2.htm (accessed 12 November 2011).

Malanczuk, P. and M. Akehurst. *Akehurst's Modern Introduction to International Law*, 7th edition. London and New York: Routledge, 1997.

Mamdani, M. *When Victims Become Killers: Colonialism, Nativism, and the Genocide in Rwanda*. Princeton: Princeton University Press, 2001.

Mandal, R. 'Some New Directions in Regional Geography'. In *Patterns of Regional Geography: An International Perspective*. Ed. R. B. Mandal. New Delhi: Concept, 1990.

Manners, I. 'Normative Power: A Contradiction in Terms?'. *Journal of Common Market Studies* 40, 2 (2002).

Maoz, Z. and B. Russett. 'Normative and Structural Causes of Democratic Peace 1946–1986'. *American Political Science Review* 87, 3 (1993).

Matheson, M. 'United Nations Governance of Postconflict Societies'. *American Journal of International Law* 95, 1 (2001).

Mayall, J. 'Non-intervention, Self-determination and the "New World Order"'. *International Affairs* 67, 3 (1991).

Mayersen, D. *The Responsibility to Prevent: Opportunities, Challenges and Strategies for Operationalisation*. Asia-Pacific Centre for the Responsibility to Protect, Brisbane, Queensland, 2010. Online: http://www.humansecuritygateway.com/documents/ APCRP_R2P_OpportunitiesChallengesStrategiesForOperationalisation.pdf (accessed 19 December 2012).

Mazrui, A. 'The Blood of Experience: The Failed State and Political Collapse in Africa'. *World Policy Journal* 12, 1 (1995).

McFaul, M. 'Democracy Promotion as a World Value'. *Washington Quarterly* 28, 1 (2004).

McInnes, C. 'A Different Kind of War? September 11 and the United States' Afghan War'. *Review of International Studies* 29, 2 (2003).

McIntosh, M and H. Alan. *New Perspectives on Human Security*. Sheffield: Greenleaf, 2007.

Meadows, D., J. Randers and W. Behrens. *The Limits to Growth: A Report for the Club of Rome's Project on the Predicament of Mankind*. New York: Potomac Associates, 1972.

Mendeleyeev. 'Why Russia Voted to Abstain on Libya "No-Fly" Resolution'. The Mendeleyev Journal (blog), 16 June 2011. Online: http://russianreport.wordpress. com/2011/03/22/russias-view-on-libya/ (accessed 15 December 2011).

Meron, T. 'On the Inadequate Reach of Humanitarian and Human Rights Law and the Need for a New Instrument'. *American Journal of International Law* 77 (1983).

———. 'The Humanization of Humanitarian Law'. *American Journal of International Law* 94, 2 (2000).

———. 'Revival of Customary Humanitarian Law'. *American Journal of International Law* 99, 4 (2005).

Merritt, R. *Foreign Policy Analysis*. D.C. Heath: Lexington Books, 1976.

Milliken, J. and K. Krause. 'State Failure, Collapse and Reconstruction: Concepts, Lessons and Strategies'. *Development and Change* 5 (2002).

Mokhtari, S. 'The New American Encounter with International Human Rights Norms: The Road After Abu Ghraib'. *Proceedings of the Annual Meeting (American Society of International Law)* 100 (2006).

Molony, S. 'Response to Rwanda "Too Little, Too Late"'. *Independent* (Ireland), 8 April 2004. Online: http://www.independent.ie/world-news/africa/response-to-rwanda-too-little-too-late-175164.html (accessed 12 December 2011).

Moore, M. 'UN Peacekeeping: A Glass Half Empty, Half Full'. *Bulletin of the Atomic Scientists* 51, 2 (1995).

Murphy, S. *Humanitarian Intervention: The United Nations in an Evolving World Order*. Philadelphia: University of Pennsylvania Press, 1996.

Nasu, H. *International Law On Peacekeeping: A Study of Article 40 of the UN Charter*. Leiden and Boston: Martinus Nijhoff, 2009.

NATO. 'NATO's Role in Relation to the Conflict in Kosovo'. 15 July 1999. Online: http://www.nato.int/kosovo/history.htm (accessed 25 December 2011).

Neack, L., J. Hey and H. Patrick. *Foreign Policy Analysis: Continuity and Change in its Second Generation*. Englewood Cliffs: Prentice Hall, 1995.

Nevins, J. 'Contesting the Boundaries of International Justice: State Countermapping and Offshore Resource Struggles between East Timor and Australia'. *Economic Geography* 80, 1 (2004).

Newman, E. 'Peacebuilding as Security in "Failing" and Conflict-Prone States'. *Journal of Intervention and Statebuilding* 4, 3 (2010).

North Atlantic Council. *Statement on Kosovo*. Washington, DC, 23–4 April 1999. Online: http://www.nato.int/docu/pr/1999/p99-062e.htm (accessed 19 December 2011).

Nyheter, D. 'Detta har hänt: striderna i Libyen'. DN.se, 21 March 2011. Online: http://www.dn.se/nyheter/varlden/detta-har-hant-striderna-i-libyen (accessed 11 September 2011).

O'Hanlon, M. 'Winning Ugly in Libya: What the United States Should Learn from its War in Kosovo'. *Foreign Affairs*, 30 March 2011.

Obama, B. *Remarks by the President on Libya: Convention Brasil 21 Center Brasilia*. Brazil, 19 March 2011. Online: http://qatar.usembassy.gov/pr-obama.html (accessed 12 December 2011).

————. Quoted in 'Not Acting in Libya "would have been a betrayal of who we are"'. CNN, 28 March 2011. Online: http://articles.cnn.com/2011-03-28/politics/us.libya_1_libya-mission-libya-policy-libyan-leader-moammar-gadhafi?_s=PM:POLITICS (accessed 12 December 2011).

————. Quoted in 'Obama on Libya: This is Not What We Wanted'. CBS News World, 4 April 2011. Online: http://www.cbsnews.com/stories/2011/03/19/501364/main20045019.shtml (accessed 12 December 2011).

Office of the United Nations High Commissioner for Human Rights. *International Covenant on Civil and Political Rights*. New York, 16 December 1966. Online: http://www.ohchr.org/EN/ProfessionalInterest/Pages/CCPR.aspx (accessed 31 July, 2011).

Ogata, S. and A. Sen. *Human Security Now*. New York: United Nations, 2003.

Oneal, J. and B. Russett. *Causes of Peace: Democracy, Interdependence, and International Organizations, 1885–1992*. Annual Meeting of the American Political Science Association, San Francisco, 2001.

Onuf, N. 'The Principle of Nonintervention, the United Nations, and the International System'. *International Organization* 25, 2 (1971).

Pellatt, K. *Nagorno-Karabakh, Abkhazia and Chechnya: Violence and Autonomy in Eurasia's Secessionist Conflicts*. Ottawa: Library and Archives Canada, 2009.

Pellet, A. 'Between Codification and Progressive Development of the Law: Some Reflections from the ILC'. *International Law FORUM du droit international* 6, 1 (2004).

Peoples, C. and N. Vaughan. *Critical Security Studies: An Introduction*. New York: Routledge, 2010.

Phillimore, R. *Commentaries upon International Law*. Littleton, CO: F. B. Rothman, 1985.

Pictet, J. 'The New Geneva Conventions for the Protection of War Victims'. *American Journal of International Law* 45, 3 (1951).

Piiparinen, T. *The Transformation of UN Conflict Management: Producing Images of Genocide from Rwanda to Darfur and Beyond.* London and New York: Routledge, 2010.

Pogge, T. 'The First United Nations Millennium Development Goal: A Cause for Celebration?'. *Journal of Human Development* 5, 3 (2004).

Pradt. *The Congress of Vienna.* London: S. Leigh, 1816.

Primakov, Y. Press statement by Russian Prime Minister. Russian Public TV, BBC Summary of World Broadcasts. Moscow, March 2009.

Prime Minister's Office Sweden. *Common Responsibility in the 1990s: The Stockholm Initiative on Global Security and Governance.* Stockholm, 22 April 1991.

Radhuyin, V. 'Sitting on the Fence'. *Frontline* 28, 8 (2011).

Rafiq, A. and R. Merrell. 'Telemedicine in Extreme Conditions: Disasters, War, and Remote Sites'. In *Telemedicine for Trauma, Emergencies, and Disaster Management.* Ed. Latifi. Norwood, MA: Artech House, 2010.

Ramcharan, B. *The International Law Commission: Its Approach to the Codification and Progressive Development of International Law.* The Hague: Nijhoff, 1977.

Ratner, S. and J. Abrams. *Accountability for Human Rights Atrocities in International Law: Beyond the Nuremberg Legacy*, 2nd edition. Oxford and New York: Oxford University Press, 2001.

Ravlo, H. and N. Gleditsch. *Colonial War and the Globalization of Democratic Values.* Copenhagen: ECPR, 2000.

Red Cross. 'Meeting of the Intergovernmental Group of Experts for the Protection of War Victims, Geneva, 23–27 January 1995, Recommendation II'. *International Review of the Red Cross* 310 (1996).

Reynolds, P. 'Huge Gaps Between Iraq Death Estimates'. BBC News, 20 October 2006. Online: http://news.bbc.co.uk/1/hi/uk/6045112.stm (accessed 12 November 2011).

Rice, S. *Remarks by Ambassador Susan E. Rice, U.S. Permanent Representative to the United Nations.* Security Council Stakeout on UN Security Council Resolution 1973. 17 March 2011. Online: http://usun.state.gov/briefing/statements/2011/158563.htm (accessed 20 September 2011).

Risse, T. and K. Sikkink. 'The Socialization of International Human Rights Norms into Domestic Practices: Introduction'. In *The Power of Human Rights and Domestic Change.* Ed. T. Risse, S. C. Ropp and K. Sikkink. Cambridge: Cambridge University Press, 1999.

Roberts, A. 'Traditional and Modern Approaches to Customary International Law: A Reconciliation'. *American Journal of International Law* 95, 4 (2001).

Rogel, C. *The Breakup in Yugoslavia and the War in Bosnia.* Westport: Greenwood Press, 1998.

———. *The Breakup of Yugoslavia and its Aftermath.* Westport: Greenwood Press, 2004.

Rogers, A. V. P. 'War Crimes Trials Under the Royal Warrant: British Practice 1945–1949'. *International and Comparative Law Quarterly* 39, 4 (1990).

Rogers, S. 'Wikileaks Iraq: Data Journalism Maps Every Death'. *Guardian*, 23 October 2010. Online: http://www.guardian.co.uk/news/datablog/2010/oct/23/wikileaks-iraq-data-journalism (accessed 1 February 2012).

———. 'Wikileaks Iraq: What's Wrong With the Data?'. *Guardian*, 25 October 2010. Online: http://www.guardian.co.uk/news/datablog/2010/oct/25/wikileaks-iraq-data (accessed 1 February 2012).

Rotberg, R. 'Failed States in a World of Terror'. *Foreign Affairs* 81, 4 (2002).

———. *When States Fail: Causes and Consequences.* Princeton: Princeton University Press, 2004.

Rothschild, E. 'What is Security?' *Daedalus* 124, 3 (1995).

RT.com. 'Russia Accuses NATO of Going Beyond UN Resolution on Libya'. Online: http://rt.com/news/russia-nato-un-resolution-libya/ (accessed 12 December 2011).

Rummel, R. *Death by Government*. New Brunswick, NJ: Transactions Publishers, 1994.

Russett, B. *Grasping the Democratic Peace: Principles for a Post–Cold War World*. Princeton: Princeton University Press, 1993.

Rustow, D. 'Transitions to Democracy: Toward a Dynamic Model'. In *Transitions to Democracy*. Ed. Lisa Anderson. New York: Columbia University Press, 1999.

Sands, P. *Principles of International Environmental Law*, 2nd edition. Cambridge and New York: Cambridge University Press, 2003.

Sassoli, M. 'State Responsibility for Violations of International Humanitarian Law'. *International Review of the Red Cross* 84, 846 (2002).

Schachter, O., M. Sørensen and H. Steiner. 'Theory and Reality in International Law'. *Order, Freedom, Justice, Power: The Challenges for International – Proceedings of the Annual Meeting (American Society of International Law)* 75 (1981).

Schimmelfennig, F. 'Introduction – The Impact of International Organizations on the Central and Eastern Eruopean States: Conceptual and Theoretical Issues'. In *Norms and Nannies: The Impact of International Organizations on the Central and East European States*. Ed. Linden. Lanham: Rowman & Littlefield, 2002.

Schindler, D. and J. Toman. *The Laws of Armed Conflicts: A Collection of Conventions, Resolutions, and Other Documents*, 4th edition. Leiden and Boston: Martinus Nijhoff, 2004.

Schnabel, A. and R. C. Thakur. 'Unbridled Humanitarianism: Between Justice, Power, and Authority'. In *Kosovo and the Challenge of Humanitarian Intervention: Selective Indignation, Collective Action, and International Citizenship*. Ed. Schnabel and Thakur. Tokyo and New York: United Nations University Press, 2000.

Schumpeter, J. *Capitalism, Socialism and Democracy*. New York: Harper, 1942.

Schwebel, S. 'The Compliance Process and the Future of International Law'. *Proceedings of the Annual Meeting (American Society of International Law)* 75 (1981).

Scott, J. 'International Law in Legal Education'. *Columbia Law Review* 4, 6 (1904).

Seely, R. *Russo-Chechen Conflict, 1800–2000: A Deadly Embrace*. New York: Frank Cass, 2005.

Setear, J. 'Treaties; Custom, Iteration, and Public Choice'. *Chicago Journal of International Law* 5, 2 (2005).

Shaw, M. 'There is No Such Thing as Society: Beyond Individualism and Statism in International Security Studies'. *Review of International Studies* 19, 2 (1994).

Silander, D. *United Nations Interim Mission in Kosovo: Standards before Status: A Policy of Catch 22*. Saarbrücken: VDM, Verlag Dr. Müller, 2009.

Sinclair, I. 'Vienna Conference on the Law of Treaties'. *International and Comparative Law Quarterly* 19, 1 (1970).

Six Nation Contact Group, *Interim Agreement for Peace and Self-Government in Kosovo*. Rambouillet, France. 23 February 1999. Online: http://www.vetevendosje.org/repository/docs/rambuje_eng.pdf (accessed 12 November 2011).

Slaughter, A-M. 'Security, Solidarity, and Sovereignty: The Grand Themes of UN Reform'. *American Journal of International Law* 99, 3 (2005).

Slomanson, W. *Fundamental Perspectives on International Law*, 5th edition. Belmont, CA: Thomson/Wadsworth, 2007.

Small, M. 'Human Security and the New Diplomacy: Protecting People, Promoting Peace'. Ed. R. G. McRae and D. Hubert. Montreal and London: McGill-Queen's University Press, 2001.

Smith, K. *European Union Foreign Policy in a Changing World*. Malden: Polity Press, 2008.

Sørensen, G. *Democracy and Democratization: Processes and Prospects in a Changing World*. Boulder: Westview Press, 1993.

Spruyt, H. 'The End of Empire and the Extension of the Westphalian System: The Normative Basis of the Modern State Order'. In *Continuity and Change in the Westphalian Order*. Ed. James A. Caporaso. Malden: Blackwell, 2000.

Strohmeyer, H. 'Collapse and Reconstruction of a Judicial System: The United Nations Missions in Kosovo and East Timor'. *American Journal of International Law* 95, 1 (2001).

Thakur, R. *The United Nations, Peace and Security: From Collective Security to the Responsibility to Protect*. Cambridge and New York: Cambridge University Press, 2006.

Tierney, S. *Accommodating National Identity: New Approaches in International and Domestic Law*. The Hague and Boston: Kluwer Law International, 2000.

Toope, S., E. Theis, J. Anaya and H. Charlesworth. 'Contemporary Conceptions of Customary International Law'. *Proceedings of the Annual Meeting (American Society of International Law)* 92 (1998).

Totten, S. P. Bartrop and S. Jacobs. *Dictionary of Genocide*. Westport: Greenwood Press, 2008.

Tutu, D. 'Taking the Responsibility to Protect'. *New York Times*, 19 February 2008. Online: http://www.nytimes.com/2008/02/19/opinion/19iht-edtutu.1.10186157.html (accessed 12 December 2011).

United Nations Charter, 1945. Online: http://www.un.org/en/documents/charter/index.shtml (accessed 1 November 2011).

United Nations Development Programme. *Human Development Report 1994*. New York: Oxford University Press, 1994.

———. *Human Development Report 1999*. New York, 1999. Online: http://hdr.undp.org/en/media/HDR_1999_EN.pdf (accessed 12 November 2011).

United Nations General Assembly. *Implications of International Response to Events in Rwanda, Kosovo Examined By Secretary-General*, Un Doc. GA/9595. New York, 1999. Online: http://www.un.org/News/Press/docs/1999/19990920.ga9595.html (accessed 12 March 2011).

———. *Responsibility of States for Internationally Wrongful Acts*, Un Doc. A/56/83. Resolution Adopted by the General Assembly on the Report of the Sixth Committee (A/56/589 and Corr.1). New York, 2002. Online: http://www.undemocracy.com/A-RES-56-83.pdf (accessed 11 November 2010).

———. *Agenda Item 55: Follow-up to the Outcome of the Millennium Summit*, Un Doc. A/59/565. New York, 2 December 2004. Online: http://www.un.org/secureworld/report (accessed 14 December 2010).

———. *2005 World Summit Outcome*, Un Doc. A/60/L.1. New York, 2005. Online: http://www.un-ngls.org/orf/un-summit-FINAL-DOC.pdf (accessed 11 November 2010).

———. *The Peacebuilding Commission*, Un Doc. A/RES/60/180. New York, 30 December 2005. Online: http://www.responsibilitytoprotect.org/index.php/component/content/article/35-r2pcs-topics/457-peacebuilding-commission-established(accessed 14 December 2010).

———. *The Current Human Rights Situation in the Syrian Arab Republic in the Context of Recent Events*, Resolution Adopted by the Human Rights Council, Un Doc. A/HRC/RES/S-16/1. New York, 29 April 2011. Online: http://www.securitycouncilreport.org/atf/

cf/%7B65BFCF9B-6D27-4E9C-8CD3-CF6E4FF96FF9%7D/Syria%20AHRC%20
RES%20S-16%201.pdf (accessed 21 December 2012).

———. *Report of the United Nations High Commissioner for Human Rights on the Situation Of Human Rights in the Syrian Arab Republic*, Un Doc. A/HRC/18/53. New York, 15 September 2011. Online: http://daccess-dds-ny.un.org/doc/UNDOC/GEN/G11/159/68/PDF/G1115968.pdf?OpenElement (accessed 20 December 2012).

———. *Human Rights Situations that Require the Council's Attention: Situation of Human Rights in the Syrian Arab Republic*, Resolution Adopted by the Human Rights Council, Un Doc. A/HRC/RES/21/26. New York, 28 September 2011. Online: http://www.unhcr.org/refworld/pdfid/50adee0d2.pdf (accessed 20 December 2012).

United Nations High Commissioner for Refugees. '2011 UNHCR Country Operations Profile – Iraq'. UNHCR.org. Online: http://www.unhcr.org/cgi-bin/texis/vtx/page?page=49e486426 (accessed 15 November 2011).

———. 'UNHCR Global Appeal 2011 (update) – Iraq'. UNHCR.org, 1 December 2010. Online: http://www.unhcr.org/4cd96bd39.html (accessed 1 November 2011).

———. *The Causes of Conflict and the Promotion of Durable Peace and Sustainable Development in Africa*, UN Doc. A/52/87-S/1998/318.

United Nations News and Media. 'Security Council Draft Resolution Against Syria Vetoed'. 4 October 2012. Online: http://www.unmultimedia.org/radio/english/2011/10/security-council-draft-resolution-against-syria-vetoed/ (accessed 20 December 2012).

United Nations Security Council. Resolution 1160 (1998), Un Doc. S/RES/1160 (1998). New York, 1998. Online: http://www.un.org/peace/kosovo/98sc1199.htm (accessed 12 June 2011).

———. Resolution 1199 (1998), Un Doc. S/RES/1199 (1998). New York, 1998. Online: http://www.un.org/peace/kosovo/98sc1199.htm (accessed 12 June 2011).

———. Draft Resolution by Belarus, India and Russian Federation, Un Doc. S/1999/328. New York, 26 March 1999. Online: http://www.securitycouncilreport.org/atf/cf/%7B65BFCF9B-6D27-4E9C-8CD3-CF6E4FF96FF9%7D/kos%20S%201999%20328.pdf (accessed 1 January 2011).

———. Resolution S/PV.3989. New York, 24 October 1999. Online: http://www.securitycouncilreport.org/atf/cf/%7B65BFCF9B-6D27-4E9C-8CD3-CF6E4FF96FF9%7D/kos%20SPV3989.pdf (accessed 1 January 2011).

———. Resolution 1706 (2006), Un Doc. S/RES/1706 (2006). Adopted by the Security Council at its 5519th meeting. New York, 31 August 2006. Online: http://daccess-dds-ny.un.org/doc/UNDOC/GEN/N06/484/64/PDF/N0648464.pdf?OpenElement (accessed 13 December 2010).

———. Resolution 1769 (2007), Un Doc. S/RES/1769 (2007). Adopted by the Security Council at its 5727th meeting. New York, 31 July 2007. Online: http://daccess-dds-ny.un.org/doc/UNDOC/GEN/N07/445/52/PDF/N0744552.pdf?OpenElement (accessed 13 December 2010).

———. *Peace and Security in Africa*. New York, 2011. Online: http://daccess-dds-ny.un.org/doc/UNDOC/GEN/N11/245/58/PDF/N1124558.pdf?OpenElement (accessed 31 July 2011).

———. Resolution 1973 (2011), Un Doc. S/RES/1973 (2011). Adopted by the Security Council at its 6498th meeting. New York, 17 March 2011. Online: http://daccess-dds-ny.un.org/doc/UNDOC/GEN/N11/268/39/PDF/N1126839.pdf?OpenElement (accessed 7 July 2011).

United Nations. 'United Nations Documents on the Development and Codification of International Law: Supplement to American Journal of International Law'. *American Journal of International Law* 41, 4 (1947).

———. *Universal Declaration on Human Rights.* 10 December 1948. Online: http://www.un.org/en/documents/udhr/index.shtml (accessed 1 November 2011).

———. *United Nations Millenium Goals.* New York, 2000. Online: http://www.un.org/millenniumgoals/poverty.shtml (accessed 1 November 2011).

———. *A More Secure World: Our Shared Responsibility. Report of the High-Level Panel on Threats Challenges and Change.* New York, 2004. Online: http://www.un.org/secureworld/report2.pdf (accessed 12 February 2011).

———. *The Work of the International Law Commission*, 7th edition. New York: United Nations, 2007.

———. Press conference on Independent International Commission of Inquiry on Syria. New York, 16 October 2012. Online: http://www.un.org/News/briefings/docs/2012/121016_Syria.doc.htm (accessed 20 December 2012).

Vaccaro, M. 'The Politics of Genocide: Peacekeeping and Disaster Relief in Rwanda'. In *UN Peacekeeping, American Policy and the Uncivil Wars of the 1990s.* Ed. William J. Durch. New York: St Martin's Press, 1996.

Wade, R. 'Failing States and Cumulative Causation in the World System'. *International Political Science Review* 26, 1 (2005).

Waldron, J. 'The Rule of International Law'. *Harvard Journal of Law and Public Policy* 30, 1 (2006).

Walker, M. *The Cold War: A History.* New York: Henry Holt, 1995.

Waller, M. and K. Drezov. *Kosovo: The Politics of Delusion.* London: Frank Cass, 2001.

Waltz, K. *Theory of International Politics.* New York: McGraw-Hill, 1979.

———. *Man, the State, and War: A Theoretical Analysis.* New York: Columbia University Press, 2001.

Weart, S. *Never at War: Why Democracies Will Not Fight Each Other.* New Haven: Yale University Press, 1998.

Weber, M. 'Power, Authority and Imperative Control'. In *The Theory of Social and Economic Organizations.* Ed. Talcott Parsons. New York: Free Press, 1964.

Weede, E. 'The Diffusion of Prosperity and Peace by Globalization'. *Independent Review* 9, 2 (2004).

Weiner, B. *The Truman Doctrine: Background and Presentation.* Ann Harbor: Claremont Graduate School, 1967.

Welsh, J. 'The 2005 International Policy Statement'. *International Journal* 61, 4 (2006).

Welsh, J. and S. Sharma. 'Policy Brief: Operationalizing The Responsibility To Prevent'. Oxford Institute for Ethics, Law and Armed Conflict (ELAC), 2012.

Wessel, R. and J. Wouters. *Multilevel Regulation and the EU: The Interplay Between Global, European, and National Normative Processes.* Leiden and Boston: Martinus Nijhoff, 2008.

Wheeler, J. and A. Bellamy, A. 'Humanitarian Intervention in World Politics'. In *The Globalization of World Politics: An Introduction to International Relations.* Ed. John Baylis and Steve Smith. Oxford: Oxford University Press, 2001.

Wheeler, N. *Saving Strangers: Humanitarian Intervention in International Society.* Oxford: Oxford University Press, 2000.

———. 'Legitimating Humanitarian Intervention: Principles and Procedures'. *Melbourne Journal of International Law* 2, 2 (2001).

Whitehead, L. 'International Aspects of Democratization'. In *Transitions from Authoritarian Rule: Comparative Perspectives*. Ed. G. O'Donnell, P. C. Schmitter, L. Whitehead. Baltimore and London: Johns Hopkins University Press, 1986.

Williams, P. *Security Studies: An Introduction*. London: Routledge, 2008.

Youngs, T. 'Kosovo: The Diplomatic and Military Options', research paper 98/93. London: House of Commons, 27 October 1998. Online: http://www.parliament.uk/documents/commons/lib/research/rp98/rp98-093.pdf (accessed 25 March 2011).

Zartman, W. *Collapsed State: The Disintegration and Restoration of Legitimate Authority*. Boulder: Lynne Rienner, 1995.

Zielonka, J. and A. Pravda (eds). *Democratic Consolidation in Eastern Europe: International and Transnational Factors, vol. 2*. Oxford and New York: Oxford University Press, 2001.

INDEX

Maps are indicated by bolded page numbers.

Abbot, Chris 52, 63
Abu Ghraib 93
Afghanistan 31, 52, 71–4
African continent 28, **30**, 90, 103;
    see also specific countries
African Union 27, 96, 114, 118, 122
Ago, Roberto 85
Ahmed, Sharif 32
Albanians 24–5, 54
A More Secure World: Our Shared
    Responsibility 53
Annan, Kofi A. 40, 50–53
Arab League 109, 112, 114, 118, 122
Arab Spring uprisings 28, 56,
    103–4, 118
Arangio-Ruiz, Gaetano 86
Argentina 64
Armenia 19–20
Article 38 (PCIJ) 80–81
Ashton, Catherine 110
Atlantic Charter 92
Austria 42
Axworthy, Lloyd 42, 51
Azerbaijan 19–20

Bahrain 64, 91
Balkan Wars 20
Ban Ki-moon 40, 48, 66–7, 109
al-Bashir, Omar 35
Belarus 64
Bellamy, Alex 2, 69

Birkelbach report 96
Blair, Tony 63, 105
Bodansky, Daniel 86
Bosnia 20, 50, 58
Bosnia–Herzegovina 23, 58–9, **59**
Bouazizi, Mohammed 126
Boutros-Ghali, Boutros 40, 96
Brandt, Willy 38
Brazil 64
Britain: see United Kingdom
Brown, Gordon 112
Brunnée, Jutta 13
Bush, George H. W. 92
Bush, George W. 93
Buzan, Barry 39, 48

Cameron, David 111, 116
Canada 42, 64
Canadian–Norwegian initiative 42
Carnegie Commission on Preventing
    Deadly Conflict 2
Carter, Jimmy 92
Caucasus 19–20
Central African Empire 49
Central African Republic 31, 33
Chad 31–3, **35**
Chataway, Teresa 52
Chayes, Abram 78
Chile 42
China: opposing NATO intervention
    in FRY 7, 62–3; opposing UN

sanctions 58; position on NATO
    intervention in Libya 113–14,
    117–21; refuting R2P concept 1–2
Churchill, Winston 92
CIA 28
civil and moral society: as a
    collective value 48; fact finding
    and educating roles of 99;
    international laws' relationship to
    7, 75; obligations accompanying
    support of 2–4, 49, 89, 95, 119,
    122, 124
civil liberties 94–5
Clinton, Bill 21, 92–3
Club of Rome Group 38
Coalition pour la Défense de la
    République (CDR) 21
Cold War, influence of 6, 14–16,
    38, 40, 91
Commission on Global Governance 41
common humanity, implications of 92
Common Responsibility in the 1990s 41
Common Security (ICDSI) 38
communism 23, 92
community law 76
community norms 93–4
Comprehensive Peace Agreement of
    2005 (Sudan) 35
Conflict, International Response, Lessons
    Learned 65
Congressional Research Service (CRS)
    report 47, 57
Congress of Vienna (1814–15) 84
Contact Group intervention
    in Kosovo 59, 61
contestation 94–5, 98
Cook, Robin 62
Copenhagen Criteria of 1993 97
corruption 18, 31, 36, 103–4
Corruption Perceptions Index
    (CPI) 28–9
Costa Rica 42
Crawford, James 86
Croatia 20, 23

Crocker, Chester 48
Crook, John 86
customary international law (CIL)
    76–7, 79–80, 88

Dahl, Robert 94–5
Dallaire, Roméo 21
Darfur 33–4, 47, 57, 73
Dayton Peace Agreement of 1995
    22–3, 58
Déby, Idriss 33
Declaration of Independence (US) 12
democracies: action on R2P vs.
    nondemocracies 119, 125;
    economic benefits of 8, 101–2;
    engaging in military conflict 100–
    101; normative power of 120;
    role of in R2P 124; underlying
    agendas of 105, 114, 121, 125; see
    also specific countries
democracy norms: characteristics
    of 94–5; emerging 90–94, 102;
    historical view of 92; imbalances
    in institutional vs. procedural
    focus 94; peace 99–101; popular
    representation 98–9; principles
    for democratic progression 96;
    prosperity 101–2; rights and
    liberties embedded in 94–5; role
    of 8; Sørensen on 95; states'
    moral duty in 89
democracy promotion: action required
    for 89, 111; changes by regions
    103; China's view of 114;
    competing interests and 121; focus
    of 8; human security and 8, 94–8,
    101; as moral responsibility 119;
    as prevention 8, 66, 101; shift
    towards 40, 89–91, 89–94; by
    US 92–3
Democratic Republic of the Congo 31
Department of Foreign Affairs and
    International Trade Canada
    (DFAIT) 42

INDEX 187

development: 9/11 terror attacks' impact on 71; in autocratic vs. democratic states 101–2; Canada's focus on 42; as environmental sector concern 44; expanded issues to consider 39–40; in failing and weak states 12, 18–19; human security thinking emerging from sector of 38; linked to security 53, 91; post—Cold War struggles 38; as preventative focus 66, 70; private sector 31; resources diverted from 71, 101; socioeconomic 102; *see also* economic development

diplomatic initiative for peace enforcement 27

displaced persons 31, 66; *see also* Internally Displaced Persons (IDPs); refugees; *specific countries*

'Doctrine of the International Community' 63

Draft Articles on the Responsibility of States for Internationally Wrongful Acts 86

Drinan, Robert 78

Eastern Zaire 50

East Pakistan (now Bangladesh) 49

East Timor 27, 28, **29**, 50, 56

economic development: benefits of democracies 8, 101–2; Cold War influence on 15–16; as conflicting priority 121; EU focus on 97; expanding impact of stressors on 18; in failing and failed states 18–19, 31–3, 101; global financial crisis 43, 71; globalization's impact on 83; as human rights concern 6, 89, 92; indicators of state condition 31; R2P and R2Prevent application 47, 65–6, 101, 107; security sector considerations 39, 41, 43–4; in

Somalia 32; by US 16, 113, 121; *see also* development

Egypt 70, 91; *see also* Arab Spring uprisings

English Bill of Rights (1689) 12

environmental sector security considerations 39, 44

Eritrea 32

Ethiopia 32

European Council 97

European Union 23, 27, 96–7

The European Union's Role in Promoting Human Rights and Democratisation in Third Countries 97

Evans, Gareth 1, 50

expansionism 84

external intervention 47, 49–51, 52

Failed States Index 31, 37

failing and failed states: atrocities in 13; challenges to 18–19; characteristics of 18–19; classification and identification of 28; development status 12; 'failed state syndrome' 5–6, 11, 17; growing problem of 5, 123; state and human security in 17–20; as triggers for humanitarian intervention 51; *see also* economics

fascism 92

Federal Republic of Yugoslavia (FRY) 23, 26, 59; *see also* Socialist Federal Republic of Yugoslavia

First Assembly of the League of Nations 80

flashpoints (current) 70

foreign policy: based on human-centered security 42; Canada's framework of 42; clash of norms in 46; entity types in 15; as a function of external sovereignty 16; humanitarian dimension in 40; initiatives 126; with Middle East 105; reorientation needed in

6, 125; state-centric focus in 4, 6, 13
Foreign Policy 31
Foreign Policy Analysis (Merritt) 15
Fourth Report of the 1999–2000 Session of the UK Foreign Affairs Committee 58
France: draft Resolution 328 (1999) rejected by 64; lack of involvement in Rwanda 21; Libyan ties 105; relationship with Chad 32–3; response to Libyan crisis 107, 110–12, 117, 120; supporting coup in Central African Empire 49; troops in UNPROFOR 23
free market systems 102
French Revolution 12
Fukuyama, Francis, on state capacity 17
fundamental freedoms: *see* human rights
Fund for Peace 28, 31

Gabon 64
Gaddafi, Muammar 57, 104–7, 110–17, 121; *see also* Libya
Gambia 64
García-Amador, F. V. 85
Gardam, Judith 82
Garrigues, Juan 52
Geneva Convention of 1864 for the Amelioration of the Condition of the Wounded in Armies in the Field 81
Geneva Convention of 1929 on the Wounded and Sick in Armies in the Field 84
Geneva Conventions on Armed Conflict of 1949 85
Geneva Conventions on the Law of the Sea (1958) 88
Genocide Convention 15, 85
globalization 6, 83, 102
Global South 83

governance dimensions 29–31, 39, 44, 56, 66
Great Britain: *see* United Kingdom
Greece 42
Guantanamo Bay 93
Guardian (UK) on Iraqi death tolls 72–3

Habré, Hissène 33
Habyarimana, Juvénal 20
Hague Convention of 1907 81, 84
Haiti 31, 50
Haq, Mahbub ul 41
Harper, Stephen 42
Hehir, Aiden 11–12
Henckaerts, Jean-Marie 81–2
High-Level Panel on Threats, Challenges and Change 52–3; *see also* UN
Holbrooke, Richard 24
human behaviour 43, 48; *see also* state behaviour
human-centric approach 12, 15, 37–44, 120, 123
Human Development Report of 1994 40–41
'Humanitarian Eight' 42
humanitarian intervention: argument for in Kosovo 24–5, 27; Balkans prompting debate on 40; concerns about 53; dangers of unregulated 11; ICISS's goal on 45; norms promoting 13, 48, 55, 124; preventative 3; reasons justifying 27, 49, 51, 63–4; selective nature of 11–12; successes at 56; *see also specific countries*
Humanitarian Intervention After Kosovo (Hehir) 11
human rights: in democracies 99; EU support of 96–7; history of 12, 75, 80, 85–6, 92; language in UN Charter 14, 40, 96; protected by human security 37; state sovereignty

relationship to 40, 46; Universal Declaration of Human Rights 52; UN Resolution 56/83 (2002) on 83, 86–7; in Western identity 91–2
human security: during and after Rawandan genocide 20–22; as appropriate priority 6; Canada's focus on 42; criticism of as an approach 70–71; definition of 39; and democracy promotion 94–8; and democratic governance 97–102; development of norms for 3, 90; domestic 43; essential characteristics of 41; and international law relationship 7; interventions supporting 47; Kosovo situation sparking debate on 27; multifaceted approach to 41; perspective on state sovereignty 13; as preventative focus 70; R2P as new vision of 55; reorientation toward human-centric focus 37; state responsibility for 3, 6, 75; state security as dependent on 3–4, 9, 37; vs. state security paradigm 4, 69, 91, 125; in weak, failing or failed states 17–20, 123
Human Security Network (HSN) 42
Hutus 20–21

Implementing the Responsibility to Protect 66
Impuzamugambi (CDR's) 21
Independent Commission on Disarmament and Security Issues (ICDSI) 38
Independent Commission on Human Security 41–2
Independent Commission on International Development Issues (ICIDI) 38
Independent International Commission of Inquiry 58
Independent International Commission on Kosovo (IICK) 65

India 1–2, 49, 64
Indonesia 90
institutional norms 94
Instructions for the Government of Armies of the United States in the Field 81
Interahamwe (MRND's) 20–21
Intergovernmental Group of Experts for the Protection of War Victims 82
Interim Agreement for Peace and Self-Government in Kosovo 61–2
Internally Displaced Persons (IDPs) 66, 72; *see also* displaced persons; *specific countries*
International Commission on Intervention and State Sovereignty (ICISS): developments in R2P 50–58; establishment of 51; future directions 71–3; humanitarian intervention unsubstantiated by 53; intervention and protection 49–50; R2P 46–9; R2P in Kosovo 58–65; R2Prevent 65–71; UN Security Council proposal 52
international community: changing perceptions of 6, 46; changing state focus 39; debate on how to protect 2 (*see also* Libya); 'Doctrine of the International Community' 63; inconsistency of response by 48, 56–7; Kosovo as precedent setting for 63; norm to protect emerging in 51; R2P as a responsive norm for 1; responsibility to act 3, 6; willingness to engage 67
International Conference for the Protection of War victims (1993) 81
International Court of Justice (ICJ) 79, 82, 86
International Covenant on Civil and Political Rights (1966) 82, 96
International Criminal Court (ICC) 35, 80, 116–17

international humanitarian law (IHL)
75, 76, 80–84, 81
international human rights law (IHRL)
75, 82
international law: community law
dependency on 76; compliance
and enforcement measures 77–8;
criticism of 75, 76; customary
international law (CIL) 76, 77,
79; governing warfare 81, 84;
and human security relationship
7; individual accountability
provisions 84, 85; influences on
77, 79–81; interpretations of
82; legal inducements of R2P
and R2Prevent 65–6; limitations
of 65; monitoring compliance
78; NATO's military action
dubious under 58; obligations
of state participants 77; private
(transnational) 76; public 76;
relevance of to state behaviour
76–80; requisite social and political
conditions 76–7; state practice 79;
substantive instruments produced
84; systemic shift in 55; treaty law
76, 78; umbrella concept in 52;
violations of 78; Westphalia Treaty
shaping 14
International Law Commission (ILC)
6, 75–6, 82–8
international legal norms 7
international relations: *see* foreign
policy
international security 43; *see also*
terrorism
intrastate conflicts 4–5, 19, 38, 43; *see
also specific countries*
Iran 70, 72–3
Iraq 31, 52–3, 68–74
Iraqi Body Count (IBC) 72–3
Ireland 42
Israel 70
Ivanov, Igor 62

Japan 42
Jordan 42
judiciary system in democracies 100
Juppé, Alain 110–11
Justinian, Roman Emperor 12

Kampuchea 49
Kang Kyung-wha 57
Kennedy, John F. 92
Kerim, Srgjan 42
Kerry, John 107
Kosachev, Konstantin 115
Kosovo **25**; Blair's objectives
regarding 63; *Conflict,
International Response, Lessons
Learned* 65; countries rejecting
draft Resolution 328 (1999)
64; criticism of international
response to 46, 50; escalation
of war in 20, 24; exclusion
from peace negotiations 24;
Interim Agreement for Peace
and Self-Government in Kosovo
61–2; intervention, protection
and war in 58–65; interventionist
force justification 63–4; lack of
preventative action in 54; NATO
in 26–7, 54, 58–9; Resolution
1160 (1998) 62, 64; UN Interim
Administration Mission in Kosovo
(UNMIK) 28; UN Resolution
1199 (1998) 58–9, 62, 64; UN
Resolution 1203 (1998) 64
Kosovo Force (KFOR) NATO's 61–2
Kosovo Report 51
Kuwait 68–9

*Larger Freedom: Towards
Development, Security and
Human Rights for All* 51–2
Latin America 90, 93
Lavrov, Sergei 115
Law of Consular Relations (1963) 88
law of treaties 76

Laws and Ordinances of Warre, Established for the Better Conduct of the Army (Cromwell) 81
League of Nations 5, 14, 27, 80
Li Baodong 113–14
Liberia 49
Libya **108**; actors in crisis of 121; China's position on intervention in 113–14, 117–21; diplomatic talks on 116–18; disagreement on use of force in 107–10; displaced persons of 109; France's response to crisis in 107, 110–12, 117, 120; Gaddafi's removal 57; great powers' response to crisis in 109–17; international dynamics surrounding 33; introduction to case study of 8; lessons learned 117–21, 125; no-fly zone over 8, 107–9, 112, 115–16, 119; normative power of democracies against 120; political unrest in 28, 56, 91; R2P as strategic argument for intervention 118–19; R2Ps application in 104; revolution and aftermath 104–6; Russia's position on intervention in 113–21; sanctions against 106–7; Transitional Council of 105, 110, 116; United Kingdom's response to crisis in 110–12; UN Security Council: R2P application and 106–9; UN Security Council Resolution 1970 (2011) on 106–7, 115–16, 118–19, 122; UN Security Council Resolution 1973 (2011) on 109–10, 113, 115–16, 119–20, 122; US response to crisis in 107–8, 110, 112–13
Lieber Code of 1863 81
Lieberman, Joe 107
Locke, John 12
Lysøen, Declaration 42

Maastricht Treaty (1993) 97
Macedonia 20
Malaysia 64
Mali 42
Mayersen, Deborah 67
McCain, John 107
Medvedev, Dmitry 116
Meron, Theodor 79–80, 82
Merrell, Ronald 73
Middle East, democartic deficiency in 91, 93, 103
military intervention: criticism of 63; as final protection 3; principles justifying 51, 53, 56, 66; Putin on 116; Rambouillet proposal on 61
Milošević, Slobodan 23–4, 62
'mobilization of shame' 77–8
Mobuto regime ousted 22
Montenegro 23, 26
Montevideo Convention (1933) 4, 14
moral codes of conduct 12
moral society: *see* civil and moral society
Mouvement Républicain National pour la Démocratie et le Développement (MRND) 20–21
mutually assured destruction (MAD) 15

Nagorno-Karabakh 19–20
Namibia 64
National Endowment for Democracy 93
NATO 6–7, 25–7, 61–4, 93, 113, 119
NATO Treaty (1949) 92
natural law 12
natural rights: *see* human rights
Nazism 92
Netherlands 64
'New Imperatives of Human Security' 41
noncitizens, international law impacting on 83, 85
noninterference norm: challenged by obligation to act 3; China's concern with violation of 114;

sovereignty norm supporting 4,
16; UN Charter upholding 5, 50,
124; violations of 50
nonstate actors, ILC need to address 87
*Norms, Institutions, and UN Reform: The
Responsibility to Protect* (Brunnée
and Toope) 13
North Africa 91
North Atlantic Treaty Organization:
see NATO
North Korea 70, 73
North-South report (ICIDI) 38
Norway 42
Nuclear Weapons Advisory Opinion
of ICJ 82, 86
Nuremberg Trials 15, 84

Obama, Barack 108, 113
Ogata, Sadako 41–2
Operationalizing the Responsibility to Prevent
(Welsh and Sharma) 67–8
Operation Allied Force 26
Operation Deliberate Force 59, 62
Ordinance for the Government of the
Army (1386) 81
Organization for Security and Co-
operation in Europe (OSCE) 61
Organization of American States
(OAS) 96
OSCE monitors in Kosovo 26
'Our Global Neighbourhood' 41

Palestine 70
Palme, Olof 38
Paris Summit to Support the Libyan
People 110
participation 94–5, 98
peace 99–101
peace enforcement 27, 44
peacekeeping operations 21, 27–8, 32,
56, 66; *see also specific countries*
Pellet, Alain 87
People, States and Fear (Buzan) 39
Pérez de Cuéllar, Javier 40

Permanent Court of International
Justice (PCIJ) 80
Philippines 90
philosophies behind human rights 12
Piiparinen, Touko 21
political indicators of state condition 31
political objectives 21
political will 3, 53, 56, 123
positive obligations of states 7–8
positivist school of thought 76–7, 80, 85
preventative action: aims of 2, 52;
barriers to 3, 6; characteristics
of 69; contextualizing 45, 65,
68, 71, 125; need to focus on 4,
6, 56; nexus between protective
action and 2; prerequisites for
effectiveness 69; reactive vs.
proactive 122
Preventing Deadly Conflict 2
prevention strategies 2; democratization
as 8, 66, 101; direct strategies
66–7; implementation questions
45, 55, 67; omitted in *Conflict,
International Response, Lessons
Learned* 65; operational 2, 66; R2P
associated 68; of strong states 69;
structural 2, 66; tools of 65, 67
Primakov, Yevgeny 62
Project of an International
Declaration Concerning the Laws
and Customs of War 81
protection and intervention 49–51; *see
also* R2P
protection strategy tools 65
protective action 2, 3
Putin, Vladimir 116

Qatar 91

R2P 46–9; action on by democracies
vs. nondemocracies 119;
challenges to 46, 57–8, 103,
122–3; democracy impacting
on 8, 124; development and

evolution of 6, 45, 50–58; disagreement on implementation of 1, 50, 54 (*see also* Libya); forcible intervention focus of 56; formal structure provided by 2; future directions 71–3, 126; *Implementing the Responsibility to Protect* 66; interpretations of 47, 56; intervention, protection and War in Kosovo 58–65; intervention and protection 49–50; lessons from Libyan crisis 117–21; limitations on 53–4; principles behind 52; as principle vs. concept vs. norm 48, 122, 126; recent applications of 1; state and international community obligations identified by 3, 46, 52, 55; as strategic argument for intervention 118; unresolved questions about 54–6, 65, 126

R2Prevent: defining 65–71; democratic norms as strategy 8, 66, 101; factors leading to neglect of 69; foundational elements of 52, 66, 125; future directions 71–3; inconsistency in response to 54; *Operationalizing the Responsibility to Prevent* 67–8; prioritizing prevention vs. protection 70; *The Responsibility to Prevent: Opportunities, Challenges and Strategies for Operationalization* 67; structural and operational prevention 2, 66; *see also* international law

Rafiq, Azhar 73

Reagan, Ronald 92, 105

refugees 8; Afghan 72; Iraqi 72; from Kosovo 26; Libyan 109; Somali 32; Sudanese 33; UN High Commissioner for Refugees (UNHCR) 72; *see also* displaced persons

representation as core state function 20, 98–9

'Responsibility of States for Internationally Wrongful Acts' 83

Responsibility to Protect report (ICISS) 46, 51

responsibility to react 47, 52, 66

responsibility to rebuild 52, 66

Rice, Susan 113

Riphagen, Willem 86

Rogozin, Dmitry 115

Roman Empire 12

Roosevelt, Franklin 92

Rosenstock, Robert 85

Rothschild, Emma 69

rule of law: as democratic norm 95; as governance dimension 29, 31; institutionalization of 92; in international relations 83; judiciary maintaining 100; supported by Amsterdam Treaty 97

Russia: attitude toward independent states in 19–20; Chechnya invaded by 20; opposing NATO intervention in FRY 7, 62, 64; opposing UN sanctions 58; position on NATO intervention in Libya 113–16, 117–21; refuting R2P concept 1–2; *see also* Soviet Union

Rwandan genocide 20–22, **22**, 46, 50–51, 97

Rwandan Patriotic Front (RPF) 20–21

Sahnoun, Mohamed 1

Salmon, Trevor 47

Saudi Arabia 91

Schnabel, Albrecht 64–5

security: biological 53; broadened perspective on 44; call for human-centered 42; as core state function 20; development link 53, 91; perception of threat in 43; preconditions for 39; reconceptualization of 39; state antagonism approach defining 14; values linked to 13

Security Studies: An Introduction (Williams) 13

Sen, Amartya 41–2

Serbia 23–6, 54, 61

Sergeyev, Igor 62

Shapiro, Jacob 72–3

Sharma, Serena 67–8

Sierra Leone 50

Slaughter, Anne-Marie 55

Slomanson, William 80–81

Slovenia 20, 23, 42, 64

social indicators of state condition 31

Socialist Federal Republic of Yugoslavia 20, 23, 26, **60**; *see also* Federal Republic of Yugoslavia (FRY)

societal sector security considerations 39, 44

socioeconomic development: *see* development

Solana, Javier 26, 62

Somalia 21, 31–2, **34**, 49–50

Sørensen, Georg 95

South Korea 90

sovereignty norm: as inadequate focus 5; internal and external components of 16; losing dominant status 90; R2P 'new direction' in 55; rights and liberties embedded in 40; state security as focus of 4; in UN Charter 14, 124; *see also* state sovereignty

Soviet Union 16–17, 19; *see also* Russia

spillover conflict 37

Stahn, Carsten 55

state behaviour: checks and balances on 99–100; community norms regulating 94; constraints on 7; influences on 43; international law' relevance to 15, 76–80, 85; standards of 91; *see also* human behaviour

state capacity 17–19

state-centric approach: alternatives to 38, 123; challenges to 87; influences behind 14; in international relations 4, 6; limitations of 39, 73; in state vs. citizen contests 12–13; *see also* China; Russia

state responsibility: broadening focus of 39; contentiousness of 83–4; historical view of 83, 86; ILC's focus on 85–6; to protect 1, 3, 6, 45; 'Responsibility of States for Internationally Wrongful Acts' 83; socioeconomic services as 19–20; UN Resolution 56/83 (2002) on 83

states: characteristics of strong 19; identification of weak and failing 28; international law applicability to 76; legitimacy 120 (see also Libya); moral duty 89; obligations regarding human rights 6, 12; positive obligations of 7–8; as trustees of the people 39; vulnerable 31; Weberian concept of successful 17; widening range of responsibilities of 39

state security: as contested concept 13; as dependent on human security 3, 9, 37; historical view of 83; justifying direct external intervention 27; pressures impacting on 18, 43; sovereignty and the state 12–16; vs. human security paradigm 4, 69, 91, 125; in weak, failing or failed 17–20

state sovereignty: challenging sanctity of 28, 50; China's concern with violation of 113–14; Cold War impact on 40; connection to human security 3, 45; human security perspective on 13; institutionalization of 5, 49, 123; international law challenging 7; Kuwait's protection based on

68; norm of 14, 90; norms clash
46, 124; R2P violating principle
of 1–2; security and 12–16;
Westphalian concept of 4
Stockholm Initiative on Global
    Security and Governance 41
Sudan 31, 33–7, **36**, 37, 57
Switzerland 42
Syria 57–8, 91, 122–3
systems theory 43

Taiwan 90
Tang Jiaxuan 62–3
Tanzania 49
Terbil, Fathi 105
terrorism: 9/11 attacks on US 27,
    52–3, 71–3, 93; by Gaddafi 105;
    global war on 74; US war on 93;
    see also international security
Thailand 42
Thakur, Ramesh 65, 71
tipping points 16
Tito, Josip 20, 23
Tokyo Tribunal 84
Tombalbaye, François 32
Toope, Stephen 13, 54–5
Transitional Broad-Based Government
    (TBBG) in Rwanda 20
transnational law 76
transparency in democracies 100
Transparency International 28–9
Treaty of Paris (1814) 84
Treaty of Rome 96
Treaty of Westphalia (1648) 4, 14, 92
Truman Doctrine 92
Tunisia 91, 126
Türk, Danilo 64
Tutsis, RPF of 20–21
Tutu, Desmond 68

Uganda 20, 49
umbrella concept in international law 52
UN: authorization for US intervention
    in Somalia 31; High-Level Panel

on Threats, Challenges and
    Change appointed 52; increasing
    peace keeping missions by 27;
    lack of action by 50; trusteeship
    system 27
UN Assistance Mission to Rwanda
    (UNAMIR) 21
UN Charter: draft Resolution
    328 (1999) concerning
    64; humanitarian acts on
    contemplated in 62; rights
    and liberties embedded in 40,
    96; sovereignty provisions and
    exceptions of 5, 14, 124
UN Development Programme
    (UNDP) 40–41
UN General Assembly: exception
    to sovereignty norm by 14;
    Resolution 56/83 (2002) 83, 86–7;
    Resolution A/HRC/ RES/21/26
    (2011) 57; Resolution A/HRC/
    RES/S-16/1 (2011) 57; Resolution
    A/RES/60/180 (2005) 54; state
    responsibility addressed by (1953)
    85; supporting state responsibility
    6; *see also* UN World Summit 2005
UN High Commissioner for Refugees
    (UNHCR) 72, 109
UN Human Rights Council (HRC) 57
UN Interim Administration Mission in
    Kosovo (UNMIK) 28
UN International Commission
    on Intervention and State
    Sovereignty (2001) 1
UN International Law Commission
    (ILC) 75
UN Operation in Somalia
    (UNOSOM) 31–2
UN Peace Building Commission 54
UN Protection Force
    (UNPROFOR) 23
UN Security Council: attempted
    reform of 52; exception to
    sovereignty norm by 14; implicit

authorization of force by 64;
position on Kosovo 24–6, 51;
and R2P application in Libya
106–9; Resolution 777 (1992)
23; Resolution 1160 (1998)
62, 64; Resolution 1199 (1998)
58–9, 62, 64; Resolution 1203
(1998) 64; Resolution 1674
(2006) 103; Resolution 1769
(2009) 47; Resolution 1894
(2009) 103; Resolution 1970
(2011) 104, 106–7, 115–16,
118–19, 127–37; Resolution
1973 (2011) 8, 104, 109–10,
113, 115–16, 119–20, 139–47;
response in Rwanda 21;
trusteeship requests by 28; *see
also* Libya
UN Transitional Administration in
East Timor (UNTAET) 28
UN Transitional Authority in Eastern
Slovenia (UNTAES) 28
UN World Summit 2005: humanitarian
intervention unsubstantiated by
53; provision to support majority
removed 52; R2P endorsed at
56–7; responsibilities articulated in
Summit Outcome document 1, 13,
47; *Summit Report* 55
Union of Resistance Forces in Chad 33
United Kingdom: Department for
International Development 28;
draft Resolution 328 (1999)
rejected by 64; peace enforcement
supported by 27; response to
Libyan crisis 110–12, 117, 120;
supporting airstrikes in Libya 107;
troops in UNPROFOR 23; UK
Foreign Affairs Committee 58
United States: authorized to
intervene in Somalia 31; in the
Balkans 23; debacle in Somalia
21; democracy promotion by
92–3; draft Resolution 328 (1999)

rejected by 64; Iraq invasion 53;
lecturing on human rights 93;
peace enforcement supported by
27; rejection of UN guidelines
53–4; relations with Libya 105;
reluctance of to act in Rwanda
21; response to crisis in Libya
107–10, 112–13, 120; support
of Habré in Chad 33; terrorism
attack of 9/11 on 27, 52–3,
71–3, 93
Universal Declaration of Human
Rights (UDHR) (1948) 52, 80, 96
universal jurisdiction doctrine 7

value-based norms 94
values 13, 48, 90
Van Rompuy, Herman 110
Vienna Conventions on Diplomatic
Relations (1961) 88
Vienna Law of Treaties (1969) 88
Vietnam 49
Vollebaek, Knut 42

war against terrorism 74, 93
war in Kosovo: *see* Kosovo
weapons of mass destruction (WMDs)
43, 68–9
Weiss, Edith Brown 87
Welsh, Jennifer 67–8
Westphalian thinking, principles
underlying 4, 92
Williams, Paul 2
Wilson, Woodrow 92
World Bank 28
World Order Models Project
(WOMP) 38
Worldwide Governance Indicators
(WGI) 29–31

Yemen 31, 91

Zaire, Rwandan war spilling into 22
Zimbabwe 31

www.ingramcontent.com/pod-product-compliance
Lightning Source LLC
Chambersburg PA
CBHW030836300326
41935CB00036B/231